Student Viewer's Handbook
TO ACCOMPANY

DESTINOS

VOLUME 1 • EPISODIOS 1–26
THIRD EDITION

Bill VanPatten
University of Illinois at Chicago

Martha Alford Marks

Richard V. Teschner
University of Texas, El Paso

With additional comprehension materials by

Matt Borden
University of Texas, Austin

Beatriz Gómez-Acuña
University of Texas, Austin

J. Elisabeth Wright
University of Texas, Austin

Thalia Dorwick
Coordinator of Print Material for The McGraw-Hill Companies, Inc.

Boston   Burr Ridge, IL   Dubuque, IA   Madison, WI   New York   San Francisco   St. Louis
Bangkok   Bogotá   Caracas   Kuala Lumpur   Lisbon   London   Madrid   Mexico City
Milan   Montreal   New Delhi   Santiago   Seoul   Singapore   Sydney   Taipei   Toronto

McGraw-Hill Higher Education

A Division of The **McGraw-Hill** *Companies*

This is an  book.

Student Viewer's Handbook I to accompany *Destinos*: An Introduction to Spanish

1 2 3 4 5 6 7 8 9 0   QPD   QPD   0 9 8 7 6 5 4 3 2

ISBN 0-07-249709-2

The editors were Thalia Dorwick, William R. Glass, Scott Tinetti, and Pennie Nichols-Alem.
The project manager was Brett Coker.
The production supervisor was Pam Augspurger.
The cover designer was Matthew Baldwin.
The photo researcher was Nora Agbayani.
The compositor was TechBooks.
Quebecor Press Dubuque was the printer and binder.

CONTENTS

Preface

TO THE INSTRUCTOR

This Student Viewer's Handbook to Accompany *Destinos* is designed to help you use *Destinos* as a supplement in a wide variety of courses, at beginning, intermediate, or advanced levels of instruction. By using the Handbook, you and your students will enjoy viewing the fifty-two half-hour episodes of the television series more and get more out of them.

How to Use the *Destinos* Series

The fifty-two episodes can be viewed one per week over two academic years, two per week over a full year, or four or five per week for a full semester or quarter, depending on the course in which the series is used.

It is a good idea to have the episodes available in the Language Lab or Media Center so that students who miss a class meeting can view the episodes they missed. If the fifty-two episodes can be made available to students in a Lab or Media Center, *Destinos* can also be used purely as a supplement out of class: Students can work on the materials on their own as a homework assignment. If time and class goals permit, the materials can then be discussed in class.

How to Use the Student Viewer's Handbook

The twenty-six chapters of this volume of the Handbook correspond to the first twenty-six episodes of the series. Here is one way to use the chapters:

- Have students do the sections called **Preparación** before coming to class. You may wish to go over the answers to **Preparación** activities in class before viewing the episode.
- Watch the episode in class with your students, then do the **¿Tienes buena memoria?** activities with the whole class.
- Have students get into pairs or small groups to do the activities in **Intercambio**. Other, personalized **Intercambio** activities may also be assigned as homework, to be discussed in class later.
- Assign the **Más allá del episodio** sections to be done at home, then go over the follow-up activities in class.

Because no answers are provided in the Handbook, most of the activities in these sections also make ideal homework assignments.

Destinos Multimedia

Two new exciting multimedia supplements are now available for use with *Destinos:* an interactive CD-ROM and a content-rich website.

- The new interactive CD-ROM to accompany *Destinos* contains additional practice with the story line of the series, vocabulary and grammar practice, as well as a writing feature that enables students to express themselves in Spanish. Please contact your local McGraw-Hill sales representative for more information, or visit our catalog page at **www.mhhe.com.**
- The new website contains a wealth of resources for students and instructors alike, including practice quizzes, cultural links and resources, as well as detailed summaries of the *Destinos* episodes and biographies of the series' characters. Go to **www.mhhe.com/destinos**, and let the adventure begin!

Composition Assignments and *Destinos*

Because *Destinos* is characterized by a strong ongoing story line, you will find that it is relatively easy to create composition assignments based on the series. The most fundamental composition topic to assign is a summary of a given episode. However, you may find that students will write better compositions if such summary assignments are based on one or more of the four units of the first half of the series: Episodes 1–6, 7–11, 12–18, and 19–26. Individual story lines within the units and throughout all twenty-six episodes also make ideal composition topics.

Extended writing assignments called **Para escribir** are also found in review episodes 6, 11, 18, and 25. These sections offer guided writing topics using a step-by-step approach, providing a framework for students so that they will write better compositions.

It is also a good idea to lay a foundation for composition assignments in general by doing the first composition as an activity for the whole class.

Testing with *Destinos*

When *Destinos* is used as a supplement, whether as the basis for activities for the whole class or as an assignment out of class, it is a good idea to include material related to the series on quizzes and exams. Here are a few suggestions for testing with *Destinos*.

- It is possible to take test items or even whole activities directly from the **¿Tienes buena memoria?** sections. This is one way to ensure that students will perform those activities carefully.
- Because *Destinos* has a strong story line and strong character development, it is relatively easy to develop true/false items about the series. Other appropriate—and easy-to-write—testing formats include matching, multiple choice, incomplete statements, and short answer questions.
- Whichever testing format you select, you should keep test items focused on the major events and characters in the series rather than on details that most students will not catch, especially if they only view each episode once. Questions about details (the name of a hotel, a particular street address, the name of a minor character, and so on) can be fun as challenging activities in class, but they will be unfair testing items for most students.
- Be sure to let students know how test items on *Destinos* will be evaluated. Is their knowledge of the story line the most important issue? Or will spelling, grammar, and vocabulary use in their answers also be evaluated?

● ● ● ● ●

Finally, as you use the series in class, remember that *Destinos* is first and foremost an exciting series to watch! Our classroom experience with the series and class tests performed by other instructors indicate that students will enjoy watching the episodes and that they will want to talk about many aspects of them. Remember to make time for such class discussion. You may be surprised by how lively it will become!

TO THE STUDENT

Welcome to *Destinos*, a series of fifty-two half-hour television shows in Spanish. As you watch the shows, you will follow an unforgettable journey that has been designed to be enjoyable as well as instructional. You will not only follow the plot of an unfolding drama but will also experience, through the powerful medium of television, some of the places in which Spanish is spoken (including the United States).

The ease with which you understand the episodes of *Destinos* will depend in part on how much Spanish you have studied, and for how long. But one aspect of the television series will also help. As you watch the series, keep in mind that in each episode there are three kinds of Spanish. Two of them are specifically designed to be comprehensible to you: the Spanish spoken by an off-screen narrator and that spoken by a character called Raquel Rodríguez, who will review the major highlights with you at the end of each episode. You should be able to understand these two kinds of Spanish easily. In addition, each episode also contains segments of more rapid conversational Spanish, that is, when the characters are speaking to each other. In most cases, the characters' actions and the context of the continuing story line will allow you to get the gist of these conversations.

This Handbook can also help you a lot. It has been designed to make viewing the first twenty-six episodes even more enjoyable, because it will help you to understand more of the Spanish you will hear in them.

Just as there are twenty-six episodes in the first half of the television series, there are twenty-six chapters in the Handbook. Most chapters have three main sections.

- You should do the section called **Preparación** (*Preparation*) before you watch each episode. This section will prepare you to view the episode by highlighting important vocabulary, previewing information and conversations from that show, as well as reviewing important information from previous shows.

- After you have watched each episode, the section called **¿Tienes buena memoria?** (*Do You Have a Good Memory?*) will help you test yourself about what you remembered from the episode. The first group of activities in this section, **¿Qué recuerdas?** (*What Do You Remember?*), will test your knowledge of information in the episode with three different activity types. The first, **Preguntas** (*Questions*), will ask you to briefly answer some questions about the episode you just watched. Usually a word or a few words will suffice as an answer. The next activity type, **¡Busca el intruso!** (*Look for the Intruder!*), will ask you to make associations based on a group of words, and then underline the word or phrase that does not belong with the others. As individual people make their own associations among various items, there may often be more than one right answer. In the final activity type in this section, **¿Cierto o falso?** (*True or False?*), you will decide whether statements about the episode are true or false.

  The second group of activities in this section is called **Actividades** (*Activities*). If you can answer most of the questions in the activities in this section, you will have understood enough of the show . . . even though you may not have understood every word.

- Finally, in the section called **Intercambio** (*Exchange*), you will have the opportunity to work with classmates as you complete activities based on a theme presented in the episode. There are also activities that you will work on as an individual, in which you discuss how a theme from the episode relates to your own life.

In addition, many chapters of the Handbook have a brief section called **Nota cultural** (*Cultural Note*), in which a wide variety of aspects of Hispanic culture are discussed. Most chapters of the Handbook also have a section called **Más allá del episodio** (*Beyond the Episode*) in which you will learn more information about some of the characters and events in the series.

Furthermore, the chapters that correspond to the review episodes of *Destinos* contain materials that will help you combine what you have learned so that you can talk about everything you have seen in the previous episodes. In addition to review activities, most review episodes have a section called **Para escribir** (*Writing*), in which you will write guided compositions about various topics. Some of the writing tasks involve summarizing the story line of *Destinos*, while others will ask you to write about your own life or the lives of those around you.

Destinos Multimedia

Two new exciting multimedia supplements are now available for use with *Destinos:* an interactive CD-ROM and a content-rich website.

- The new interactive CD-ROM to accompany *Destinos* contains additional practice with the story line of the series, vocabulary and grammar practice, as well as a unique writing feature that enables you to express yourself in Spanish. Please contact your instructor for more information, or visit our catalog page at **www.mhhe.com.**
- The new website contains a wealth of resources for you, including practice quizzes, cultural links and resources, as well as detailed summaries of the *Destinos* episodes and biographies of the series' characters. Go to **www.mhhe.com/destinos**, and let the adventure begin!

• • • • •

And now it's time to begin the series. If you have not yet seen the first show, turn to page 1 of this Handbook, look at the unit opener, then do the **Preparación** section in **Episodio 1**. Then, only after you have finished, watch the first show. Here is how the story begins.

An old man has retired to his hacienda outside a small town close to Mexico City. With the wealth he has accumulated since leaving Spain at the end of its bloody Civil War, he is restoring the hacienda to its original sixteenth-century splendor. But his health has begun to fail, and now he hopes to live out the remainder of his years peacefully, in the tranquillity of the Mexican countryside.

Then a letter arrives—a letter in which a woman from Spain makes claims about the old man's past. . . .

Destinos

Episodios 1–26

The story begins at La Gavia, a historic estate near Toluca, Mexico . . .

1

La carta

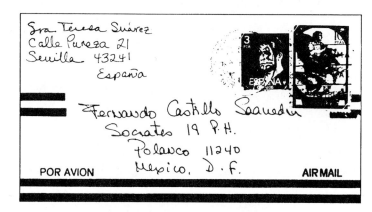

> Sra. Teresa Suárez
> Calle Pureza 21
> Sevilla 43241
> España
>
> Fernando Castillo Saavedra
> Sócrates 19 P.H.
> Polanco 11240
> Mexico. D.F.
>
> POR AVION   AIR MAIL

The interactive CD-ROM to accompany *Destinos* contains additional practice with the video story line and will help you improve your skills in Spanish.

BEFORE VIEWING . . .

Be sure to complete the preview section (called **Preparación**) in **Episodio 1** before viewing **Episodio 1** (the video segment that corresponds to **Episodio 1** in this Handbook).

Preparación

You are about to watch **Episodio 1** from *Destinos*. At times you will hear narration in English that will explain things and help you follow along, and you will also hear a lot of Spanish. You will be able to understand much of what you hear because several kinds of Spanish are used. There is

- Spanish spoken directly to you by the narrator, which you will learn to understand with relative ease
- Spanish spoken directly to you by a special character, who will review the highlights of the video episode for you at the end of each show
- Spanish spoken by the characters to one another, which at first will be more difficult for you to understand.

As you watch the video episodes, especially at the beginning of the series, you should focus in particular on the Spanish spoken to you by the narrator and the special character. Just relax and listen, and you'll be surprised by how much you can understand.

As for the Spanish spoken by the characters to each other, just try to get the gist (general idea) of it. As you continue with the series, you will find yourself understanding more and more of that type of Spanish.

Throughout the Handbook, the **Preparación** section is intended to start you thinking about the program and speculating about what may happen in the next video episode. So now, even before you watch the first episode, take a few moments to speculate about what it may be about. Look at the cover of this Handbook and at the **Episodio 1** opening page (with its titles and visual material). Think about what the series title, *Destinos*, might mean. If you guessed either *destinies* or *destinations*, you were right. The title of the series is a play on both words.

VOCABULARIO

This vocabulary box will precede the activities in the **Preparación** sections. The box contains some, but not all, of the important words found in the episode.

Los sustantivos (Nouns)

la abogada   lawyer
la carta   letter
la hacienda   estate, hacienda
el médico   doctor
el patriarca   patriarch, male head of the family
el secreto   secret

Los adjetivos (Adjectives)

mexicoamericano/mexicoamericana   Mexican-American

Actividad A.

Where do you think the first episode of *Destinos* will take place?

1.   _____ in the United States
2   _____ in Argentina
3.   _____ in Mexico
4.   _____ in Spain

Actividad B.

What do you think the principal setting will be?

1.   a restaurant
2.   a hacienda
3.   a university campus
4.   a hotel

Actividad C.

What do you think will set the story in motion?

1.   a letter
2.   a telephone call
3.   a telegram
4.   a crime

When you have finished watching **Episodio 1**, come back and see how accurate your first guesses were. Read through the activities again at that time and change your answers if you wish.

. . . AFTER VIEWING

¿ **T** ienes buena memoria?

In this repeating section of the Handbook you will review important information from the episode that you have just watched.

¿QUÉ RECUERDAS?

Actividad A. Preguntas (*Questions*)
Briefly answer the following questions about **Episodio 1**.

1. ¿Quién es don Fernando Castillo Saavedra? _____

2. ¿Cómo se llama la hacienda donde vive don Fernando? _____

3. ¿En qué nación está situada (*is located*) la hacienda? _____

4. ¿Quién es Julio Morelos? _____

5. ¿Cuántos hijos tiene don Fernando? _____

6. ¿Cómo se llaman los hijos de don Fernando? _____

7. ¿Dónde vive Raquel Rodríguez? _____

8. ¿Cuál es su (*her*) profesión? _____

Actividad B. ¡Busca el intruso! (*Look for the intruder!*)
For each group of names, places, or words, underline the one that does not belong with the others.

1. don Fernando, Julio, Raquel, Ramón

2. abogada, hijo, padre, secreto

3. Miami, Nueva York, Los Ángeles, La Gavia

4. profesor, abogada, médico, mexicoamericana

5. Carlos, Mercedes, Juan, Ramón

Actividad C. ¿Cierto o falso? (*True or false?*)
Indicate whether the following sentences are **Cierto (C)** or **Falso (F)**.

C F 1. Mercedes tiene tres hermanos.
C F 2. Don Fernando es médico.
C F 3. La Gavia es la hija de don Fernando.
C F 4. Don Fernando guarda (*is keeping*) un secreto importante.
C F 5. Raquel es abogada.

ACTIVIDADES

Actividad A. ¿Quiénes son?
Now that you have watched **Episodio 1** of *Destinos*, look at the following photos and match them with the brief descriptions. As you do this activity, you will be reading short, relatively easy sentences in Spanish. You should guess at the meaning of words you don't immediately understand.

a.

b.

c.

1. _____ Raquel es abogada. Vive en Los Ángeles.
2. _____ Fernando es el paciente de Julio, el médico.
3. _____ Es una persona muy misteriosa.

Actividad B.   ¿Quién es don Fernando?

The word **don** is a title of respect used with a man's first name. Which of the following statements describe don Fernando? Indicate **Sí** or **No**, according to what you now know about the character.

Sí	No	1.	Es profesor de literatura.
Sí	No	2.	Es miembro de la familia Castillo Saavedra.
Sí	No	3.	Necesita un doctor.
Sí	No	4.	Vive en La Gavia, una hacienda.
Sí	No	5.	Tiene una carta importante.

Más allá del episodio: La Gavia

La Gavia es el nombre de una hacienda mexicana. Es la residencia principal de don Fernando Castillo Saavedra, el patriarca de la familia Castillo. Es una hacienda de la época colonial. Está situada¹ al suroeste de la Ciudad de México, cerca de² la ciudad industrial de Toluca.

Don Fernando compró³ La Gavia en ruinas con la idea de restaurar la hacienda. Es un lugar histórico, pero también es muy importante para don Fernando.

La Gavia es una hacienda muy grande. Tiene una entrada majestuosa y una capilla muy bonita. En la hacienda hay también un patio muy agradable y una biblioteca impresionante.

¹ Está... *It is located*   ² cerca... *close to*   ³ *bought*

La entrada de La Gavia

La capilla de la familia Castillo Saavedra

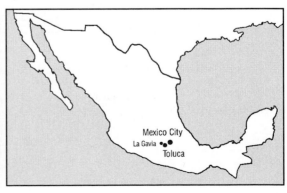
Mexico City
La Gavia
Toluca

El secreto

The interactive CD-ROM to accompany *Destinos* contains additional practice with the video story line and will help you improve your skills in Spanish.

BEFORE VIEWING . . .

Be sure to complete the preview section (called **Preparación**) in **Episodio 2** before viewing **Episodio 2** (the video segment that corresponds to **Episodio 2** in this Handbook).

Preparación

As you prepare to watch **Episodio 2** from *Destinos*, remember the three kinds of Spanish you will hear: Spanish spoken directly to you by the narrator, Spanish spoken to you by Raquel, and the Spanish that the characters speak to each other. As you continue with the program, you will find that you understand more and more of all three kinds of Spanish.

VOCABULARIO

Los verbos (Verbs)	Los sustantivos		Las palabras adicionales (Additional Words)	
perdonar to pardon	**la compañía**	company (*business*)	**está muerto/a**	is dead
	el director	head, leader; director	**ya murió**	already died
	la Guerra Civil (española)	(Spanish) Civil War		

Actividad A.

At the end of **Episodio 1**, you saw don Fernando crush a letter in his hand. Answer the following questions about the letter. As you read the questions, remember what you know about don Fernando and try to make logical guesses. There are no right or wrong answers so far.

1. ¿De dónde es la carta?
    _____ de España
    _____ de los Estados Unidos
    _____ de la Argentina
    _____ de otra parte de México

2. El narrador dice: «Don Fernando tiene un secreto importante. El secreto está en una carta... una carta importante.» ¿Cuál es el secreto de la carta? (¡OJO! **tiene que ver con** = *has to do with*)
    _____ El secreto tiene que ver con la vida privada de don Fernando.
    _____ El secreto tiene que ver con asuntos legales.
    _____ El secreto tiene que ver con la compañía de don Fernando.

Actividad B.

During **Episodio 1**, don Fernando says to Ramón, "Llama a tus hermanos. Y a tu tío Pedro." If **llamar** means *to call*, can you guess who Ramón will be calling in this episode?

Ramón va a llamar
_____ a otros médicos.   _____ a una abogada.
_____ a unos amigos.   _____ a otras personas de la familia.

When you have finished watching **Episodio 2**, come back and see how accurate your first guesses were. Read through **Actividades A** and **B** again at that time and change your answers if you wish.

Actividad C.

Read the following phone call that Ramón will make to his brother Carlos during **Episodio 2**. Knowing that **Hoy vino...** means that someone *came today*, can you guess what Ramón is telling Carlos? (*Hint:* Remember what you saw in **Episodio 1**.)

Ramón le dice a Carlos que
a. _____ hoy vino una abogada.
b. _____ hoy vino el médico para ver a don Fernando.
c. _____ hoy vino Juan.

CARLOS: ¡Ramón, qué milagro! ¿Cómo estás?
RAMÓN: Bien. ¿Y tú?
CARLOS: Bien.... Con mucho trabajo. ¿Qué pasa?
RAMÓN: Te tengo malas noticias...
CARLOS: ¿De papá?
RAMÓN: Sí. Hoy vino el médico y... ¿Puedes venir mañana, a La Gavia?
CARLOS: Sí. Claro que sí.
RAMÓN: Bien. Tengo que llamar a Juan. Te veré mañana. Adiós.
CARLOS: Bien. Te veo mañana.

Now read the conversation again. Knowing that **¿Puedes... ?** means *Can you . . . ?*, what do you think that Ramón is asking Carlos to do? What does Carlos answer?

Ramón desea que Carlos venga a
a. _____ un hospital.
b. _____ la hacienda.
c. _____ Los Ángeles.

Carlos dice que _____ sí _____ no.

...AFTER VIEWING

¿Tienes buena memoria?

¿QUÉ RECUERDAS?

Actividad A.   Preguntas
Briefly answer the following questions about **Episodio 2**.

1.   ¿Quién es Pedro Castillo Saavedra? _____

2.   ¿Cómo se llama la esposa de Ramón? _____

3.   ¿Quién es Maricarmen? _____

4.   ¿Cuántos hijos tienen Carlos y Gloria? _____

5.   ¿Cómo se llaman los hijos de Carlos y Gloria? _____

6.   ¿Cuántos hijos tienen Juan y Pati? _____

7.   Y el esposo de Mercedes, ¿vive o ya murió? _____

8.   ¿Quién es Rosario? _____

9.   ¿Cuál es el secreto de don Fernando? _____

10.   ¿Quién escribió (*wrote*) la carta que don Fernando tiene? _____

Actividad B.   ¡Busca el intruso!
For each group or pair of names or places, underline the one that does not belong with the others.

1.   Ramón y Consuelo, Fernando y Pedro, Juan y Carlos, Ramón y Juan

2.   Juanita, Maricarmen, Rosario, Carlitos

3.   don Fernando y Mercedes, Juan y Pati, Ramón y Maricarmen, Carlos y Juanita

4.   Guernica, Miami, Sevilla, La Gavia

5.   Gloria, Mercedes, Pati, Consuelo

Actividad C.   ¿Cierto o falso?

Indicate whether the following sentences are **Cierto (C)** or **Falso (F)**.

C   F   1.   Pedro y Raquel son médicos.

C   F   2.   Carlos y Gloria no tienen hijos.

C   F   3.   La madre de Ramón y Mercedes está muerta.

C   F   4.   Don Fernando tiene tres nietos (*grandchildren*).

C   F   5.   Juan y Pati no tienen hijos.

ACTIVIDADES

Actividad A.   La familia de don Fernando

Today you met all of the known relatives in don Fernando's immediate family, plus a few other people. Review what you know about them by matching the people on the left with their descriptions on the right. Don't be discouraged if you can't get all of the items correct this time. You will be working with the same characters throughout the whole series. This is only your first chance to practice their names.

1. _____ Ramón   a.   hijo de don Fernando; director de una compañía
2. _____ Pedro   b.   esposa de don Fernando y madre de sus cuatro hijos
3. _____ Juan   c.   hija de don Fernando; vive en La Gavia
4. _____ Carlos   d.   la esposa secreta de don Fernando
5. _____ Mercedes   e.   hijo de don Fernando; vive en La Gavia
6. _____ Rosario   f.   hermano de don Fernando; profesor en México
7. _____ Carmen   g.   hijo de don Fernando; profesor en Nueva York

¡Un desafío! ¿Tienes una memoria muy buena?

1. _____ Gloria   a.   médico de la familia
2. _____ Pati   b.   esposa de Carlos
3. _____ Consuelo   c.   esposa de Juan
4. _____ Lupe   d.   cocinera
5. _____ Maricarmen   e.   hija de Consuelo y Ramón
6. _____ Julio   f.   secretaria de Carlos
7. _____ Ofelia   g.   antigua estudiante de Pedro
8. _____ Raquel   h.   esposa de Ramón

Actividad B.   ¿Dónde vive?

Not all of the characters live and work with don Fernando. Complete each statement by indicating where each person lives and what he or she does for a living.

     Los lugares: la Ciudad de México, La Gavia, Los Ángeles, Miami, Nueva York

     Las profesiones: Es director de la Compañía Castillo Saavedra, S.A.*
                       Es administrador/administradora de la hacienda.
                       Es profesor de literatura en la universidad.
                       Es profesor de derecho en la universidad.
                       Es abogada de derecho internacional.

     MODELO: Carlos vive en _____. Es _____. →
               Carlos vive en Miami. Es director de la Compañía Castillo Saavedra, S.A.

---

*Castillo Saavedra, S.A. es la compañía de don Fernando. S.A. (Sociedad Anónima) significa *Inc.* en inglés.

1. Carlos vive en _____. Es _____.

2. Ramón vive en _____. Es _____.

3. Mercedes vive en _____. Es _____.

4. Juan vive en _____. Es _____.

5. Pedro vive en _____. Es _____.

6. Raquel vive en _____. Es _____.

Actividad C.   El secreto

At the family conference called by don Fernando, the patriarch revealed the information contained in the letter he received from Spain. Which of the following possibilities does he suggest? ¡OJO! There may be more than one right answer.

_____ Don Fernando tiene otra hacienda.
_____ Don Fernando tiene otra esposa.
_____ Don Fernando tiene otro hermano.
_____ Don Fernando tiene otro hijo.

Nota cultural: Las familias hispánicas

It is more typical of Hispanic families for many members of the extended family (all of the relatives, not just the immediate family) to live under the same roof. Widowed grandparents and unmarried aunts and uncles, in particular, may stay in the family home. Unmarried children tend to live with their parents much longer, in some cases for their whole lives. As is the case with Ramón, even married family members may still live under the same roof as their parents. This custom is changing somewhat in modern Hispanic society, especially in urban areas.

Regardless of whether it is a cause or a result of these living arrangements, there is a certain closeness in Hispanic families. How does this compare with your own experience?

Intercambio

This repeating section is a lesson-culminating activity that will allow you to speak more in depth about the video story line, its characters, your classmates, and yourself.

In this activity you will try to get members of the class to guess which *Destinos* characters you are talking about. Try to stump your classmates!

Paso (Step) **1**

Think of two characters and prepare two statements that describe each one. Ask your instructor for help with new vocabulary items if you need them.

MODELO: Esta persona no vive en La Gavia. Tiene esposa pero no tiene hijos. ¿Quién es?

_____

_____

_____

_____

Paso 2

Your instructor will call on students to read their statements. The student whose character description is identified by the *least* number of people wins!

Más allá del episodio: Juan y Pati

Juan Castillo, con Pati, su esposa

Juan y Pati son esposos. Viven en un apartamento en el Soho, un barrio¹ de la ciudad de Nueva York. Juan es profesor de literatura latinoamericana en la Universidad de Nueva York (NYU). Pati también es profesora en la Universidad de Nueva York, pero no de literatura. Su especialización es el teatro y ha sido² la directora de obras como³ *Bodas de sangre* (*Blood Wedding*) (del dramaturgo español Federico García Lorca). El montaje⁴ fue⁵ de la compañía «Hispanic Theater of New York».

En este momento,⁶ el matrimonio de Juan y Pati es inestable y tenso. Los dos trabajan⁷ y las responsabilidades de sus respectivas carreras académicas aumentan la tensión entre ellos. También, sus personalidades están en conflicto: Los dos son muy ambiciosos y hay rivalidad entre ellos. El futuro de su matrimonio es incierto...

¹*neighborhood, district* ²*ha... has been* ³*obras... works like* ⁴*production* ⁵*was* ⁶*En... Right now, Currently*
⁷*Los... Both of them work*

Un viaje a Sevilla (España)

La Catedral de Sevilla

El comienzo

>
> The interactive CD-ROM to accompany *Destinos* contains additional practice with the video story line and will help you improve your skills in Spanish.

BEFORE VIEWING . . .

Preparación

VOCABULARIO

Los verbos

busca he/she looks for
llega he/she arrives
viaja he/she travels

Los sustantivos

el apellido last name
el barrio neighborhood
el comienzo beginning
la dirección address
el mercado market
el nombre (first) name

Los adjetivos

preocupado/preocupada worried
turístico/turística tourist

Actividad A.

In **Episodio 1** of *Destinos* you met Raquel Rodríguez. Indicate whether the following statements about Raquel are **Cierto (C)** or **Falso (F)**.

C F 1. Raquel es hija de don Fernando.
C F 2. Es abogada.
C F 3. Vive y trabaja en Los Ángeles.
C F 4. Es mexicoamericana.
C F 5. Cree que Rosario vive en España.

Actividad B.

In **Episodio 2** you learned information about a trip Raquel will take. Because this episode is called **El comienzo**, it is a safe bet that her trip will start in this episode.

Where will Raquel go and for what reason? What information does she already have? ¡OJO! There may be more than one appropriate answer.

1. Raquel va a viajar a
    _____ España.
    _____ la Argentina.
    _____ Puerto Rico.

2. Raquel va a buscar a
    _____ Rosario, la primera esposa de don Fernando.
    _____ Carmen, la segunda esposa de don Fernando.
    _____ la persona que escribió la carta.
    _____ otro hijo de don Fernando.

3. Raquel probablemente sabe
    _____ el nombre del hijo de Rosario y don Fernando.
    _____ el nombre de la persona que escribió la carta.
    _____ el nombre de la calle donde la persona vive.

Actividad C.

Read the following conversation that Raquel will have with the receptionist at her hotel in Spain. **¿Dónde está... ?** means *Where is . . . ?* Now that you know that, what does Raquel ask about?

RAQUEL: Perdone.
RECEPCIONISTA: Eh, sí, señorita.
RAQUEL: ¿Ud. sabe dónde está la calle Pureza?
RECEPCIONISTA: Sí. Está en el Barrio de Triana.
RAQUEL: ¿Está muy lejos?
RECEPCIONISTA: Un poco.

Raquel pregunta dónde está
a. Rosario.
b. la calle Pureza.
c. el hijo de Rosario y don Fernando.

Now read the conversation again. **¿Está lejos?** means *Is it far away?* Now that you know that, what information does the receptionist give to Raquel?

RAQUEL: Perdone.
RECEPCIONISTA: Eh, sí, señorita.
RAQUEL: ¿Ud. sabe dónde está la calle Pureza?
RECEPCIONISTA: Sí. Está en el Barrio de Triana.
RAQUEL: ¿Está muy lejos?
RECEPCIONISTA: Un poco.

El recepcionista dice que la calle Pureza
a. está lejos, un poco lejos.
b. no está lejos.
c. está en el Barrio de Triana.
d. no está en la ciudad.

¿**T**ienes buena memoria?

¿QUÉ RECUERDAS?

Actividad A.   Preguntas

Briefly answer the following questions about **Episodio 3**.

1. ¿A qué ciudad viaja Raquel? _____

2. ¿Cómo llega Raquel al Barrio de Triana, en autobús o en taxi? _____

3. Raquel busca a una persona. ¿A quién busca? _____

4. ¿Cómo se llaman los nietos de Teresa Suárez? _____

5. ¿Dónde vive la señora Suárez? _____

6. ¿Con quién habla Raquel en el mercado de Triana? _____

7. ¿Cuáles son dos de los países (*countries*) cerca de España? _____

8. ¿En qué parte de España está la región de Andalucía, en el norte o en el sur? _____

_____

Actividad B.   ¡Busca el intruso!

For each name or place, underline the one that does not belong with the others.

1. el mar Cantábrico, el Golfo Pérsico, el Océano Atlántico, el mar Mediterráneo

2. el País Vasco, Cataluña, Andalucía, Sevilla

3. la Giralda, el Barrio de Triana, La Gavia, la Barbería Los Pajaritos

4. Raquel, Elena, Jaime, Miguel

5. España, Portugal, África, Francia

Actividad C.   ¿Cierto o falso?

Indicate whether the following sentences are **Cierto (C)** or **Falso (F)**.

C F 1. Raquel busca a don Fernando en España.
C F 2. La Giralda es el nombre del hotel donde se aloja (*is staying*) Raquel.
C F 3. Jaime es el hermano menor (*younger*) de Miguel.
C F 4. Teresa Suárez ya murió.
C F 5. España es un país europeo.

ACTIVIDADES

Actividad A.   ¿De quién se habla?

Indicate whether the following statements refer to Elena Ramírez (**E**) or to Teresa Suárez (**T**), her mother-in-law (**su suegra**).

E   T   1. Vive en Madrid ahora.
E   T   2. Tiene dos hijos jóvenes.
E   T   3. Su hijo tiene esposa y dos hijos.
E   T   4. Está en el mercado cuando llega Raquel a su barrio.
E   T   5. Es la abuela de Miguel y Jaime.

Actividad B.   ¿Cuánto saben?

Don Fernando's family knew nothing about the existence of Rosario. Based on what you have seen and heard in **Episodio 3**, do the following new characters have any information to give Raquel about the case?

a. Es posible.
b. No sabe nada.
c. Probablemente no sabe nada.

1. _____ Miguel Ruiz
2. _____ Elena Ramírez
3. _____ el esposo de Elena
4. _____ el taxista

Nota cultural: Los apellidos hispanos

You have probably noticed in previous lessons that the Castillo family is sometimes called **la familia Castillo Saavedra** and sometimes just **la familia Castillo**. In most Hispanic countries people use two last names (**apellidos**). The first is the name of the father, the second that of the mother. It is correct to call a person by the first of the two names (the name of one's father) or by both names. Thus, both **la familia Castillo** and **la familia Castillo Saavedra** are authentic usages.

Miguel and Jaime, who are the sons of Miguel Ruiz and Elena Ramírez, have the last names **Ruiz Ramírez**. Elena's son, Miguel, is known either as **Miguel Ruiz** or as **Miguel Ruiz Ramírez**. It would not be correct to call him **Miguel Ramírez**.

A married woman can add the preposition **de** before her husband's last name. So **Teresa Suárez** could also be called **Teresa Suárez de Ruiz**. However, in Spain it is very common for a woman to use only her maiden name: **Teresa Suárez**, **Elena Ramírez**. Elena's full married name is **Elena Ramírez de Ruiz**.

Intercambio

In this activity you will interview a classmate and ask some basic questions about someone in his or her family, then compare that person with a character from *Destinos*.

Paso 1

The class should be divided into two groups: those who will interview and those who will be interviewed. For those who will be interviewed, think of a member of your own extended family who has the most in common with Raquel Rodríguez. Write that person's name and family relation down on a sheet of paper. For those who interview, prepare a series of questions you could ask to compare that person to Raquel. Ask your instructor for help if you need it. You should prepare at least eight questions!

> MODELOS: Esta (*This*) persona, ¿dónde vive?
> ¿Tiene un trabajo? ¿Dónde?
> ¿Tiene esposo o esposa? ¿Cómo se llama?

Paso 2

For those who interview, write up a brief comparison of your classmate's relative and Raquel. You must make at least five comparisons.

> MODELO: El pariente* de Cathy vive en San Francisco. No vive en Los Ángeles, como Raquel. Es profesora, no es abogada. Como Raquel, no tiene esposo…

_____

_____

_____

_____

_____

Paso 3

Read your description to the class. Then listen to your instructor's comments.

Más allá del episodio: La familia Ruiz

Elena y Miguel, con sus dos hijos

Elena Ramírez es la madre de Miguel y Jaime, los dos chicos que Raquel conoce[1] en la calle Pureza. Con dos hijos, Elena tiene mucho trabajo. Jaime, especialmente, le da problemas.

Jaime es un niño con mucha energía. Es el menor de los dos hijos y le gusta ser el centro de atención. No es muy buen estudiante y Elena habla con frecuencia con su maestro[2] y el director de su escuela. Este año,[3] Jaime tiene muchas dificultades en la clase de matemáticas.

En cambio,[4] Miguel es un hijo modelo y Elena está muy orgullosa[5] de él. Miguel es inteligente, estudioso... y sus maestros hablan muy bien de él. Como hermanos típicos, a veces Jaime y Miguel no se llevan bien... y Elena tiene que intervenir en sus peleas.[6]

¿Y el padre de los chicos? ¿Cómo es él? ¿Y cómo es la relación que tiene con Elena, Jaime y Miguel?

[1]*meets*   [2]*teacher*   [3]*Este... This year*   [4]*En... On the other hand*   [5]*proud*   [6]*fights*

* ¡OJO! The word **pariente** is a false cognate. It means *relative*, not *parent*.

Perdido

The interactive CD-ROM to accompany *Destinos* contains additional practice with the video story line and will help you improve your skills in Spanish.

BEFORE VIEWING . . .

 **reparación**

VOCABULARIO

Los verbos

comprar   to buy

Los sustantivos

la asignatura	subject (*school*)
el colegio	grade/high school
el gato	cat
el pájaro	bird
el perro	dog
el pez (*pl.* **peces**)	fish

Los adjetivos

perdido/perdida lost

Las palabras adicionales

sabe (algo)	he/she knows (something)
no sabe nada	he/she doesn't know anything

Actividad A.
In the last episode of *Destinos* you followed Raquel to Spain. What do you remember about her trip? Complete the following statements.

1. Raquel está ahora en... Barcelona / Sevilla / Madrid.
2. Tiene una carta escrita por... Teresa Suárez / Pedro Castillo / don Fernando.
3. Busca a... Miguel Ruiz / Elena Ramírez / Teresa Suárez.
4. En la calle, habla primero con... dos chicos / dos esposos / dos taxistas.
5. Dicen que la señora Suárez vive ahora en... Barcelona / Málaga / Madrid.
6. Caminan al mercado y Raquel habla con... Teresa Suárez / Elena Ramírez / Mercedes.
7. Elena es... la madre / la abuela / la hermana ...de los chicos.
8. Elena... tiene / no tiene / también desea ...información sobre Rosario.

Actividad B.
What do you think will happen in this episode? Try to predict what will happen by answering the following questions.

1. In **Episodio 3** you learned that Teresa Suárez is currently living in Madrid. Do you think that Raquel will be able to make contact with her? If so, how?
   a. _____ Teresa Suárez no desea hablar con Raquel.
   b. _____ Raquel no habla con Teresa Suárez en este episodio.
   c. _____ Raquel habla con Teresa por teléfono.

2. You also learned that Elena Ramírez knows nothing about the letter that Sra. Suárez wrote to don Fernando. Do you think her husband knows something?
   a. _____ El esposo de Elena no sabe nada.
   b. _____ El esposo sabe algo.

Actividad C.
Read the following conversation that Raquel will have with Miguel Ruiz, Elena's husband. **Ya hablé** means *I already spoke*. Now that you know that, with whom did Miguel speak and what did he learn?

a. _____ Miguel habló con Teresa Suárez.
b. _____ Miguel habló con Rosario.
c. _____ Miguel no sabe nada.
d. _____ Miguel sabe algo interesante.

RAQUEL: Miguel, ¿Elena le ha contado lo de la carta?
MIGUEL: Sí, y además ya hablé con mi madre por teléfono.
RAQUEL: ¿Y qué dijo? ¿Mencionó algo de Rosario?
MIGUEL: Realmente no.
RAQUEL: ¿Dijo algo de mi cliente, don Fernando?
MIGUEL: No. No dijo nada.
RAQUEL: Mi cliente, don Fernando, quiere saber qué pasó con Rosario. ¿Podría yo hablar por teléfono con su madre?
MIGUEL: No creo. Mi madre prefiere que Ud. vaya a Madrid.

Now read the conversation again. **Vaya** means *go*. Now that you know that, how will Raquel and Teresa Suárez make contact?

a. _____ La señora Suárez desea hablar con Raquel por teléfono.
b. _____ La señora Suárez desea hablar con Raquel en Sevilla.
c. _____ La señora Suárez desea hablar con Raquel en Madrid.

. . . AFTER VIEWING

¿**T**ienes buena memoria?

¿QUÉ RECUERDAS?

Actividad A. Preguntas
Briefly answer the following questions about **Episodio 4**.

1. ¿Cómo se llama el esposo de Elena Ramírez? _____

2. ¿Adónde tiene que ir (*has to go*) Raquel para hablar con Teresa Suárez? _____

3. ¿Cuál es la asignatura favorita de Miguel? _____

4. ¿Cuál es la asignatura favorita de Jaime? _____

5. ¿Qué tipos de animales hay en el mercadillo de los animales? _____

_____

6. ¿Qué tipo de animal compra la familia de Jaime? _____

7. ¿Cómo se llama el nuevo animal de Jaime? _____

8. ¿Por qué corre (*runs*) Jaime al final del **Episodio 4**? _____

_____

Actividad B. ¡Busca el intruso!
For each group of items below, underline the one that does not belong with the others.

1. la cerveza, el jerez, el vino, la tortilla española

2. las matemáticas, las ciencias naturales, el colegio, la educación física

3. los peces tropicales, las aceitunas, los pájaros, las tortugas

4. la cervecería, la Catedral de Sevilla, la pastelería, el mercadillo

Actividad C. ¿Cierto o falso?
Indicate whether the following sentences are **Cierto (C)** or **Falso (F)**.

C F 1. Miguel es un buen estudiante.
C F 2. Raquel tiene que (*has to*) viajar a Barcelona.
C F 3. El esposo de Elena se llama Jaime.
C F 4. En el **Episodio 4**, Raquel habla con Teresa Suárez por teléfono.
C F 5. Miguel Ruiz no sabe nada de Rosario.

ACTIVIDADES

Actividad. En este episodio
All of the following events took place during the two days shown in **Episodio 4**, but . . .
in what order did they occur? Put them in order, from 1 to 3 or 4 in each group.

Por la noche

a. _____ Miguel revela su conversación con su madre.

b. _____ Raquel llama a Pedro Castillo por teléfono, y habla con él.

c. _____ Raquel decide viajar a Madrid, en tren.

Al día siguiente

a. _____ La familia entra en una pastelería.

b. _____ Miguel padre compra un perro.

c. _____ Osito se escapa y se pierde.

d. _____ La familia lleva a Raquel al mercado de los animales.

Nota cultural: En las universidades hispánicas

After completing their high-school degree (called **el bachillerato**), students in most Hispanic countries who enter the university must immediately select a major and follow a prescribed series of courses (with few electives). Courses tend to last for a full year, with obligatory examinations at the end of the course.

Observaciones del Profesor	Alumno _____
	Asignatura ___ NATURALEZA _____
	Curso 5ª , Un. 4ª , Obj. 1.2.2.
	Fecha _____ - Noviembre _____
	Calificación [ ]

1.- ¿ Qué órganos forman el aparato circulatorio ?

2.- ¿ Qué elementos forman la sangre ?

3.- Las _____ son los vasos sanguíneos que conducen la sangre desde los órganos hasta el corazón.

Las _____ son los vasos sanguíneos que conducen la sangre desde el corazón a todos los órganos del cuerpo.

Intercambio

Paso 1

In pairs, use the following questions to interview each other. You may add questions if you like and may consult your instructor for help. Jot down all information you get from your partner because you will need it later.

1. ¿Cuál es tu especialización (*major*)?

   _____

2. ¿Qué clases tienes este semestre (trimestre)?

   _____

3. ¿Cuál es tu clase favorita?

   _____

4. ¿Quién es tu profesor favorito (profesora favorita)?

   _____

Paso 2

With the notes you took in **Paso 1**, write a short paragraph in which you talk about your partner's college experience. Be prepared! Your instructor may call on you to read the information out loud.

_____

_____

_____

_____

_____

_____

Más allá del episodio: Raquel Rodríguez

Raquel usa su computadora con frecuencia.

Raquel Rodríguez es una abogada mexicoamericana. Es soltera.[1] Es una mujer muy inteligente. Es sensible,[2] sincera y generosa con sus amigos y colegas. También tiene mucha imaginación. A veces,[3] es un poco impaciente. En sus ratos libres,[4] le gusta ir de compras[5] y leer novelas. Los padres de Raquel viven en Los Ángeles. Están jubilados.[6] Raquel es hija única[7] y su madre se mete mucho[8] en su vida. Las dos se pelean[9] con frecuencia. Pero Raquel quiere[10] mucho a sus padres y los visita regularmente. Raquel también tiene familia en México.

Raquel conoció[11] a Pedro Castillo en México. El bufete[12] donde Raquel trabaja tiene una sucursal[13] allí. Pedro ha tenido[14] mucho contacto con esa oficina y siempre ha admirado[15] el trabajo de Raquel. Por eso, Pedro se puso en contacto con Raquel cuando don Fernando reveló el secreto de la carta. Ella aceptó el caso inmediatamente.

Raquel está muy emocionada[16] porque éste es su primer viaje a España. Pero, ¿va a encontrar[17] a Teresa Suárez, la mujer que le escribió una carta a don Fernando? ¿y a Rosario, la primera esposa de don Fernando?

[1]*single* [2]*sensitive* [3]*A... Sometimes* [4]*ratos... free time* [5]*ir... to go shopping* [6]*ya no trabajan* [7]*hija... no tiene hermanos* [8]*se... gets very involved* [9]*se... fight* [10]*loves* [11]*met* [12]*law office* [13]*branch office* [14]*ha... has had* [15]*ha... has admired* [16]*excited* [17]*va... is she going to find*

La despedida

> The interactive CD-ROM to accompany *Destinos* contains additional practice with the video story line and will help you improve your skills in Spanish.

BEFORE VIEWING . . .

Preparación

VOCABULARIO

Los verbos

encuentra(n)	he/she finds (they find)
sale(n)	he/she leaves (they leave)
va(n)	he/she goes (they go)
vende(n)	he/she sells (they sell)

Los sustantivos

los caramelos	candy/candies
el ciego	blind man
el cupón de la lotería	lottery ticket

Actividad A.

Although Raquel has not yet unraveled the secret of the letter, she has accumulated some information and, being a lawyer, has kept careful records of it. How much do you remember about the details of the case? In simple sentences, answer the following questions about Raquel's investigation.

1. ¿Cómo se llama la persona que escribió la carta?
2. ¿Dónde vive esa persona?
3. ¿Desea hablar con Raquel?
4. ¿Adónde necesita ir Raquel para hablar con ella?
5. ¿Sabe algo de Rosario la familia Ruiz?
6. ¿Cómo debe ir Raquel a Madrid?

Actividad B.

At the end of **Episodio 4**, the entire Ruiz family disappeared along with Raquel into the narrow streets of **el Barrio de Santa Cruz**. What do you think will happen in this video episode? In each group, choose the statement that best expresses what you expect to see.

1. _____ Jaime encuentra a su perro.
   _____ Hay un accidente y Osito está muerto.

2. _____ Jaime se pierde también en el Barrio de Santa Cruz.
   _____ Raquel se pierde también.

3. _____ Raquel sale para Madrid.
   _____ Raquel decide quedarse (*to stay*) en Sevilla otro día.

Actividad C.

Read the following conversation between Raquel and Elena Ramírez in the Barrio de Santa Cruz. **¿Dónde nos encontramos?** means *Where shall we meet?* Now that you know that, try to find the name of their meeting place.

1. Elena dice que van a encontrarse en
   a. _____ otra calle.
   b. _____ un café.
   c. _____ La Giralda.

ELENA: Yo voy por esta calle. Y Ud., vaya por ésa.
RAQUEL: Sí, sí. Pero... espere. ¿Dónde nos encontramos?
ELENA: En la Giralda... a las once y media.
RAQUEL: Sí, está bien, pero... ¿dónde está la Giralda?
ELENA: Allí, en aquella torre.
RAQUEL: De acuerdo. Y buena suerte.
ELENA: Gracias.

Now read the conversation again. Knowing that Raquel and Elena have arranged to meet, can you determine approximately at what time they will meet? *Hint*: Look for a number.

2. Elena y Raquel van a encontrarse aproximadamente
   a. _____ a las dos.
   b. _____ a las once.

... AFTER VIEWING

¿**T**ienes buena memoria?

¿QUÉ RECUERDAS?

Actividad A. Preguntas

Briefly answer the following questions about **Episodio 5**.

1. ¿Quién está en la plaza cuando Jaime encuentra a Osito? _____

2. ¿Cómo gana la vida (*earns a living*) el señor que habla con Jaime y Raquel? _____
   _____

3. ¿Por qué no trabaja los domingos este señor? _____

4. Raquel le compra algo a Jaime. ¿Qué compra? _____

5. ¿Cuándo sale Raquel para Madrid, el domingo o el lunes? _____

6. ¿Va Raquel a Madrid en coche, en avión o en tren? _____

7. ¿Quién está en la foto que Miguel le da (*gives*) a Raquel? _____

8. ¿Para quién es la foto? _____

Actividad B. ¡Busca el intruso!

For each group of names, places, or words below, underline the one that does not belong with the others.

1. la Giralda, el Hotel Doña María, el Alcázar, la Catedral de Sevilla

2. el cupón, O.N.C.E., el perro, la lotería

3. Teresa Suárez, Elena, Miguel padre, don Fernando

4. el restaurante, la cervecería, la estación de trenes, la pastelería

Actividad C. ¿Cierto o falso?

Indicate whether the following statements are **Cierto (C)** or **Falso (F)**.

C F 1. El ciego vende caramelos.
C F 2. Osito es el nuevo gato de Jaime.
C F 3. La O.N.C.E. es una organización que vende cupones de lotería en España.
C F 4. Antes de ir (*Before going*) a Madrid, Raquel va primero (*first*) a Barcelona.
C F 5. La foto que tiene Raquel es para Rosario.

ACTIVIDADES

Actividad A. Por la mañana

The events of the morning in Sevilla involve primarily three characters: Raquel, Jaime, and a new character, **el ciego**. On the next page, match those characters with the statements that describe them or indicate what they do in the video episode. ¡OJO! More than one name may be possible for each statement.

1. _____ Corre por las calles del barrio.

2. _____ Habla con un niño en la calle.

3. _____ Encuentra al perro en la Plaza de las Tres Cruces.

4. _____ Habla con el ciego.

5. _____ Vende cupones de la lotería.

6. _____ Necesita estar en la Giralda a las once y media.

7. _____ Dice que tener un perro es una gran responsabilidad.

8. _____ Compra caramelos.

9. _____ Se pierde.

10. _____ Entra en la Catedral.

Actividad B. Por la tarde y al día siguiente

All of the following events took place after everyone was found in **Episodio 5**, but . . . in what order did they occur? Put them in order, from 1 to 7.

a. _____ Raquel compra un billete en el Rápido (= un tren muy rápido).
b. _____ Desean visitar el Alcázar.
c. _____ Al día siguiente, llegan a la estación del tren.
d. _____ Desgraciadamente, el Alcázar está cerrado.
e. _____ Cenan en un restaurante elegante.
f. _____ El tren sale de la estación.
g. _____ Todos dicen adiós.

Nota cultural: Hablando de la hora...
(*Talking about time . . .*)

Although phrases in two languages may be roughly equivalent, cultural differences often make that correspondence less exact. For example, the Spanish phrase **de la tarde** does not exactly correspond to *in the afternoon*, the English equivalent offered above. Because lunch in Hispanic countries is generally served at 2:00 (or later) and dinner at 10:00 (or later), **la tarde** is often viewed as lasting until the dinner hour. Thus, in Spanish one speaks of **las ocho de la tarde**, which would be *8:00 in the evening* in English.

Another difference between English and Spanish time-telling systems is the more common use of the 24-hour clock in Hispanic countries. Note in the photo how the visiting hours for **La Giralda** are indicated. (When the time given is after 12:00 noon, simply subtract 12 to get the hour: 15:00 → 3:00 P.M.) Times in transportation schedules and TV listings are generally given using the 24-hour system.

Intercambio

In this activity, you will compare your class schedule with those of your classmates.

Paso 1

Using the chart below, write out your class schedule.

	lunes	martes	miércoles	jueves	viernes
8.00					
9.00					
10.00					
11.00					
12.00					
1.00					
2.00					
3.00					
4.00					
5.00					

Paso 2

Walking about the room, try to find at least three people who each have at least one class subject that you have. Also find out at what time your classmates have those classes. Keep track of the information in the chart from **Paso 1**.

MODELO: ¿Tienes una clase de biología? ¿Sí? ¿A qué hora?
¿Tienes una clase de arte? ¿No? Gracias.

Paso 3

Write out three statements about what you discovered.

MODELO: Mary y yo tenemos una clase de biología. Ella va a la clase a las 9.00 los martes y jueves pero yo voy a las 11.00 los lunes y miércoles…

_____

_____

_____

Más allá del episodio: Don Fernando Castillo Saavedra

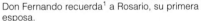
Don Fernando recuerda[1] a Rosario, su primera esposa.

Para su familia, don Fernando es una persona buena y generosa. Pero cuando era joven, era un hombre muy duro y ambicioso. Cuando llegó a México, después de[2] la Guerra Civil española, no tenía nada. En pocos años se convirtió en un gran industrial, pero… hay muchas personas que no tienen precisamente buenos recuerdos[3] de él.

Don Fernando adora a su familia. También le gusta mucho su papel[4] de patriarca de la familia. Tiene gran influencia sobre sus hijos.

Es curioso, pero don Fernando nunca habla de su pasado. Nace[5] en Bilbao, una ciudad en el norte de España. Se casa[6] muy joven con Rosario. Después de la boda, los dos viven en Guernica. Cuando comienza la Guerra Civil, Fernando es soldado del ejército[7] republicano. Después del bombardeo de Guernica, busca desesperadamente a Rosario, pero no la encuentra. Cree que Rosario está muerta. Por eso se va a Madrid y al final de la Guerra toma un barco con destino a México.

Don Fernando nunca le habló de Rosario a Carmen, su segunda esposa, ni[8] al resto de su familia. Pero Carmen siempre creyó que él tenía un gran secreto —¿un gran amor?— en España. Los hijos no sospechaban nada. Cuando don Fernando recibió una carta de España, decidió buscar a Rosario. Así[9] comenzó la búsqueda[10] de Raquel.

---

[1] *remembers* [2] *después… after* [3] *memories* [4] *role* [5] *He is born* [6] *Se… He marries* [7] *army* [8] *nor* [9] *Thus, In that way* [10] *search, quest*

¿Maestra?

The interactive CD-ROM to accompany *Destinos* contains additional practice with the video story line and will help you improve your skills in Spanish.

BEFORE VIEWING . . .

Preparación

VOCABULARIO

Los sustantivos

el bocadillo	sandwich (*Spain*)
el maestro/la maestra	grade-school teacher
el reportero/la reportera	reporter, journalist

Actividad A.

In previous episodes of *Destinos* you have followed Raquel's investigation to Spain. What do you remember about her investigation and trip? Select the correct statement in each group.

1. a. _____ En Sevilla, Raquel habla con uno de los hijos de Teresa Suárez.
    b. _____ En Sevilla, Raquel habla con Teresa Suárez.

2. a. _____ Raquel sale de Sevilla para Madrid.
    b. _____ Raquel sale de Madrid para Sevilla.

3. a. _____ Raquel va en avión.
    b. _____ Raquel va en tren.

Actividad B.

What do you think will happen in this video episode? Try to predict what will happen by answering the following questions.

1. Raquel will speak to this person on the train. Who do you think he is?
    _____ Es reportero.
    _____ Es el conductor del tren.

2. What do you think this person wants?
    _____ Desea entrevistar a Raquel.
    _____ Desea viajar con Raquel en su compartimiento.

Actividad C.

Here is part of a conversation that Raquel will have with someone on the train. Read through the conversation to get a general idea of what it is about.

—Aquí estoy en el Rápido de Sevilla a Madrid. Conmigo está la ganadora del premio especial de la Organización Nacional de Ciegos.
—¿La lotería?
—Ud. estará muy contenta de su buena suerte.
—Perdone, pero no sé de qué habla.
—Esta maestra de primaria es la Sra. Díaz. Su clase de sexto grado le compró un cupón y...

Now read the conversation again. **Su buena suerte** means *your good luck*. Now that you know that, can you guess the meaning of the words **ganadora** and **premio**?

1. La palabra **ganadora** significa
    a. _____ *a person who lives in Granada.*
    b. _____ *winner.*

2. La palabra **premio** significa
    a. _____ *primary.*
    b. _____ *prize.*

3. Based on your guesses so far, on the title of this video episode (called **¿Maestra?**), and on what you have learned in **Actividad C**, what do you think is happening?
    a. _____ El hombre cree que Raquel es otra persona.
    b. _____ El hombre sabe algo de don Fernando y busca más información, como Raquel.

. . . AFTER VIEWING

¿**T**ienes buena memoria?

¿QUÉ RECUERDAS?

Actividad A. Preguntas

Briefly answer the following questions about **Episodio 6**.

1. ¿Quién es Alfredo Sánchez? _____

2. ¿A quién busca Alfredo? _____

3. Raquel no quiere hablar con el reportero sobre su cliente. ¿Por qué? _____
    _____

4. ¿Adónde va Raquel cuando el tren llega a Madrid? _____

5. ¿Por qué hace una llamada (*makes a call*) Alfredo al final del episodio? _____
    _____

Actividad B. ¡Busca el intruso!

For each group of names, places, or words below, underline the one that does not belong with the others.

1. la reportera, la maestra, la abogada, la peseta
2. la lotería, el premio, la maestra, la novela
3. el bocadillo, el vino tinto, el reportaje, las aceitunas
4. don Fernando, el caso secreto, el premio, Raquel

Actividad C. ¿Cierto o falso?

Indicate whether the following statements are **Cierto (C)** or **Falso (F)**.

C F 1. Alfredo y José María son empleados (*employees*) del tren.
C F 2. Durante (*During*) el viaje a Madrid, Raquel lee una novela española.
C F 3. El reportero no encuentra a la persona que busca en el tren.
C F 4. En la estación de trenes en Madrid, Raquel toma un taxi a su hotel.
C F 5. Antes de tomar el taxi, Raquel llama a México por teléfono para hablar
         con Pedro.

ACTIVIDADES

Actividad A. Los nuevos personajes

The most important new character in this video episode appears to be the reporter. What do you remember about the interaction between him and Raquel? Complete the following statements. ¡OJO! There may be more than one right answer in some cases.

1. El reportero se llama... Federico Suárez / Alfredo Sánchez.
2. Alfredo cree que Raquel es... la ganadora de un premio / una reportera para la tele-
    visión / una maestra de primaria.

3. Alfredo... encuentra / no encuentra ...a la maestra de primaria durante este episodio.
4. Raquel... acepta / rechaza ...el interés que tiene el reportero en el caso de don Fernando.
5. El reportero... desea investigar más / acepta la negativa de Raquel.

Actividad B.   En este episodio

All of the following events took place during the trip shown in **Episodio 6**, but . . . in what order did they occur? Put them in order, from 1 to 4 in each group.

En el compartimiento de Raquel
a. _____ Raquel dice que no es la ganadora del premio.
b. _____ Un reportero desea entrevistar a Raquel.
c. _____ Raquel escribe en su computadora. Está sola.
d. _____ Otro señor entra en el compartimiento.

Luego
a. _____ Raquel dice que el caso es un secreto.
b. _____ El tren llega a la estación.
c. _____ El reportero pregunta mucho sobre el caso de Raquel.
d. _____ Raquel y el reportero comen algo.

En la estación del tren
a. _____ Raquel sale en taxi.
b. _____ Ve el sobre de la carta.
c. _____ El reportero acompaña a Raquel a un taxi.
d. _____ El reportero llama a su oficina.

Repaso de los Episodios 1–5

Actividad.   Resumen

Complete the following summary of the first five video episodes of *Destinos* with words from the following lists. ¡OJO! Not all of the words will be used.

Nombres: Jaime, don Fernando, Teresa Suárez, Miguel, Rosario, Ramón

Miembros de la familia: el esposo, el hijo, el hermano, el tío

Lugares: México, España, La Gavia, Sevilla, Madrid

Verbos: toma, investiga, vende, vive, compra, encuentra, saben

Otras palabras: algo, nada, siempre

En México, un hombre muy viejo está gravemente enfermo. Se llama _____.[1]

Este señor recibe una carta y la carta tiene un gran secreto. El señor revela el secreto a su familia: que su primera esposa, _____,[2] no murió en la Guerra Civil española.

Pedro, el _____[3] de don Fernando, llama a Raquel Rodríguez. Raquel va a viajar a _____,[4] a la ciudad de _____,[5] para buscar a _____,[6] la persona que escribió la carta. Pero la señora ya no _____[7] allí. Raquel habla con Elena Ramírez y con su _____,[8]

Miguel Ruiz, quien es también un _____⁹ de Teresa Suárez. Ellos no

_____¹⁰ nada de la historia de Rosario.

    El domingo Raquel acompaña a la familia al mercadillo de los animales. Los hijos de Miguel

y Elena quieren un perro y su padre _____¹¹ uno. ¿Y qué pasa? El perro se

escapa y _____¹² se pierde en las calles de Sevilla buscándolo. Raquel corre

por las calles también y finalmente _____¹³ a Jaime. Los dos hablan un poco

con un hombre ciego que _____¹⁴ cupones de la lotería.

    Por fin Raquel y Jaime se reúnen con el resto de la familia. Al día siguiente Raquel

_____¹⁵ un tren para Madrid. Allí vive la señora Suárez con otro hijo. Raquel

todavía no sabe _____¹⁶ de Rosario.

Para escribir

In this repeating section of the Student Viewer's Handbook you will practice writing. You will narrate events (at first, in the present and, eventually, in the past), describe people and events, and express opinions about many things.

    In this activity you will develop a written description of your family. You will be writing for someone who knows nothing about your family. Based on the description of your family, the reader should be able to draw an accurate representation of your family tree. The length of this first composition should be no more than 100 words.

Thinking About What You Will Write

As writers, we seldom plunge into the act of writing without first giving some thought to what we want to put on paper. In order to write this composition, think about what you want to say about your family. Who will you describe? What information about those people will you provide? Here is a partial list that you may use to check off the information you will include. You should also add any other ideas that you think would be important to include.

_____ immediate family only
_____ immediate and extended family
_____ in-laws
_____ pets
_____ names and ages
_____ information about where the person lives, works, or studies

Organizing Your Composition

Now that you have some idea of what you want to write, you should think about how you will organize your information. Here are several sequences that you may use to organize the information in your description. Which of the sequences do you prefer and why? Is a combination of sequences better than just one? Can you think of some other way(s) to organize the information?

1.   Begin with a brief overview of the family in general and then describe individual family members.
2.   Begin with the description of a particular family member and his or her relationship to you, then continue on to other family members.

3. Use the family members' ages as an organizing principle.
4. Begin with a description of yourself and then describe other family members.

Drafting

Paso 1
Now draft your compostion. At this stage, you should not worry too much about grammar and spelling. Your goal is to get your ideas down on paper.

Paso 2
After you have completed your draft, look over what you have done. Have you included all the information you wanted to include? Can the reader draw your family tree based on what you've written?

Finalizing Your Composition
If you are satisfied with the information contained in your draft, it is time to look it over for language and style.

Paso 1
Think about the tone and style of your writing. Have you avoided using personal statements such as "**Bobby es mi pariente favorito**" or have you included some of these statements in order to give the composition a bit more feeling? What do you think the reader would enjoy more?

Paso 2
Now review your composition to check for some of the grammar points you have learned in class thus far. Depending on the grammar you have learned, you may need to check for some of the following things:

*   Do your adjectives agree in number and gender with the nouns they modify?
*   Are all the endings on your verbs correct?
*   Have you omitted subject pronouns once the subject referent is established?

If you wish, you and a classmate may exchange drafts to review each other's language.

Paso 3
Prepare a clean final copy for your instructor.

Un viaje a Madrid (España)

La Plaza Mayor de Madrid

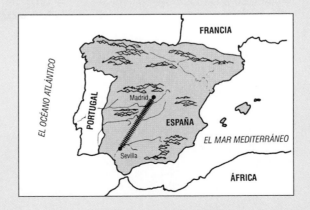

La cartera

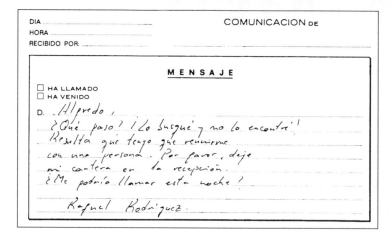

DIA	COMUNICACION DE
HORA	
RECIBIDO POR:	

M E N S A J E

☐ HA LLAMADO
☐ HA VENIDO

D. *Alfredo,*
¿Qué pasó? ¡Lo busqué y no lo encontré!
Resulta que tengo que reunirme
con una persona. Por favor, deje
mi cartera en la recepción.
¿Me podría llamar esta noche?

Rafael Rodríguez.

The interactive CD-ROM to accompany *Destinos* contains additional practice with the video story line and will help you improve your skills in Spanish.

BEFORE VIEWING . . .

Preparación

VOCABULARIO

Los verbos

dejar to leave (*something*) behind

pierde he/she loses

Los sustantivos

la cartera wallet
la habitación bedroom
el jersey sweater (*Spain*)

Actividad A.

In the last episode of *Destinos* Raquel left
Sevilla by train, on her way to Madrid to meet
Sra. Suárez. What happened on the train?
Indicate what you remember by identifying
these two men.

1. _____ Viaja con Raquel en su
   compartimiento.
2. _____ Es reportero de la televisión.

a.   b.

Now indicate whether the following statements
about **Episodio 6** are **Cierto (C)** or **Falso (F)**.

C F 1. El reportero cree que Raquel es otra persona.
C F 2. El reportero no sabe por qué Raquel está en España.
C F 3. El señor que viaja en el compartimiento con Raquel se llama Alfredo
          Sánchez.
C F 4. El reportero no tiene ningún interés en el caso que investiga Raquel.

Actividad B.

What do you think will happen in this episode of *Destinos?* Indicate whether the following events are **Probable (P)** or **Improbable (IMP)**.

P IMP 1. Raquel finalmente conoce a la Sra. Suárez.
P IMP 2. El reportero sigue a Raquel porque quiere saber algo más del caso.
P IMP 3. El reportero encuentra a la maestra que ganó el premio de la lotería.
P IMP 4. El reportero es persistente. Por fin Raquel le dice algo del caso que
             investiga.

Actividad C.

Here is one of the new characters you will meet in **Episodio 7**. Look at the photo and
read the brief description. Then indicate who you think the man might be.

Este hombre es de Sevilla, pero ahora vive en Madrid. Tiene dos hermanos. Uno vive en
Barcelona; el otro vive en Sevilla y es guía turístico. ¿Quién será?

1. _____ Es el asistente que trabaja con el reportero.
2. _____ Es el recepcionista del hotel donde se aloja Raquel en Madrid.
3. _____ Es un hijo de la Sra. Suárez; vive en Madrid con ella.
4. _____ Es el hijo de don Fernando y Rosario.

Actividad D.

Here is part of a conversation that Raquel will have with a bellhop (**un botones**) at her
Madrid hotel. Read through the conversation to get a general idea of what it is about.

BOTONES: ¡Qué pena lo de la cartera! Ojalá la encuentre pronto.
RAQUEL: Gracias. Un amigo está buscando el taxi ahora mismo. ¿Me puede hacer el favor
        de dejar un mensaje con el recepcionista?
BOTONES: Con mucho gusto, señorita.
RAQUEL: Cuando vuelva mi amigo, que me llame por teléfono.
BOTONES: ¿Y cómo se llama su amigo?
RAQUEL: Alfredo Sánchez. Bueno, realmente no es mi amigo. Es un reportero que
        conocí en el tren.

Now read the conversation again. **Dejar** means *to leave*. Now that you know that, can you guess the meaning of the word **mensaje**?

La palabra **mensaje** significa

a. _____ *messenger*.

b. _____ *message*.

Based on your guesses so far, on the title of this video episode, and on what you have learned in **Actividad D**, what do you think will happen to Raquel?

a. _____ Raquel pierde su cartera.

b. _____ Raquel encuentra la cartera de otra persona, una persona muy importante para el caso.

. . . AFTER VIEWING

¿Tienes buena memoria?

¿QUÉ RECUERDAS?

Actividad A. Preguntas

Briefly answer the following questions about **Episodio 7**.

1. ¿Qué cosa pierde Raquel en el taxi? _____

2. ¿Quién busca el taxi con el objeto perdido? _____

3. ¿Cómo se llama el hijo de Teresa Suárez que vive con ella en Madrid? _____

4. ¿Quién es el hombre que viajó (*traveled*) con Raquel en el tren? _____

5. ¿En qué hotel se aloja (*is staying*) ese hombre? _____

6. ¿Por qué va Alfredo Suárez al hotel de Raquel? _____

7. Hay otro hombre que espera a Raquel en la recepción del hotel. ¿Quién es? _____

_____

8. ¿Adónde va Raquel a cenar su primera noche en Madrid? _____

Actividad B. ¡Busca el intruso!

For each group of names, places, things, or actions, underline the one that does not belong with the others.

1. la Puerta de Alcalá, el Palacio de Comunicaciones, la Giralda, la Plaza de las Cibeles

2. Raquel Rodríguez, Mercedes Castillo, el Sr. Díaz, Alfredo Sánchez

3. una corbata, una blusa, una falda, un vestido

4. la habitación, el hotel, el botones, la cartera

5. hablar por teléfono, vender la lotería, dejar un mensaje, llamar a alguien (*someone*)

Actividad C. ¿Cierto o falso?

Indicate whether the following statements are **Cierto (C)** or **Falso (F)**.

C F 1. A Raquel no le gusta Madrid porque no es una ciudad muy bella *(beautiful)*.

C F 2. Raquel quiere invitar a Alfredo a tomar algo.

C F 3. Al final del episodio, Raquel recibe *(receives)* su cartera.

C F 4. Federico quiere invitar a Raquel a cenar en casa de él.

C F 5. Alfredo y Raquel no se ven *(see each other)* en el hotel esa noche.

ACTIVIDADES

Actividad A. ¿Quién... ?

In **Episodio 7** you met some new characters and there is some confusion about who is who! Show that you know the characters by matching the following characters with their brief description.

1. _____ Federico Ruiz   a. un reportero
2. _____ Alfredo Sánchez   b. otro hijo de la Sra. Teresa Suárez
3. _____ el Sr. Díaz   c. el botones que toma el mensaje de Raquel
                              d. un maestro de primaria

Now match the following characters with the statements that describe them or that relate what they do in the episode. ¡OJO! More than one name may be possible for each statement.

a. Federico Ruiz   d. Raquel Rodríguez
b. Alfredo Sánchez   e. Teresa Suárez
c. el Sr. Díaz

1. _____ Pierde su cartera.
2. _____ Encuentra la cartera perdida.
3. _____ Busca a Raquel en el hotel.
4. _____ Quiere conocer a Raquel.
5. _____ Está alojado/a en el Hotel Príncipe de Vergara.
6. _____ Espera a una persona en el hotel.

Actividad B. ¿Qué pasa?

At this point, you know more about what happened this evening at the Hotel Príncipe de Vergara than some of the characters do! Answer the following questions about the slightly confusing events that happened in **Episodio 7**.

1. ¿Por qué no recibe Raquel su cartera en este episodio?
   a. _____ Porque Alfredo dice que no puede llegar al hotel hasta mañana.
   b. _____ Porque Raquel no puede encontrar a Alfredo y decide irse con Federico.

2. ¿A quiénes confunde el botones cuando escribe la nota?
   a. _____ Confunde a Alfredo Sánchez con Federico Ruiz.
   b. _____ Confunde al Sr. Díaz con Alfredo Sánchez.

3. ¿Qué confusión hay con el Sr. Díaz en la recepción?
   a. _____ Creen que es una *señora*.
   b. _____ No tienen su reservación.

Nota cultural: La comida española

Tapas (Spanish *hors d'œuvres*) have recently become popular in the United States. Consequently, you probably weren't surprised to see a number of the characters in *Destinos* having **tapas**. Olives (**las aceitunas**) and portions of **tortilla española** are typical Spanish snacks; others include **jamón serra-no** (cured Spanish ham, similar to prosciutto) and **calamares fritos** (fried squid rings).

Having a snack and a drink of some kind in the late afternoon—a soft drink or mineral water, hot tea, an alcoholic beverage—is a popular Hispanic custom. In a previous episode you have seen some of the characters having **un fino** (a dry Spanish sherry), which can be accompanied by the toast **¡Salud!** (*To your health!*). As you will see, the specific food items and beverages for the afternoon snack vary from country to country.

Finally, note that places like **la Cervecería Giralda** from **Episodio 4** do not have the negative connotations they can have in other cultures. You may recall that Miguel and Elena's children accompanied their parents to the pub.

Intercambio

In this activity you will practice talking about clothing that you and your classmates wear.

Paso 1

Observe your classmates and their clothes. In the chart below, jot down the number of items of clothing you see in class today.

La ropa que llevamos hoy			
bluejeans	otros tipos de pantalones	faldas	vestidos
jerseys	sudaderas (*sweatshirts*)	camisas	camisetas
blusas	zapatos de cuero (*leather*)	zapatos de tenis	zapatos para correr (*running*)
zapatos de otro tipo	¿ ?	¿ ?	¿ ?

Paso 2

Write down the three most popular articles of clothing you have noticed. Then using the following phrases or others you can think of, prepare a statement about each to explain why they are so popular.

ser cómodo/a (*comfortable*)   durar (*to last*) mucho
ser barato/a (*inexpensive*)   ir bien con cualquier tipo de ropa
ser fácil de lavar (*wash*)   estar de moda (*in style*)

1. _____

2. _____

3. _____

Paso 3

Read your statements to the class. How many of your classmates say the same thing as you?

Más allá del episodio: Alfredo Sánchez

Un reportero que tiene grandes ambiciones

Alfredo Sánchez trabaja para la televisión española. Tiene todas las cualidades necesarias para ser un buen reportero: es una persona dinámica y ambiciosa... ¡y además[1] es muy curioso! Está siempre en busca de[2] un nuevo caso.

Alfredo es madrileño[3] y, para él, Madrid es la ciudad ideal para un reportero. Allí viven muchas personas importantes en la vida[4] política y artística de España. Siempre es posible encontrar algún escándalo o alguna intriga para hacer un buen reportaje.

A Alfredo le gusta mucho el periodismo,[5] pero en estos momentos se siente un poco frustrado en su vida profesional. Según[6] él, no avanza lo suficientemente de prisa[7] en su carrera. Su jefe[8] le ha prometido[9] un ascenso si puede conseguir una entrevista exclusiva con la maestra que ganó un premio en la lotería. Por otra parte, la revista[10] ¡Hola! también desea una entrevista exclusiva....

Alfredo tiene mucho interés en Raquel, en su viaje, en su cliente y en la persona que ella busca. Cuando ve el nombre Fernando Castillo en el sobre[11] que tiene Raquel, llama inmediatamente a un contacto que tiene. Desea saber más acerca de este señor Castillo. Ahora tiene un poco de información: Don Fernando Castillo Saavedra, un poderoso industrial mexicano que busca a una persona en España... ¿Será[12] una persona de su pasado? ¿una historia de amor? ¿una intriga internacional? Alfredo está seguro de que aquí hay algo interesante.... Pero ¿a quién le dará[13] su exclusiva, a la televisión o a la revista ¡Hola!?

[1]*besides* [2]*en... in search of* [3]*de Madrid* [4]*life* [5]*journalism* [6]*According to* [7]*no... he's not getting ahead quickly enough* [8]*boss* [9]*le... has promised him* [10]*magazine* [11]*envelope* [12]*Could it be* [13]*will he give*

El encuentro

The interactive CD-ROM to accompany *Destinos* contains additional practice with the video story line and will help you improve your skills in Spanish.

BEFORE VIEWING . . .

**reparación**

VOCABULARIO

Los verbos		Los sustantivos		Los adjetivos	
casar(se)	to get married	la guerra	war	agradecido/a	thankful
nace	he/she is born			segundo/a	second
				vivo/a	alive

Actividad A.

In the last video episode of *Destinos*, you watched a "comedy of errors" that occurred at Raquel's hotel. Things were lost, everyone was looking or waiting for someone else, and identities were confused. To be sure that you have understood the details, match these statements with the characters who made them.

a. Raquel Rodríguez   c. el Sr. Díaz
b. Federico Ruiz   d. Alfredo Sánchez

1. _____ «¡Huy! No encuentro mi cartera.»
2. _____ «No se preocupe. José María y yo se la vamos a buscar.»
3. _____ «Perdón. Hay un error. La tarjeta está a nombre de la Sra. Díaz.»
4. _____ «Ya he conseguido su cartera.»
5. _____ «Por ser tan amable, lo invito a tomar algo.»
6. _____ «Mi madre está muy agradecida y quiere invitarla a cenar con nosotros en casa esta noche.»

¡Un desafío! Can you also indicate with whom each character is speaking?

Actividad B.

The title of this episode, **El encuentro**, refers to the fact that Raquel will finally talk to Teresa Suárez. What questions is Raquel likely to ask her? Indicate whether it is **Probable (P)** or **Improbable (IMP)** that Raquel will ask these questions.

P   IMP   1. ¿Por qué vive Ud. ahora en Madrid?
P   IMP   2. ¿Dónde está Rosario ahora?
P   IMP   3. ¿Cuándo murió el Sr. Ruiz, su esposo?
P   IMP   4. ¿Cómo sabe Ud. que don Fernando fue el esposo de Rosario?
P   IMP   5. ¿Cómo se llama el hijo de Rosario y don Fernando?

Now formulate two more questions that Raquel might ask Sra. Suárez. How do you think Sra. Suárez will answer all of these questions?

Actividad C.

In this activity you will learn about some key words and phrases that will enhance your understanding of **Episodio 8**.

Paso 1

Read the following excerpt from Raquel's conversation with Teresa Suárez.

SRA. SUÁREZ: La última carta que recibí de ella fue cuando se casó de nuevo.
RAQUEL: ¿Se casó de nuevo?
SRA. SUÁREZ: Pues, sí. Rosario era muy atractiva... muy simpática. Y como creía que Fernando había muerto...
RAQUEL: Sí, sí. Lo comprendo. ¿Y con quién se casó?
SRA. SUÁREZ: Con un hacendado...

Now read the following sentences.

Don Fernando se casó con Rosario en 1935.
Don Fernando se casó con Carmen en 1942.
Teresa Suárez se casó con Juan Ruiz en 1941.

What do you think the phrase **se casó** means? If you guessed *got married*, you were right.

Paso 2
Look at this document, then answer the questions that follow.

This document is called **un certificado de nacimiento**. What kind of document do you think it is?

a. _____ an invitation to a function of some kind
b. _____ a letter
c. _____ a birth certificate
d. _____ a marriage license

Paso 3
As you know, Sra. Suárez is much older than Raquel. After Raquel has asked her questions, Teresa has a few of her own. Read this excerpt from their continuing conversation, and pay particular attention to the phrase **cuando yo tenía su edad**.

SRA. SUÁREZ: ¿Es Ud. pariente de Fernando?
RAQUEL: No. Soy abogada. La familia de él me pidió que investigara el paradero de Rosario.
SRA. SUÁREZ: Así que tampoco es amiga cercana de la familia...
RAQUEL: Realmente no. Conozco bien a Pedro, el hermano de don Fernando.
SRA. SUÁREZ: Una señorita como Ud. tan atractiva, bien educada... ¡Y abogada! Eso era casi imposible cuando yo tenía su edad. Y ahora es tan corriente.

Now answer the following question. What do you think Teresa means when she says **cuando yo tenía su edad**?

a. _____ When I met my husband . . .
b. _____ When I was your age . . .
c. _____ When I left my home . . .

. . . AFTER VIEWING

¿Tienes buena memoria?

¿QUÉ RECUERDAS?

Actividad A.   Preguntas
Briefly answer the following questions about **Episodio 8**.

1. ¿En qué ciudad nace el hijo de Rosario y don Fernando? _____

2. ¿Cómo se llama ese hijo? _____

3. ¿A qué país se va a vivir Rosario después de la Guerra Civil en 1939? _____

4. ¿Cómo se llama el segundo esposo de Rosario? _____

5. ¿Qué cosa le da la Sra. Suárez a Raquel para Rosario? _____

6. Raquel necesita algo de Sevilla. ¿Qué es? _____

7. ¿A qué país tiene que viajar Raquel ahora? _____

Actividad B.   ¡Busca el intruso!

For each group of names, places, and items, underline the one that does not belong with the others.

1. los edificios modernos, la ciudad cosmopolita, el centro político, la influencia árabe
2. Guernica, Madrid, Sevilla, Buenos Aires
3. Rosario, Teresa Suárez, Miguel Ruiz, Federico Ruiz
4. Carlos, Ángel, Federico, Ramón

Actividad C.   ¿Cierto o falso?

Indicate whether the following statements are **Cierto (C)** or **Falso (F)**.

C   F   1. Rosario y su hijo viven en Venezuela ahora.
C   F   2. Raquel tiene algo para la Sra. Suárez.
C   F   3. Don Fernando es el segundo esposo de Rosario.
C   F   4. Raquel va a visitar el taller de Federico al día siguiente.
C   F   5. Teresa Suárez no tiene noticias (*news*) nuevas de Rosario.

ACTIVIDADES

Actividad A.   ¿Quién lo hizo?

The following statements summarize the main events of **Episodio 8**. Who carried out each one? ¡OJO! More than one name may be possible for each statement.

¿Quién... ?

a. Raquel
b. Teresa
c. Federico

1. _____ Finalmente conoce a la Sra. Suárez.
2. _____ Hace varias preguntas.
3. _____ Dice que Rosario vive en la Argentina.
4. _____ Dice que don Fernando está en el hospital.
5. _____ Tiene una carta de Rosario.
6. _____ Toma un fino y cena.
7. _____ Cuenta la historia del perro perdido.
8. _____ Lleva a Raquel a su hotel.
9. _____ Llama a Elena Ramírez.
10. _____ Recibe un TELEX.

Actividad B. ¿Quién lo va a hacer?

In **Episodio 8** the character made a number of plans for the near and distant future. Indicate who is going to do each of the following by matching the names on the left with the plans on the right.

1. _____ Raquel
2. _____ el Sr. Díaz
3. _____ Federico
4. _____ Alfredo Sánchez

a. Va a conseguir un certificado de nacimiento.
b. Va a ver a Raquel mañana.
c. Va a darle una foto a la Sra. Suárez.
d. Va a visitar un taller de guitarras.
e. Tiene que viajar a la Argentina.
f. Va a visitar un museo famoso.
g. Va a darle una cartera a Raquel.

Actividad C. ¿Qué más sabes ahora?

Raquel is finally finding out something about Rosario.

Paso 1

Indicate which of the following pieces of information Teresa Suárez gives Raquel.

1. _____ el nombre del segundo esposo de Rosario
2. _____ el número de teléfono de Rosario
3. _____ la fecha en que Rosario se casó con don Fernando
4. _____ la dirección de Rosario en la Argentina
5. _____ el cumpleaños de Rosario
6. _____ el nombre del hijo de Rosario y don Fernando

Paso 2

Now complete the following version of Raquel's review. Choose words and phrases from this list.

murió	la Argentina	un hijo	se casó
no murió	México	una hija	no se casó

La Sra. Suárez me cuenta la historia de Rosario. Rosario _____[1] durante la Guerra Civil española. Tampoco murió don Fernando. Pero los dos creían que el otro había muerto. Rosario sí tuvo _____[2] llamado Ángel. Rosario y su hijo fueron a vivir a _____.[3] Allí Rosario _____[4] de nuevo. Su segundo esposo se llama Martín Iglesias.

Nota cultural: Nos podemos tutear

As you know, Raquel uses **usted** with people she does not know well. In this video episode of *Destinos*, however, you heard one speaker "negotiate" for a less formal way of speaking. Do you remember who that was? As you listen, try to determine the word the speaker uses to describe informal use.

The words Federico used to express *using **tú** with each other* were **tutearse** or **tratarse de tú**. If someone asks you to do that, you will want to begin addressing him or her by using the second-person singular verb forms, just as Raquel shifts from **trabaja** to **trabajas**.

When everyone was in Teresa's kitchen, Federico tried to make Raquel feel at home with a frequently used phrase: **Está en su casa**. Now that Federico and Raquel address each other with **tú**, he would say: **Estás en tu casa**.

I ntercambio

Paso 1

By now you have some ideas about Raquel. Using the interrogative words you know, make up five questions you would like to ask Raquel to find out more information about her. Use at least three different question words.

MODELO: ¿Por qué no tienes marido?

_____

_____

_____

_____

_____

Paso 2

Pass the questions to the person on your right. That person will try to answer those questions based on what he or she thinks of Raquel. You will answer questions from the person on your left. When you are finished, return the questions with answers to the person on your left.

Paso 3

One or two people will read their questions and answers out loud. If you have a similar question, raise your hand and tell the class how the person to your right answered. Are you all in agreement about Raquel and her life?

M ás allá del episodio: Rosario del Valle Iglesias

Rosario, la primera esposa de don Fernando

«**R**osario, ¿eres tú?» Don Fernando recuerda[1] a una joven y hermosa mujer... la persona con quien se casó hace muchos años.[2] Para Teresa Suárez, Rosario es una compañera... la buena amiga de su juventud[3]... la amiga que perdió después de la Guerra Civil.

Después del bombardeo de Guernica, Rosario buscó a Fernando desesperadamente por todas partes, pero no lo encontró. La casa, la oficina del banco, las casas de los amigos... casi todo el pueblo fue destruido. Finalmente tuvo que aceptar que Fernando murió.

¿Qué podía hacer? La ciudad estaba en ruinas y la Guerra Civil continuaba. Rosario estaba sola, embarazada,[4] sin familia ni amigos. Decidió alejarse[5] de Guernica y comenzó un largo y difícil viaje. Llegó a Sevilla y encontró una pequeña casa en el barrio de Triana. Allí conoció a Teresa Suárez, su vecina,[6] y se hicieron buenas amigas.

El hijo de Fernando que esperaba nació unos meses[7] después. Llamó al niño Ángel, por ser un rayo de esperanza en medio de su dolor.[8] Al terminar[9] la guerra, la vida[10] era muy difícil y Rosario no tuvo fuerzas para esperar tiempos mejores.[11] Decidió alejarse de nuevo, para olvidar el gran amor de su vida y la tragedia de su país. Y, lo más importante de todo, para empezar una nueva vida por su hijo. Pero... ¿adónde ir?

[1] remembers [2] hace... many years ago [3] youth [4] pregnant [5] to go far away [6] neighbor [7] unos... several months [8] por... because he was a ray of hope in the midst of her pain [9] Al... When . . . was over [10] life [11] tiempos... better times

Estaciones

The interactive CD-ROM to accompany *Destinos* contains additional practice with the video story line and will help you improve your skills in Spanish.

BEFORE VIEWING . . .

**reparación**

VOCABULARIO

Los verbos	**Los sustantivos**		**Los adjetivos**
recibir to receive	**la agencia de viajes**	travel agency	**increíble** incredible
	la estación	season	
	el invierno	winter	
	el otoño	autumn	
	la primavera	spring	
	el taller	shop (*for manufacturing or repair*)	
	el verano	summer	

Actividad A.

Episodio 8 was important in terms of the progress of Raquel's investigation. For the first time, Raquel has learned some concrete information about the case she is investigating. How much do you remember about the progress she made? Indicate whether the following statements are **Cierto (C)** or **Falso (F)**. If Raquel still does not know a particular piece of information, indicate **no se sabe todavía (NSS)**.

1. Raquel descubre que Rosario
    C F NSS   a. no murió en la guerra.
    C F NSS   b. no tuvo un hijo.
    C F NSS   c. se fue a vivir a la Argentina.
    C F NSS   d. nunca se casó de nuevo.
    C F NSS   e. murió en la Argentina.

2. Al final del **Episodio 8**, Raquel
    C F NSS   a. llama a Elena Ramírez.
    C F NSS   b. necesita saber la dirección de Rosario en Buenos Aires.
    C F NSS   c. quiere un certificado de nacimiento.
    C F NSS   d. tiene la cartera perdida.
    C F NSS   e. recibe una carta.

Actividad B.

At the end of the last video episode Raquel received a TELEX. What do you think the TELEX is about? Choose the description that best expresses your expectations.

```
GA
27063
08111
27063 NHBAM E
↵
27063 NHBAM E
27064 NHPVM E

     QUERIDA RAQUEL:
FERNANDO ESTA PEOR. ME URGE COMUNICARME CONTIGO.
 LLAMAME AL HOSPITAL INGLES 3-95-72-83

          SALUDOS, PEDRO
```

1. _____ Es un TELEX de Pedro. Le dice a Raquel que don Fernando está muy mal. Ella debe llamar a la familia Castillo inmediatamente.

2. _____ Es un TELEX de la oficina de Raquel en Los Ángeles. Ella tiene que volver a la oficina lo más pronto posible.

3. _____ Es un TELEX del hotel Doña María, en Sevilla. Tienen algunas cosas que Raquel dejó en el hotel.

. . . AFTER VIEWING

¿**T**ienes buena memoria?

¿QUÉ RECUERDAS?

Actividad A.   Preguntas

Briefly answer the following questions about **Episodio 9**.

1. ¿De quién es el TELEX que Raquel recibe en el hotel? _____

2. ¿Qué noticias hay en el telegrama? _____

3. ¿Qué cosa le da Alfredo a Raquel? _____

4. ¿Quién es la persona que ganó el premio de la lotería? _____

5. ¿Dónde compra Raquel el billete de avión (*plane ticket*)? _____

6.   Cuando es otoño en España, ¿qué estación es en la Argentina?   _____

7.   ¿Qué compra Raquel en El Corte Inglés?   _____

8.   ¿Cómo está don Fernando hoy, bien o mal?   _____

Actividad B.   ¡Busca el intruso!

For each group of items, underline the one that does not belong with the others.

1.   la estación del metro, la cartera, el mercado, la farmacia

2.   las tunas, las guitarras, los zapatos, los estudiantes universitarios

3.   el desayuno, el billete, la reserva, la agencia de viajes

4.   el invierno, la primavera, el verano, el taller

5.   amarillo, morado, otoño, verde

Actividad C.   ¿Cierto o falso?

Indicate whether the following statements are **Cierto (C)** or **Falso (F)**.

C   F   1.   Raquel va a viajar a Buenos Aires inmediatamente.
C   F   2.   Don Fernando ya murió.
C   F   3.   Raquel canta con los amigos de Federico.
C   F   4.   En la Argentina, la primavera empieza en el mes de septiembre.
C   F   5.   Raquel compra ropa para su viaje a la Argentina.

ACTIVIDADES

Actividad A.   ¿Quién lo hace?

Match the following events or actions from the video episode with the person or persons associated with them. ¡OJO! More than one character may be associated with each item.

a.   Teresa Suárez
b.   Raquel Rodríguez
c.   el Sr. Díaz
d.   Federico Ruiz
e.   Alfredo Sánchez

1.   _____ Va a un taller de guitarras para ver a Federico.
2.   _____ Le da algo a Raquel.
3.   _____ Escucha música.
4.   _____ Quiere saber más acerca de un caso interesante.
5.   _____ Revela la información correcta acerca de un caso.
6.   _____ Compra ropa.
7.   _____ Aprende algo acerca de un caso.
8.   _____ Va a una agencia de viajes.

Actividad B.   Problemas nuevos y viejos

In **Episodio 9** a number of situations either escalated or were resolved or averted. Did you catch the most important details about them?

Acerca de don Fernando

C   F   1.   Está en el hospital.
C   F   2.   Ya murió.
C   F   3.   Ahora está mucho mejor.

Acerca de «la maestra»

C   F   4.   La maestra que ganó el premio es maestro.
C   F   5.   El Sr. Díaz es el maestro.
C   F   6.   Alfredo ya no quiere saber la historia del cupón.

Acerca de Raquel

C   F   7.   No tiene reservación para la Argentina.
C   F   8.   No tiene ropa apropiada para la Argentina.

Nota cultural: Un café, por favor

When Raquel ordered coffee (**un café**, **nada más**), the waiter poured it immediately from the pot that he had in his hand. Raquel could also have ordered her coffee by saying **un café solo**.

The waiter had to return with Alfredo's order, which was somewhat different: **Y un café con leche, por favor.** In many parts of the Spanish-speaking world, very strong coffee (almost like espresso) is mixed with warm or hot milk (**leche**). The milk is served on the side and added by the customer, to his or her taste.

Intercambio

Paso 1

Using all the Spanish you know now, write six statements about what you do on a typical day.

MODELO: Trabajo por la tarde, después de mis clases.

_____

_____

_____

_____

_____

Paso 2

Using **Paso 1** as your base, interview people until you find someone who shares two or more activities with you. The person who finds someone with the most in common activities wins!

MODELO: ¿Trabajas por la tarde? ¿Sí? ¡Yo también!

Más allá del episodio: Teresa Suárez

La mujer que le escribió una carta a don Fernando

Teresa Suárez conoció a Rosario en Sevilla. Las dos vivían en el barrio de Triana. Se hicieron[1] amigas rápidamente. Teresa estaba recién casada[2] y podía comprender muy bien el dolor[3] de su amiga, que pensaba mucho en su esposo muerto. Con frecuencia cuidó al[4] pequeño Ángel mientras Rosario trabajaba.

Teresa nació[5] en Jerez de la Frontera, pero sus padres se trasladaron[6] a Sevilla cuando era pequeña. En Sevilla, conoció a Juan Ruiz, se casaron y tuvieron tres hijos. Teresa no estudió en la universidad y nunca trabajó fuera de[7] casa. Siempre se dedicó a la familia. Su esposo murió hace años[8] y desde entonces vive en Madrid.

Ahora que sus hijos son grandes,[9] su vida ha cambiado bastante.[10] Ya no ve con frecuencia a Julio, el hijo que vive en Barcelona. Desgraciadamente, Teresa no se lleva bien con[11] su esposa. A ella le gusta meterse en los asuntos de sus hijos, y eso no le gusta mucho a la esposa de Julio.

El hijo menor de Teresa, Federico, todavía vive con ella. Esto le gusta mucho porque Federico es su hijo favorito. También quiere mucho a Miguel y a su familia y los visita con frecuencia. Miguel y Jaime adoran a su abuela. Sobre todo les gustan las cenas deliciosas que les prepara: una paella exquisita, una tortilla de patatas sabrosa....

---

[1]Se... *They became* [2]recién... *recently married* [3]*pain* [4]cuidó... *she took care of* [5]*was born* [6]se... *moved* [7]fuera... *outside of* [8]hace... *some years ago* [9]*grown* [10]ha... *has changed a great deal* [11]no... *she doesn't get along with*

10

Cuadros

The interactive CD-ROM to accompany *Destinos* contains additional practice with the video story line and will help you improve your skills in Spanish.

BEFORE VIEWING . . .

reparación

VOCABULARIO

Los verbos

despedirse (i) (de) to say good-bye (*to*)
pasarlo bien/mal to have a good/bad time

Los sustantivos

la barba	beard
el consejo	(*piece of*) advice
el corazón	heart
el cuadro	painting
el museo	museum
el novio/la novia	boyfriend/girlfriend
el ojo	eye
el pelo	hair
el pintor/la pintora	painter
la tarjeta postal	postcard

Los adjetivos

alto/a	tall
bajo/a	short
delgado/a	thin
gordito/a	plump, fat

Actividad A.

During the last video episode of *Destinos*, several situations were "wrapped up" and others continued to develop. Indicate whether the following statements about the episode are **Cierto (C)** or **Falso (F)**.

C   F   1.   Don Fernando está muy mal; está ahora en el hospital.
C   F   2.   Raquel pierde su cartera de nuevo.
C   F   3.   Raquel necesita comprar ropa porque en la Argentina es otoño.
C   F   4.   Alfredo convence a Raquel de que el caso de don Fernando debe presentarse en la televisión.
C   F   5.   Elena llama a Raquel para decirle que no puede obtener el certificado de nacimiento de Ángel Castillo.

Actividad B.

In this video episode you will see Raquel's last night and day in Madrid. Based on what you learned in the last episode and on your intuition, what do you think she will do?

Sí   No   1.   ¿Va a ver a Alfredo y al Sr. Díaz una vez más?
Sí   No   2.   ¿Va a conocer a la novia de Federico?
Sí   No   3.   ¿Va a despedirse de la Sra. Suárez?

El título de este episodio es «Cuadros». ¿Qué lugar crees que Raquel va a visitar en este episodio?

4.   a.   _____ la casa de un artista
     b.   _____ un museo
     c.   _____ una galería de arte

Actividad C.

You have seen in other video episodes that Sra. Suárez has a tendency to comment on the actions of others. Read the advice she gives Raquel as they say good-bye. **El corazón** means *heart*.

SRA. SUÁREZ: Gracias, Raquel. Que tenga muy buen viaje.
RAQUEL: Gracias, señora.
SRA. SUÁREZ: Si vuelve otra vez a Madrid, ya sabe que aquí tiene unos amigos.
RAQUEL: Muchas gracias.
SRA. SUÁREZ: Y algo más. Hay algo más en la vida que el trabajo. Hay que dedicarle tiempo al corazón.

What kind of advice do you think Sra. Suárez is offering?

1.   La Sra. Suárez le da a Raquel consejos sobre

     _____ su vida profesional.   _____ su vida personal.

2.   Parece que la Sra. Suárez cree que Raquel piensa demasiado en

     _____ su trabajo.   _____ sus padres.

3.   La Sra. Suárez probablemente cree que Raquel debe buscar

     _____ más clientes.   _____ un novio.

. . . AFTER VIEWING

¿**T**ienes buena memoria?

¿QUÉ RECUERDAS?

Actividad A.   Preguntas
Briefly answer the following questions about **Episodio 10**.

1. ¿Cómo se llama la novia de Federico Ruiz? _____

2. ¿Qué tipo de baile (*dance*) enseña ella? _____

3. ¿Qué cosa le da Raquel a la Sra. Suárez? _____

4. ¿Qué consejo le da la Sra. Suárez a Raquel? _____

5. ¿Cómo se llama el museo que visita Raquel? _____

6. ¿A quién ve Raquel en el museo? _____

7. ¿Qué hace Raquel cuando está en el Parque del Retiro? _____

8. ¿Qué recibe Raquel cuando regresa al Hotel Príncipe de Vergara? _____

_____

Actividad B.   ¡Busca el intruso!
For each group of names or items that follows, underline the one that does not belong with the others.

1. El Greco, las figuras delgadas, las escenas religiosas, las escenas ordinarias

2. *Las Meninas*, Velázquez, las escenas religiosas, la familia real

3. las escenas horribles, el período negro, Goya, los ojos expresivos

4. Velázquez, Goya, Picasso, El Greco

Actividad C.   ¿Cierto o falso?
Indicate whether the following statements are **Cierto (C)** or **Falso (F)**.

C   F   1. A la Sra. Suárez no le gusta Osito.
C   F   2. Raquel, Teresa Suárez, Federico y su novia cenan juntos.
C   F   3. El período negro de Goya se caracteriza por las escenas horribles en sus cuadros.
C   F   4. Raquel no quiere pasar más tiempo en Madrid.
C   F   5. Raquel habla con Elena Ramírez por teléfono desde el hotel.

ACTIVIDADES

Actividad A. ¿Qué hicieron?

Indicate the statements that are true for each of the following characters you saw in **Episodio 10**.

Raquel

1. _____ por fin le da la foto de Miguel y Jaime a la Sra. Suárez.
2. _____ no ve al reportero y al Sr. Díaz otra vez.
3. _____ todavía no tiene el certificado de nacimiento de Ángel Castillo.

Federico

4. _____ tiene una novia que es pintora.
5. _____ no tiene la oportunidad de despedirse de Raquel.

La Sra. Suárez

6. _____ va con Raquel a la escuela de baile donde trabaja la novia de Federico.
7. _____ se despide de Raquel y le da un consejo.

Actividad B. El Greco y Velázquez

Look at the painting on the left of San Jerónimo by El Greco. Indicate the appropriate word or phrase in each pair. Now compare the painting of San Jerónimo with *Las Meninas*, on the right, by Velázquez. What physical differences do you notice between the people in the paintings?

3. con barba/
   sin (*without*)
   barba

4. de pelo corto, no largo/
   de pelo largo, no corto

1. alto/bajo

5. ojos expresivos/
   ojos tristes

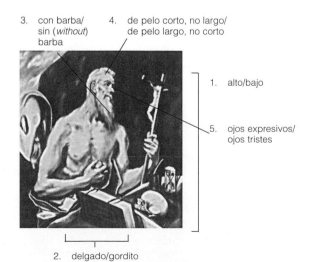

2. delgado/gordito

Las Meninas, Velázquez

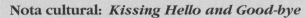

Nota cultural: *Kissing Hello and Good-bye*

In Spain, as well as in other parts of the Hispanic world, people frequently kiss hello and good-bye. This form of greeting is practiced by women with other women and by men with women, but not usually by men with other men.

As you have probably noticed in the video episode, in Spain the kiss is a double one. Women embrace lightly and touch cheeks, first one side, then the other, as they make a soft kissing sound. The same sequence can be followed by a man with a woman, depending on the closeness of the relationship between them. In this video episode, Raquel and Federico shake hands and embrace as they kiss, even though they do not know each other all that well.

In other parts of the Hispanic world a single kiss is more common. The question of whether or not to embrace is an individual one, depending on how comfortable one is with the other person.

Intercambio

In this activity, you will discuss physical traits of family members.

Paso 1

Interview someone in the class, asking questions about his or her mother's and father's physical traits. You may ask your instructor for help if you need it. (If your partner is an adopted child [**un hijo adoptivo/una hija adoptiva**] or does not remember his or her parents, ask him or her questions about family members he or she *does* know, even if they are of his or her adoptive family.)

descripción de la mamá	descripción del papá	¿otro miembro de la familia?

Paso 2

Now describe who your partner most closely resembles, the mother or the father (or another family member). Write up your reasons, using the following models. The verb phrase **se parece a** means *he/she resembles*.

MODELOS: _____ se parece más a su papá porque... En ciertas cosas, se parece a su mamá. Por ejemplo, ...

_____ no se parece ni a su mamá ni a su papá porque...

Más allá del episodio:
Manuel Díaz

Manuel Díaz, el maestro ganador del premio de la lotería.

Manuel Díaz es un maestro como muchos otros. Lleva una vida ordenada y sencilla.[1] Vive en un pequeño apartamento, con un gato muy viejo que se llama Tigre. Sigue desde hace años[2] la misma rutina y detesta las situaciones inesperadas.[3]

El Sr. Díaz es una persona muy reservada. No le gusta hablar de sí mismo.[4] Cuando está con personas que no conoce bien, prefiere hablar de temas generales. Vive solo[5] y tiene muchas manías. Su ropa, por ejemplo, tiene que estar siempre bien planchada,[6] y no soporta[7] la música moderna. Pero a pesar de[8] esas manías, es muy simpático, especialmente cuando se le conoce bien.[9]

A Manuel le gusta mucho la literatura. Ha leído[10] casi todos los clásicos por lo menos dos veces. También es apasionado del arte, especialmente de la pintura clásica. Sus pintores favoritos son Goya y Velázquez.

Hasta ahora, su único lujo[11] ha sido[12] la ópera. No se pierde ni[13] una representación. Ahora que tiene un poco de dinero, va a poder realizar finalmente uno de sus sueños.[14] Visitar los grandes teatros del mundo, como la Escala de Milán, el Metropolitano de Nueva York o el teatro Colón de Buenos Aires. ¿Ya tiene el viaje planeado? ¿Va a ver a Raquel en la Argentina?

---

[1]*simple* [2]*desde... for many years* [3]*unexpected* [4]*de... about himself* [5]*alone* [6]*ironed* [7]*no... he can't stand* [8]*a... in spite of* [9]*se... you get to know him well* [10]*Ha... He has read* [11]*luxury* [12]*ha... has been* [13]*No... He never misses even* [14]*dreams*

11

La demora

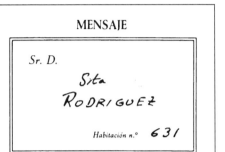

MENSAJE

Sr. D.

Sita
RODRIGUEZ

Habitación n.º **6 3 1**

The interactive CD-ROM to accompany *Destinos* contains additional practice with the video story line and will help you improve your skills in Spanish.

BEFORE VIEWING . . .

Preparación

VOCABULARIO

Los verbos	Los sustantivos	Los adjetivos
subir (a) to go up to (*a place*)	**la demora** delay	**cansado/a** tired
	el vuelo flight	

Actividad A.

As you know, the opening narration of each video episode consists of a summary of what happened in the previous episode. First read the following sentences that are based on the opening review in **Episodio 11**. Then indicate whether they are **Cierto (C)** or **Falso (F)**, based on what you remember about that episode.

C F 1. Raquel conoce a María, la novia de Federico.
C F 2. Cena con ellos y con la Sra. Suárez, pero no se despide todavía.
C F 3. Antes de salir para Buenos Aires, Raquel va al Museo del Prado.
C F 4. Allí ve algunas obras de artistas españoles muy importantes: El Greco, Murillo y Picasso.
C F 5. Al final de su visita al Museo del Prado, Raquel se encuentra con Alfredo y el Sr. Díaz.

C   F   6.   Cuando Raquel vuelve a su hotel, hay un mensaje para ella, de la agencia de viajes.

C   F   7.   Raquel trata de comunicarse con la agencia de viajes. Por fin puede hablar con ellos.

C   F   8.   Decide ir a la agencia para preguntar qué pasa con su reservación.

Actividad B.

Here is a message that the hotel receptionist will give to Raquel in this video episode. What problem is Raquel going to encounter, according to the message?

```
DIA ........................          COMUNICACION DE
HORA ......................          ........................................
RECIBIDO POR: .........          ........................................

                    M E N S A J E

☐ HA LLAMADO
☐ HA VENIDO

D.   Estimada Sta. Rodriguez :
        Sentimos Mucho Informarle Que Hemos Tenido
Problemas El Reservar Su Asiento En El Vuelo 897 Para
Buenos Aires , Haga El Favor De Llamarnos lo
Mas Pronto Posible   2-52-73-61

        Roberto Ruiz
        Agencia Aguila
```

_____ La agencia perdió su billete.

_____ La agencia no puede confirmar su reservación.

If you were Raquel, what would you do? Keep in mind that Raquel is a bit tired from all of her traveling and from all of the experiences she has had in the last few days.

Yo creo que

a. _____ Raquel debe ir directamente al aeropuerto. Allí puede tomar un café y esperar su vuelo.

b. _____ Raquel debe preguntarle al recepcionista si ella puede subir a su habitación.

c. _____ Raquel debe visitar otros lugares interesantes o históricos, por ejemplo, otros museos.

. . . AFTER VIEWING

¿Tienes buena memoria?

¿QUÉ RECUERDAS?

Actividad A.   Preguntas

Briefly answer the following questions about **Episodio 11**.

1.   ¿Qué pasa con el vuelo de Raquel a Buenos Aires? _____

2.   ¿A qué hora va a salir el vuelo? _____

3.   ¿Qué hace Raquel cuando regresa al hotel? _____

Actividad B.   ¡Busca el intruso!

For each group of names or items that follows, underline the one that does not belong with the others.

1.   el reportero, el maestro, el hotel, la abogada

2.   el maestro, el Sr. Díaz, el cupón de lotería, Raquel

3. la habitación, el hotel, el tren, el botones
4. la guitarra, Elena Ramírez, el certificado de nacimiento, Raquel
5. la demora, el botones, el vuelo, el billete

Actividad C.   ¿Cierto o falso?
Indicate whether the following sentences are **Cierto (C)** or **Falso (F)**.

C F 1. Raquel habla con Rosario en Madrid.
C F 2. Alfredo Sánchez habla con la maestra en Madrid.
C F 3. El vuelo de Raquel tiene una demora de diez horas.
C F 4. Raquel duerme la siesta (*takes a nap*) en el hotel.
C F 5. En la Argentina Raquel espera encontrar a Rosario y a su hijo.

ACTIVIDADES

Actividad A.   En este episodio

All of the following events took place during Raquel's last few hours in Madrid, but . . . in what order did they occur? Put them in order, from 1 to 6.

Raquel
a. _____ Descansa unas horas.
b. _____ Se entera de que hay una demora.
c. _____ Va a la agencia de viajes para resolver el problema.
d. _____ Se despierta cuando suena el teléfono.
e. _____ Va al aeropuerto y sale para la Argentina.
f. _____ Vuelve al hotel y sube a su habitación.

Actividad B.   ¡Un desafío!
¿Tienes una memoria muy buena? Can you recall any of these details from this video episode and previous ones?

1. ¿Cómo se llama el hotel de Raquel en Madrid? _____

2. ¿Cuál es el número de la habitación de Raquel? _____

3. ¿Qué cosa le da Raquel a la Sra. Suárez? _____

4. ¿Qué cosa le da la señora a Raquel? _____

5. ¿A qué hora sale el vuelo de Raquel para la Argentina? ¿Y cuál es el número del

    vuelo? _____

Repaso de los episodios 7–10

Actividad A.   El sueño de Raquel: Primera parte
Complete the following summary of the first part of Raquel's dream with words from the following lists. ¡OJO! Some words will be used more than once. Others may not be used at all.

Verbos: buscar, conocer, creer, dar, deber, decir, empezar, encontrar, ir, llegar, poder, revelar, salir, tomar, volver

Cosas: la cartera, la corbata, el mensaje

Personas: el botones, el cliente, el recepcionista, el reportero

Otras palabras: pero, porque, pronto

Después de volver al hotel, Raquel sube a su habitación y toma una siesta. Mientras duerme, _____[1] a soñar con lo que ha pasado desde que salió de Sevilla.

Primero, toma el tren de Sevilla a Madrid. En el tren, _____[2] a dos señores. Uno se llama Alfredo Sánchez y es _____[3] de televisión. Alfredo _____[4] a una maestra para entrevistarla. Alfredo _____[5] que Raquel es la maestra, pero Raquel le _____[6] que no, que está equivocado. En el coche-comedor del tren, Alfredo _____[7] a hacerle preguntas a Raquel acerca de su investigación, pero Raquel no _____[8] nada del caso.

Cuando por fin llega a su hotel en Madrid, Raquel descubre que ha dejado su _____[9] en el taxi. Alfredo y su asistente _____[10] a buscarla. Por fin (ellos) la _____,[11] pero Raquel no está cuando ellos _____[12] al hotel.

Al día siguiente, Raquel y Alfredo se encuentran en el hotel y Alfredo le _____[13] al Raquel el objeto perdido. Mientras _____[14] un café, Alfredo intenta convencer a Raquel una vez más de que el caso de don Fernando _____[15] ser muy interesante para un reportaje de televisión. _____[16] Raquel le dice que no, que ella _____[17] respetar el secreto profesional de su _____.[18]

Actividad B. El sueño de Raquel: Segunda parte

Choose the appropriate completion for each sentence.

Raquel también sueña con la Sra. Suárez.
1. Raquel va a la casa de la Sra. Suárez porque
    a. _____ la Sra. Suárez la llama por teléfono y la invita.
    b. _____ el hijo de la Sra. Suárez va al hotel y la invita.
2. Durante la conversación con la Sra. Suárez, Raquel se entera de que, después de la guerra, Rosario se fue a vivir a
    a. _____ Sevilla.
    b. _____ la Argentina.
    c. _____ México.
3. La Sra. Suárez también le dice a Raquel que Rosario
    a. _____ se casó de nuevo con un rico hacendado.
    b. _____ se casó de nuevo con un político importante.
4. Según (*According to*) Teresa Suárez, don Fernando y Rosario tuvieron
    a. _____ un hijo.
    b. _____ una hija.

5. Según la dirección que tiene Raquel, Rosario vive
   a. _____ cerca de Buenos Aires.
   b. _____ cerca de Bariloche.

Para escribir

In this activity you will write a short narration in which you describe your daily routine to someone who is not familiar with it. You want to tell the reader as much as you can about what you do and also include some interesting information about yourself. Your narration should be no fewer than 150 and no more than 250 words long.

Thinking About What You Will Write

In order to write this narration, the first thing you must do is to think about what daily activities you will include. Make a list of verbs that have to do with your daily routine. You will not necessarily use them all in your narration, but that is OK. For the moment, you are just trying to create a bank of ideas from which to draw.

Organizing Your Thoughts

Now think about the order in which you will present your daily routine. You will probably choose a chronological order. What kind of day will you describe? A weekday on which you go to the university or to work? A Saturday or Sunday on which your routine may be substantially different from that of weekdays?

Drafting

Paso 1

Now draft your narration. At this stage, you should not worry about grammar and spelling. Your goal is to get your ideas down on paper.

Paso 2

After you have completed your draft, look over what you have done. Are you still satisfied with the activities you selected? Do you want to add some and delete others? Do you want to go into more detail about some aspects of your routine? Have you included at least one interesting detail about yourself or your life? Keep in mind that you are writing for someone who doesn't know anything about you.

Finalizing Your Narration

If you are satisfied with the information contained in your draft, it is time to look it over for language and style.

Paso 1

First, look at your narration for style. Does the narration flow, or is it disjointed and choppy? Does it contain words and phrases that connect events, or is it mostly an accumulation of sentences?

Here is a list of words and phrases that can help make your narration flow more smoothly.

también	also	**por eso**	that's why; therefore
pero	but	**y**	and

These words and phrases can help you express the sequence of events in your routine smoothly.

primero	first	**por la mañana**	in the morning
luego	then, next	**por la tarde**	in the afternoon
después	later (on)	**por la noche**	in the evening
por fin	finally		

Paso 2

Review your composition for the following language elements as well.

- Gender of nouns
- Adjective agreement
- Agreement of subjects and verbs

Paso 3

Prepare a clean copy of the final version of your narration for your instructor.

Un viaje a la Argentina

El Obelisco de Buenos Aires conmemora la fundación de la ciudad.

67

12

Revelaciones

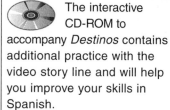

The interactive CD-ROM to accompany *Destinos* contains additional practice with the video story line and will help you improve your skills in Spanish.

BEFORE VIEWING . . .

Preparación

VOCABULARIO

Los verbos		Los sustantivos	
desaparecer (desaparezco)	to disappear	**el ataque cardíaco**	heart attack
mudarse	to move (*from one residence or city to another*)	**la estancia**	ranch
		el marinero	sailor
		el medio hermano	half brother
		el padrastro	stepfather

Actividad A.

In the last video episode of *Destinos* Raquel left Madrid by plane, on her way to Buenos Aires to continue her search for Rosario. Indicate whether the following statements about the events immediately preceding her departure are **Cierto (C)** or **Falso (F)**.

C   F   1.   Raquel pierde su vuelo.

C   F   2.   Hay una demora y el vuelo no sale cuando debe.

C   F   3.   Raquel habla con don Fernando por teléfono.

C F   4. Raquel se duerme en su habitación.
C F   5. Piensa en el consejo de la Sra. Suárez.
C F   6. Sabe dónde Rosario vive en la Argentina.

Actividad B.

Here are photographs of some of the places and events you will see in **Episodio 12**. What do you think is happening in each?

1. Raquel está en
    a. _____ un parque.
    b. _____ un cementerio.
    c. _____ una estancia.

2. Toma una fotografía de
    a. _____ Rosario.
    b. _____ un monumento.
    c. _____ una tumba.

3. Raquel toca a la puerta en
    a. _____ una estancia.
    b. _____ una casa en Buenos Aires.

4. La persona que contesta es
    a. _____ Martín Iglesias.
    b. _____ Rosario.
    c. _____ una persona desconocida.

. . . AFTER VIEWING

¿**T**ienes buena memoria?

¿QUÉ RECUERDAS?

Actividad A.   Preguntas

Briefly answer the following questions about **Episodio 12**.

1. ¿Qué problema tiene Raquel al llegar al Hotel Alvear? _____

    _____

2. ¿Cuánto cuesta por día la habitación de Raquel en el Hotel Alvear? _____

3. ¿Por qué va Raquel a la estancia? _____

4. ¿Cómo se llama el gaucho que Raquel conoce? _____

5. ¿Cómo se llama el segundo hijo de Rosario? _____

6. ¿Qué profesión tiene él? _____

7. ¿Está viva Rosario o ya murió? _____

8. ¿Dónde está Ángel Castillo del Valle ahora? _____

Actividad B.   ¡Busca el intruso!

For each group of names, places, or items, underline the one that does not belong with the others.

1. $200 por día, la estancia Santa Susana, la suite, la habitación doble

2.   la Casa Rosada, la estancia Santa Susana, la música folklórica, los gauchos

3.   el médico, el gaucho, el dentista, el psiquiatra

4.   Rosario del Valle Iglesias, Martín Iglesias, Ángel Castillo, Raquel Rodríguez

Actividad C.   ¿Cierto o falso?

Indicate whether the following statements are **Cierto (C)** or **Falso (F)**.

C   F   1.   La ciudad de Buenos Aires es un puerto marítimo.
C   F   2.   Rosario vive en Buenos Aires.
C   F   3.   A Ángel Castillo le gustaba (*liked*) estudiar ciencias económicas.
C   F   4.   El segundo hijo de Rosario sabe dónde vive su hermano.
C   F   5.   Raquel necesita la ayuda de un psiquiatra ahora.

ACTIVIDADES

Actividad A.   ¿Quién es?

In **Episodio 12** you met these new characters. Identify them and tell where they work, then indicate why they are important to Raquel's investigation.

1.   Este hombre se llama
     a.   _____ Cirilo.   b.   _____ Francisco.   c.   _____ Esteban.
2.   Es
     a.   _____ botones.   b.   _____ chofer.   c.   _____ gaucho.
3.   Trabaja en
     a.   _____ el hotel.   b.   _____ Buenos Aires.   c.   _____ la estancia
                                                                         Santa Susana.
4.   Es un personaje importante porque
     a.   _____ le dice a Raquel que Rosario se mudó a la capital y le da su dirección.
     b.   _____ le dice a Raquel que Rosario ya murió.

5.   Este hombre se llama
     a.   _____ Enrique Casas.   b.   _____ Ángel Castillo.   c.   _____ Arturo Iglesias.
6.   Es
     a.   _____ profesor.
     b.   _____ médico (psiquiatra).
     c.   _____ abogado.
7.   Trabaja en
     a.   _____ su casa.   b.   _____ el hotel.   c.   _____ la universidad.
8.   Es un personaje importante porque
     a.   _____ quiere ayudar a Raquel a buscar a Rosario.
     b.   _____ es hijo de Rosario y medio hermano de Ángel Castillo.

Actividad B.   La historia de Ángel

As you know, Raquel has learned that Rosario has died. Her investigation must continue, however, and Arturo is willing to share information with her. The following events all form part of Ángel's story as told by Arturo, but . . . in what order did they occur? Put them in order, from 1 to 7. *Note:* All of the verbs are in the past tense.

a. _____ Martín murió de un ataque cardíaco.
b. _____ Ángel dejó los estudios y se dedicó a pintar.
c. _____ Ángel discutió con su padrastro.
d. _____ Martín, Rosario y el joven Arturo fueron a Buenos Aires para visitar a Ángel.
e. _____ Martín y Rosario supieron (*found out*) algo que no le gustó a Martín.
f. _____ Ángel se embarcó como marinero.
g. _____ Ángel se fue a la capital para estudiar ciencias económicas.

Nota cultural: The *vos* forms

In some countries, particularly in Argentina, Uruguay, and most of Central America, the pronoun **vos** is used instead of **tú**. Most verb forms used with **vos** are the same as the **tú** verb forms. However, in the present tense the endings **-ás**, **-és**, and **-ís** are generally used: **trabajás**, **comés**, **vivís**. Stem vowels do not change: **podés**, **querés**, **dormís**.

> Y vos, ¿qué **querés** hacer esta tarde?
> ¿**Vivís** en México?

Just as you heard **vosotros** forms in Spain, when Spaniards addressed each other, you will hear **vos** forms in the video episodes that take place in Argentina and whenever Argentine characters are talking.

Intercambio

In this activity, you will talk about Raquel's and your instructor's past activities.

Paso 1
What do you think your instructor and Raquel (or another *Destinos* character) have both done in the past? What have they done differently? Write six statements in which you talk about their past activities. Note: You are not expected to know about Raquel's or your instructor's pasts; your statements only need to be plausible.

> MODELO: Raquel estudió en la Universidad de California, Los Ángeles. Pero mi profesor(a) estudió en la Universidad de Wisconsin.

Paso 2
In groups of three, share your statements. Of all the statements, select eight that you like the most.

Paso 3
Each group should read its statements out loud. Your instructor will respond accordingly. Who seems to know more about your instructor? Is everyone in agreement about the plausibility of statements about Raquel?

Más allá del episodio: Martín Iglesias

Martín Iglesias, poco antes de morir

Martín Iglesias tenía[1] una estancia próspera en su país, la Argentina. Cuando terminó la Guerra Civil española, Martín era joven y muy trabajador.[2] Vio en España una gran oportunidad. Pensó que los productos de su estancia tendrían[3] un buen mercado allí. Por eso se fue a España, primero a Madrid y luego a Barcelona.

Martín tenía también otro motivo para viajar a España. Quería buscar a una hermana de su madre que vivía en Sevilla. Sólo tenía una vieja dirección y el nombre del hospital en que su tía trabajaba antes de la guerra. Llegó a la casa de la dirección, pero nadie conocía a esa señora. Uno de los vecinos[4] le dio la dirección del hospital. Fue allí, en ese mismo hospital, donde Martín conoció a Rosario.

Rosario ayudó a Martín a buscar a la hermana de su madre. Desde el principio[5] a Rosario le gustó mucho la manera de ser del argentino. También comprendió muy bien su búsqueda.[6] ¡Ella sabía mucho de búsquedas imposibles! Desgraciadamente, después de varios días, descubrieron que la tía de Martín había muerto. Su familia vivía ahora en el sur de Francia.

Martín ya no tenía motivos para estar más tiempo en Sevilla. Empezaba a hacer los preparativos para regresar a la Argentina. Y pasaba mucho tiempo —todo el tiempo que podía— con Rosario.

Martín era muy serio y algo estricto, pero tenía un gran corazón. Rosario le habló de sus cosas, de su pasado,[7] de su hijo... y Martín la escuchó con atención. Comprendió que el corazón de su amiga estaba lleno de dolor.[8] Ella no podía olvidar... todavía. Pensó que un gran cambio[9] sería una buena idea. Martín le habló mucho de su país y de su familia. Trató de[10] convencerla. «Estoy seguro[11] de que podés rehacer[12] tu vida en la Argentina» le repetía varias veces. «Te vas a sentir como en casa.»

Por fin Martín tuvo que volver. Rosario pensó mucho en las cosas que Martín le había dicho.[13] Por fin decidió irse a la Argentina, con su hijo. Le escribió una larga carta a Martín y se embarcó. Cuando llegó a Buenos Aires, Rosario no pudo contener las lágrimas[14] cuando vio a Martín. Por primera vez en mucho tiempo lloraba de alegría.[15] Pero ¿cómo reaccionó Ángel? ¿Le gustó la Argentina? ¿Aceptó a Martín?

---

[1] *had* [2] *hardworking* [3] *would have* [4] *neighbors* [5] *Desde... From the beginning* [6] *search, quest* [7] *past* [8] *estaba... was filled with pain* [9] *change* [10] *Trató... He tried to* [11] *sure* [12] *remake, make over* [13] *le... had told her* [14] *no... couldn't hold back her tears* [15] *lloraba... she was crying for joy*

13

La búsqueda

The interactive CD-ROM to accompany *Destinos* contains additional practice with the video story line and will help you improve your skills in Spanish.

BEFORE VIEWING . . .

Preparación

VOCABULARIO

Los verbos		Los sustantivos		Los adjetivos	
almorzar (ue)	to have lunch	**el barco**	boat	**fresco/a**	fresh
comenzar (ie)	to begin	**la búsqueda**	search		
comer	to eat	**el puerto**	port		
probar (ue)	to try; to taste	**la tienda**	store		
reconocer (reconozco)	to recognize				
recordar (ue)	to remember				

Actividad A.

Indicate whether the following events took place (**Sí, ocurrió**) or not (**No, no ocurrió**) in the previous episode.

Sí No 1.   No hay habitación para Raquel en el hotel de Buenos Aires.

Sí No 2.   En la estancia, un joven le dice a Raquel que Rosario murió hace años.

Sí No 3.   Un gaucho le dice que Rosario se mudó a la capital.

Sí No 4. Con el chofer, Raquel busca un número en la calle Gorostiaga.
Sí No 5. En una casa, Raquel conoce a un amigo de Rosario.
Sí No 6. Arturo le da a Raquel la nueva dirección de Rosario y de su hermano Ángel.

Actividad B.

As you prepare to watch this video episode, think about its title, **La búsqueda**. What does the title suggest to you? What does a search for a person entail? Indicate the most logical completion for the following sentences.

1. Mientras buscan a Ángel, Raquel y Arturo
    a. _____ hablan con muchas personas.
    b. _____ hablan con pocas personas.

2. Raquel y Arturo comienzan la búsqueda
    a. _____ en la estación central de policía de Buenos Aires.
    b. _____ en el lugar donde Arturo vio a su hermano por última vez.

3. Las personas que van a saber algo de Ángel, probablemente, son
    a. _____ los dependientes y dueños de negocios.
    b. _____ los viejos marineros.

Actividad C.

In this video episode, Raquel and Arturo will meet a man who is suspicious of strangers. Read part of their conversation, trying to get the gist of it. Then indicate which of the following sentences is an accurate summary of the conversation.

a. _____ José cree que Héctor es el hermano de Arturo.
b. _____ José no conoce a Ángel pero sí sabe el nombre de una persona que posiblemente lo conoció.

SEÑOR: Yo soy José, sí, señor.
ARTURO: Disculpe la molestia. Mario nos dijo que tal vez Ud. puede conocer a Ángel Castillo, mi hermano.
SEÑOR: ¿Ángel Castillo?
ARTURO: Sí, es mi hermano. Perdimos contacto hace muchos años. Tenía amigos acá. Pintaba. Le gustaban los barcos.
SEÑOR: Lo siento. No lo conozco. ¿Ya hablaron con Héctor?
ARTURO: No. ¿Quién es?
SEÑOR: Sí. Tienen que hablar con Héctor. Él ha vivido siempre en este barrio. Conoce a todo el mundo. Seguro que conoció a su hermano.
RAQUEL: ¿Y dónde podemos encontrar a Héctor?

José is suspicious. For this reason, it is likely that he does not trust strangers. What do you think will happen after Raquel asks her question?

a. _____ José les da la dirección de Héctor en seguida.
b. _____ José piensa un momento y luego les da la dirección de Héctor.
c. _____ José les dice que él va a buscar a Héctor.
d. _____ José no quiere darles más información.

. . . AFTER VIEWING

¿**T**ienes buena memoria?

¿QUÉ RECUERDAS?

Actividad A.   Preguntas

Briefly answer the following questions about **Episodio 13**.

1.   ¿Qué cosa tiene Arturo cuando llega al hotel de Raquel? _____

2.   ¿Dónde comienzan su búsqueda Raquel y Arturo? _____

3.   ¿Qué les dice la señora de la tienda a Raquel y Arturo? _____

_____

4.   ¿Qué son australes? _____

5.   ¿Quién es José y dónde lo encuentran Raquel y Arturo? _____

_____

6.   ¿Cuándo van a hablar Raquel y Arturo con Héctor? _____

7.   ¿Por qué llama Raquel por teléfono a México? _____

_____

8.   ¿Adónde van a cenar Raquel y Arturo esa noche? _____

Actividad B.   ¡Busca el intruso!

For each group of names, places, or items, underline the one that does not belong with the others.

1.   la Pampa, el Chaco, la Patagonia, la Amazonia

2.   Héctor, Ángel, Arturo, José

3.   el salmón, los langostinos, los calamares, los mejillones

4.   el barco, el marinero, el austral, el puerto

Actividad C.   ¿Cierto o falso?

Indicate whether the following statements are **Cierto (C)** or **Falso (F)**.

C   F   1.   Ángel Castillo está en el Brasil ahora.
C   F   2.   El hombre de la pescadería no conoce a Ángel.
C   F   3.   Héctor es amigo de José.
C   F   4.   En el restaurante La Barca, Raquel y Arturo comen brochettes.
C   F   5.   Cuando Raquel llama a México, habla con don Fernando.

ACTIVIDADES

Actividad. ¿Quiénes son? ¿Y qué hicieron?

Paso 1

As you probably predicted, Arturo and Raquel talk to a number of people in the course of their search for Ángel. Based on what you have seen in this video episode, who is the one person most likely to lead them eventually to Ángel?

a. _____ José, el marinero
b. _____ la dependienta de la tienda de comestibles
c. _____ Mario, el dueño de la tienda de antigüedades
d. _____ el vendedor de pescado
e. _____ Héctor, otro marinero
f. _____ doña Flora, la esposa de José
g. _____ Arturo

Paso 2

Now indicate which of the people in **Paso 1** made the following contributions to the search for Ángel.

1. _____ Mencionó a la señora del negocio de al lado. ¿Por qué? Ella conoce a todo el mundo.
2. _____ Pensó en José. Llevó a Raquel y Arturo a la casa donde vive con su esposa.
3. _____ Encontró una foto de Ángel a los veinte años.
4. _____ Atendió a una clienta. Luego miró la foto varias veces pero no reconoció a Ángel.
5. _____ Mencionó dos lugares donde podían encontrar a José, en el bar o en el barco.
6. _____ Buscó a Héctor y sabe dónde va a estar mañana por la noche.

Paso 3

Select the statement that best describes what the next step in the search for Ángel will be.

a. _____ Héctor va a ir a la casa de Arturo.
b. _____ Arturo y Raquel van a buscar a Héctor en una fiesta.
c. _____ José va a hablar con Héctor para ver si conoce a Ángel.

Nota cultural: ¿Cómo se dice... ?

As you have already learned, the names for some foods are different in different parts of the Spanish-speaking world. Listen again as Arturo and Raquel discuss what Arturo is going to prepare for dinner.

Did you notice that, as they discuss the main course, Arturo and Raquel use slightly different words to describe it? Arturo uses a more French pronunciation, **unas brochettes**, while Raquel uses the term more frequently used in most of the Spanish-speaking world, **las brochetas**. Neither term is more "correct" than the other; they are merely different. You will find out what **brochetas** are in the next video episode.

You should also note that neither Arturo nor Raquel is confused or upset by the difference in terminology. Spanish is an international language, and there are differences in pronunciation, in vocabulary, and in usage throughout the Spanish-speaking world. These differences do not generally make communication difficult.

Intercambio

In this activity, you will talk about things you might have done in the past.

Paso 1

Describe four activities from the following list that you have (supposedly) done in the past. You may add information to the phrase and expand on the idea if you like. Make sure at least one of the activities is *not* true. Embellish where you can!

MODELO: Una vez comí ostras crudas (*raw*). ¡Qué deliciosas!

1. preparar langosta
2. pescar (*to fish*) salmón
3. conocer a una persona famosa
4. escribir un poema de amor (*love*)
5. recibir un poema de amor
6. llegar tarde a un examen
7. mentir (*to lie*) a un professor/una profesora
8. ¿ ?

Paso 2

Make your statements to the class. Can they tell which statements are true and which ones are not?

Más allá del episodio: Ángel Castillo

Ángel Castillo, el hijo de don Fernando y Rosario

Ángel era[1] muy pequeño cuando su madre se casó con Martín Iglesias. Para el niño, la transición a la Argentina fue muy difícil: abandonar a sus amigos españoles, el largo viaje, la llegada a Buenos Aires, tener que adaptarse a otras costumbres...

Además[2] Ángel ya no era el único[3] rey de la casa. Nunca aceptó por completo a su nuevo padre. Martín era muy ordenado y algo estricto. Verdaderamente quiso[4] ser un buen padre, pero muchas cosas los separaba. Desde pequeño[5] Ángel fue muy inquieto y poco disciplinado. El nacimiento de su nuevo hermano fue otra cosa difícil de aceptar. Rosario no fue severa con él. Pensaba que sólo era cuestión de tiempo. Además... Ángel le recordaba a[6] su padre, a su primer esposo... ¡a Fernando!

Rosario y Martín tenían grandes planes para Ángel. El muchacho, sin embargo,[7] nunca fue un buen estudiante. La única materia que le gustaba era el dibujo. Pasaba horas y horas en la estancia pintando. Un día hizo un retrato[8] muy bonito de Cirilo tocando la guitarra. Todos admiraban su talento, pero para sus padres la pintura sólo era un pasatiempo.[9] Tenía que comenzar una carrera seria.

Ángel empezó entonces a estudiar Ciencias Económicas en la Universidad de Buenos Aires. Rápidamente se aburrió de[10] los estudios y volvió a su pasión, la pintura. Empezó a frecuentar el medio[11] artístico de la ciudad y a llevar una vida bohemia. Pintó mucho en esa época, especialmente las calles pintorescas de La Boca y el puerto. Los barcos le fascinaban. Trató de[12] vender sus cuadros, pero sin mucho éxito. Un día su familia descubrió su engaño.[13] Después de una violenta pelea[14] su padrastro murió. ¿Qué hizo entonces Ángel? ¿Es cierto lo que[15] cree Arturo?

---

[1]*was* [2]*Besides* [3]*only* [4]*he tried* [5]*Desde... From a very young age* [6]*le... reminded her of* [7]*sin... nevertheless* [8]*hizo... he did a portrait* [9]*hobby* [10]*se... he got bored with* [11]*environment, culture* [12]*Trató... He tried to* [13]*deception* [14]*fight* [15]*lo... what*

En el extranjero

BEFORE VIEWING . . .

Preparación

VOCABULARIO

Los verbos
llevarse (bien/mal) to get along (well/badly)
preparar to prepare

Los sustantivos
la carne meat

Los adjetivos
divorciado/a divorced
juntos/as together
solo/a alone

Las palabras adicionales
en el extranjero abroad

Actividad A.

In the last video episode of *Destinos* Raquel and Arturo started their search for Ángel. What do you remember about the search? Complete the following statements.

1. Entre las cosas de su madre, Arturo encontró
   a. _____ una carta.
   b. _____ una pintura.
   c. _____ una foto... de Ángel.

2. En el Barrio de la Boca, Raquel y Arturo hablaron con
    a. _____ pocas personas.
    b. _____ varias personas.
    c. _____ muchas personas.

3. Por fin encontraron a un marinero que
    a. _____ conoció a Ángel.
    b. _____ tenía la dirección de Ángel.
    c. _____ les dio el nombre de otro marinero.

4. Arturo invitó a Raquel a
    a. _____ cenar en su casa.
    b. _____ ir al teatro.
    c. _____ ir a un parque.

Actividad B.

In this video episode Raquel and Arturo will meet and talk with Héctor. Read part of their conversation, trying to get the gist of it.

RAQUEL: ¿Se quedó a vivir en el extranjero?
HÉCTOR: Sí. No recuerdo bien qué país era... ¿saben? Creo que era Puerto Rico, pero no estoy seguro. Era un país en el Caribe... no sé si Puerto Rico, pero estoy seguro que era en el Caribe... Sí, posiblemente Puerto Rico.
RAQUEL: ¿Y la carta?
HÉCTOR: ¡Claro! ¡La carta! La tengo que buscar.
ARTURO: Es muy importante para mí.
HÉCTOR: Sí, comprendo. Mire, Ud. sabe dónde encontrarme. Necesito un par de días para buscar la carta.
ARTURO: Bueno, se lo agradezco muchísimo.
HÉCTOR: No hay de qué. Ángel era mi amigo.

Para pensar...*

¿Qué importancia puede tener el Caribe en esta historia? ¿Qué no recuerda muy bien Héctor? ¿Y por qué está interesada Raquel en una carta que tiene Héctor?

. . . AFTER VIEWING

¿Tienes buena memoria?

¿QUÉ RECUERDAS?

Actividad A.   Preguntas

Briefly answer the following questions about **Episodio 14**.

1. ¿Qué comida le prepara Arturo a Raquel? _____

_____

Para pensar... means *Something to think about . . .* This repeating feature of the episodes, which can occur in any section, will suggest things for you to think about as you view the video episodes or work with the Handbook.

2. ¿A quién llama Raquel desde su hotel? _____

3. ¿Por qué van Raquel y Arturo a la cantina Piccolo Navio? _____

4. ¿Por qué salen de la cantina Raquel, Arturo y Héctor? _____

5. ¿Qué tipo de relaciones existían (*were there*) entre Héctor y Ángel? _____

6. Héctor dice que Ángel se fue en un barco de carga. ¿Adónde iba (*was going*) el

   barco? _____

7. ¿Qué cosa le da Héctor a Arturo? _____

Actividad B.   ¡Busca el intruso!

For each group of names, places, or items, underline the one that does not belong with the others.

1. el chorizo, la panceta, el tomate, la carne de cerdo

2. un héroe nacional, la Revolución de 1812, San Martín, Río de la Plata

3. el trabajo, Héctor, la fiesta, la cantina Piccolo Navio

4. el extranjero, la pintura, el Caribe, Puerto Rico

Actividad C.   ¿Cierto o falso?

Indicate whether the following statements are **Cierto (C)** or **Falso (F)**.

C   F   1. A Raquel le gustan mucho las brochetas.
C   F   2. Arturo nunca se ha casado (*has never been married*).
C   F   3. Raquel habla por teléfono con su madre.
C   F   4. Héctor canta y baila en la cantina Piccolo Navio.
C   F   5. Arturo le da a Raquel una pintura que Ángel pintó.

ACTIVIDADES

Actividad A.   ¿Cuánto recuerdas?

Paso 1

All of the following events happened in **Episodio 14**, but . . . in what order did they occur? Put them in order, from 1 to 6. The understood subject of most of the sentences is **Arturo y Raquel**.

a. _____ Fueron al Piccolo Navio.
b. _____ Tomaron café y miraron unas fotos.
c. _____ Se sentaron a cenar en el jardín.
d. _____ Comieron brochetas y hablaron.
e. _____ Raquel llamó a su madre por teléfono.
f. _____ Conocieron a Héctor y hablaron con él.

Paso 2

Raquel found out some things about Arturo in this video episode. What were they? Indicate whether the statements are **Cierto (C)** or **Falso (F)**.

C   F   1. Arturo vive solo.
C   F   2. Se casó una vez pero está divorciado.
C   F   3. Su esposa volvió a su país natal, el Perú.
C   F   4. Su profesión no es muy importante para él.

Actividad B.   El amigo de Ángel

So far, Héctor has been able to provide a little bit of information, and perhaps he might be of even more help later on. What do you remember about Héctor and the information he has given Arturo and Raquel? ¡OJO! More than one answer may be possible in some cases.

1. Héctor se acuerda muy bien de Ángel porque Ángel
   a. _____ lo ayudó cuando era niño.   c. _____ era su amigo.
   b. _____ vivió en el barrio.

2. También dice Héctor que recibió una carta de Ángel
   a. _____ hace dos días.   c. _____ hace muchos años.
   b. _____ hace unas semanas.

3. Héctor cree que Ángel
   a. _____ se casó muy joven.
   b. _____ se preocupaba mucho por su padre, don Fernando.
   c. _____ se fue a vivir en el extranjero, en Puerto Rico.

Nota cultural: Los brindis

As Arturo and Raquel have a glass of wine before dinner, they exchange a toast used throughout the Spanish-speaking world, with minor variations. You may have heard the toast on other occasions, and you can probably guess its general meaning.

   ¡Salud, dinero y amor! Y tiempo para disfrutarlos.*

   A shorter toast is simply **Salud**, the equivalent of *To your health*. It is considered polite to use it even prior to drinking water, as in **Episodio 12** when Arturo brought up glasses of water for them both on the rooftop and began to tell Raquel about his city.

Intercambio

Paso 1

Fill in the following calendar with today's day in the right-hand column and then the previous four days. For example, if today is Wednesday, you write **miércoles** in the right-hand column, **martes** in the column immediately left, **lunes** in the next, and so on. Then, list any and all meats you have eaten for the meals indicated for today and the last four days. (Note: if you are a vegetarian, write **ninguna carne** in the blanks.)

					hoy:
desayuno					
almuerzo					
cena					

---

*A frequent variation is: **Y tiempo para gozarlos.**

Paso 2

Now, ask questions in Spanish to find five classmates who ate what you ate prior to today. Jot down their names and the meat they ate in the chart from **Paso 1**. Be sure to have the information regarding day and meal!

MODELO: ¿Comiste jamón esta semana (la semana pasada)? ¿En qué día? ¿Para qué comida del día? Gracias.

Paso 3

Write out four statements about what you and the classmates you interviewed ate. Turn the statements in to your instructor.

MODELO: Roberto y yo comimos jamón. Pero yo lo comí el martes para el desayuno y Roberto lo comió el lunes para el almuerzo.

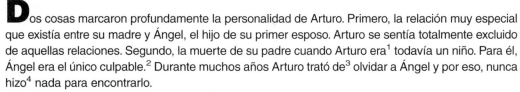

Más allá del episodio: Arituro Iglesias

Arturo Iglesias, el hijo de Rosario y Martín

Dos cosas marcaron profundamente la personalidad de Arturo. Primero, la relación muy especial que existía entre su madre y Ángel, el hijo de su primer esposo. Arturo se sentía totalmente excluido de aquellas relaciones. Segundo, la muerte de su padre cuando Arturo era[1] todavía un niño. Para él, Ángel era el único culpable.[2] Durante muchos años Arturo trató de[3] olvidar a Ángel y por eso, nunca hizo[4] nada para encontrarlo.

Desde pequeño, Arturo siempre tuvo un carácter mucho más reflexivo que su medio hermano. Le gustaba mucho la sicología. Ya de adolescente decidió ser psiquiatra. Le gustaba la idea de ayudar a los demás,[5] pero no era ésta la única razón. Por sus propios conflictos internos en cuanto a[6] su hermano, le interesó mucho la cuestión de «la vida interior» del ser humano.

Arturo fue un buen estudiante. Terminó sus estudios de psiquiatría siendo el número uno de su clase. Rosario estaba muy orgullosa[7] de él. Le regaló[8] una cámara fotográfica y un viaje a Europa, ¡el sueño[9] de Arturo desde siempre! Así descubrió sus dos pasatiempos favoritos, la fotografía y los viajes.

Unos años más tarde, cuando Arturo era ya un psiquiatra de cierto prestigio en Buenos Aires, viajó a Lima para un congreso.[10] En una conferencia,[11] conoció a Estela Vargas, la amiga de un colega y en aquella época estudiante de sicología. Fue una atracción muy fuerte.[12] Arturo regresó a Buenos Aires pero él y Estela se escribían y se telefoneaban con frecuencia. Vivieron unas relaciones muy intensas a pesar de[13] la distancia. Todo era muy romántico, breves estancias[14] en el Perú o la Argentina, flores, mensajes, regalos.... Pronto decidieron casarse. La boda[15] fue en Lima con una ceremonia muy bonita. Los novios se fueron a Italia de luna de miel.[16]

El primer año todo fue muy bien. Pero poco a poco las relaciones se deterioraron. Entre su consulta y las clases en la universidad, Arturo tenía poco tiempo para su esposa. Llegó a estar obsesionado con su trabajo. Ella, por su parte, no trabajaba —nunca terminó su carrera— y no tenía muchos amigos en Buenos Aires. Se sentía muy sola. Además, extrañaba[17] mucho a su familia. Al cabo de cinco años de matrimonio, se divorciaron. ¿Crees que Arturo todavía piensa mucho en Estela?

[1]*was* [2]*responsible* [3]*trató... tried to* [4]*did* [5]*los... others* [6]*en... about* [7]*estaba... was very proud* [8]*Le... She gave him as a gift* [9]*dream* [10]*convention* [11]*lecture* [12]*strong* [13]*a... in spite of* [14]*stays* [15]*wedding* [16]*de... for a honeymoon* [17]*she missed*

15

Culpable

The interactive CD-ROM to accompany *Destinos* contains additional practice with the video story line and will help you improve your skills in Spanish.

BEFORE VIEWING . . .

Preparación

VOCABULARIO

Los verbos

andar en mateo	to take a carriage ride
ir de compras	to go shopping
tener vergüenza	to be embarrassed, ashamed

Los sustantivos

la bolsa	purse, handbag
el cuero	leather
el/la malabarista	juggler
el presentimiento	premonition
el regalo	present, gift

Los adjetivos

aburrido/a	boring
culpable	guilty
divertido/a	fun
preocupado/a	worried

Actividad A.

In the last video episode of *Destinos* Raquel and Arturo were finally able to make some progress in their search for Ángel. How much do you remember about **Episodio 14**? Complete the following statements.

1. En casa de Arturo, Raquel pasó una noche muy
    a. _____ aburrida.   b. _____ agradable.   c. _____ triste.

2. Al día siguiente, en la cantina Piccolo Navio, Raquel y Arturo conocieron a este hombre. Se llama

a. _____ José.   b. _____ Héctor.   c. _____ Ángel.

3. Este hombre era amigo de Ángel. Les dice a Raquel y Arturo que Ángel se fue a vivir a un país

a. _____ del Caribe.   b. _____ de Europa.   c. _____ de África.

4. El hombre tiene algo que da la dirección de Ángel. Es

a. _____ un telegrama.   b. _____ un libro.   c. _____ una carta.

5. Para buscarla, necesita

a. _____ unos minutos.   b. _____ un par de días. c. _____ una semana.

6. Al final de su conversación, este hombre le da algo a Arturo como recuerdo de su hermano Ángel. Es

a. _____ una foto.   b. _____ un cuadro.   c. _____ un poema.

Para pensar...

¿Crees que hay una atracción mutua entre Raquel y Arturo? ¿Siente ella algo por él? Y él, ¿qué piensa de esta abogada norteamericana?

Actividad B.

In this video episode Arturo will express his concerns about Ángel's fate.

Paso 1

Read part of a conversation between Arturo and Raquel without looking ahead in this activity. Then answer this question. Which of the following statements best describes Arturo's mood in this conversation?

a. _____ Arturo está contento.
b. _____ Arturo está preocupado.
c. _____ Arturo está aburrido.

RAQUEL: ¿En qué piensas?
ARTURO: En Ángel. ¿Qué quería de la vida? ¿Qué buscaba?
RAQUEL: ¿Te sientes bien? ¿Qué te pasa?
ARTURO: No te preocupes. No es nada.
RAQUEL: Ya verás. Pronto podrás hablar con tu hermano... Arturo, dime por favor qué es lo que te pasa.
ARTURO: Me tenés que perdonar, Raquel. Es que...
RAQUEL: ¿Sí... ?
ARTURO: Tengo un mal presentimiento... ¿Qué pasa si Ángel... ?

Paso 2

Now read the conversation again. Then answer the questions.

1. You should be able to understand the meaning of **¿Te sientes bien?** But what about **¿Qué te pasa?** What does Raquel want to know?
   a. _____ Where are you going?
   b. _____ What are you thinking about?
   c. _____ What's the matter?

2. The verb form **dime** is a command. Knowing that **me** means *me* or *to me* in English, what you do you think Raquel is saying when she uses this verb form? (*Hint:* **Di** does not look very much like the infinitive from which it derives. Let the context in which **dime** is used be your guide.)

3. According to the context and to Arturo's mood, what do you think the word **presentimiento** means?

   a. _____ premonition   b. _____ thought   c. _____ headache

---

Para pensar...

¿Qué presentimiento tiene Arturo? ¿Qué quiere decir él cuando le dice a Raquel «¿Qué pasa si Ángel... ?» ¿A qué o a quién se refiere el título de este episodio?

. . . AFTER VIEWING

¿**T**ienes buena memoria?

¿QUÉ RECUERDAS?

Actividad A.   Preguntas

Briefly answer the following questions about **Episodio 15**.

1. ¿Por qué está pensativo (*pensive*) Arturo? ¿Qué le pasa? _____

2. ¿Qué espectáculo ven Arturo y Raquel en la calle Florida? _____

3. ¿Cuáles son algunas de las frutas utilizadas en el espectáculo? _____

   _____

4. ¿Por qué quiere Raquel comprar ropa nueva? _____

   _____

5. ¿Cuándo van a encontrarse con Héctor Raquel y Arturo? _____

6. ¿Por qué compra Arturo fruta, queso y vino al día siguiente? _____

7. ¿Cuáles son dos de las cosas que hacen Raquel y Arturo en el Parque del Rosedal? _

   _____

8. ¿Qué *no* quiere hacer Arturo en el parque? ¿Por qué? _____

Actividad B.   ¡Busca el intruso!

For each group of names, places, or items, underline the one that does not belong with the others.

1. la calle Florida, el espectáculo de la fruta, el gran Jaime Bolas, el barrio italiano

2. la manzana, la frutilla, la naranja, el melón

3. la bolsa, la chaqueta, el presentimiento, el cuero

4. las compras, el Parque del Rosedal, el bote, el *picnic*

Actividad C. ¿Cierto o falso?

Indicate whether the following statements are **Cierto (C)** or **Falso (F)**.

C F 1. Raquel compra una bolsa de cuero.
C F 2. A Arturo no le gusta mucho Raquel.
C F 3. A Arturo le gusta mucho ir al Parque del Rosedal.
C F 4. Arturo compra una chaqueta de cuero.
C F 5. Raquel y Arturo cenan en la cantina Piccolo Navio.

ACTIVIDADES

Actividad A. ¿A quién se refiere?

Identify the character described in each sentence.

a. Ángel Castillo
b. Arturo Iglesias
c. Raquel Rodríguez
d. Héctor Condotti

1. _____ Después de hablar con Héctor, está muy pensativo.
2. _____ Va a buscar la carta que Ángel le escribió hace muchos años.
3. _____ Probablemente tiene que hacer un viaje al Caribe.
4. _____ Tiene vergüenza en el parque y no quiere andar en mateo.
5. _____ Se fue a vivir al Caribe. Ahora tendrá unos 52 años.
6. _____ Se siente culpable porque nunca buscó a su hermano.

Actividad B. ¿Qué pasó?

The following paragraphs are a summary of what Raquel and Arturo did in **Episodio 15**. Complete the paragraph with phrases from the following list.

tuvieron un *picnic*
fue a la Cuadra
compró una bolsa de cuero
decidieron ir a un parque
llamó a Arturo
encontró la carta
no le gustó mucho
no le interesó mucho
recibió un regalo de Arturo

Raquel visitó varias tiendas con Arturo y _____.[1] Más tarde, _____,[2] un centro comercial. Allí compró una blusa y unos pantalones. Luego regresó a su hotel. Mientras tanto, Héctor _____[3] para decirle que _____.[4] Pero no puede ver a Arturo y Raquel hasta mañana. Esto _____[5] a Raquel. Empieza a ponerse un poco impaciente y quiere terminar pronto la investigación.

Para pasar el resto del día, Raquel y Arturo _____,[6] aunque la idea _____[7] a Arturo. Pero lo pasaron muy bien. Anduvieron en bote y en mateo y también _____[8] con la comida que Arturo llevaba en la canasta. Por la noche, Raquel _____,[9] una linda chaqueta de cuero. Parece que sí hay una atracción entre Arturo y Raquel, ¿no?

Nota cultural: Tiendas y parques

In this video episode Raquel and Arturo visit a number of well-known places in Buenos Aires. It is obvious from the video episode that Buenos Aires is a cosmopolitan city on a par with Paris, Madrid, New York, and other major cities and capitals. In addition to its wide boulevards and many public buildings, Buenos Aires is also home to

- **La calle Florida**, an elegant pedestrian mall with expensive shops, designer boutiques, and restaurants that serve many ethnic foods as well as the varieties of **parrillada** (*grilling*) for which Argentina is famous. Additional shopping options in Buenos Aires include **centros comerciales**, that is, shopping centers like **la Cuadra** (which have begun to spring up in all major cities in the Spanish-speaking world), and smaller, less expensive **boutiques**, found in many neighborhoods.
- **El Rosedal**, the large park and recreational area in the center of Buenos Aires. It is similar to Central Park in New York, **el Parque Chapultepec** in Mexico City, and **el Retiro** in Madrid. All of these parks are particularly crowded on the weekends. They are sites for family gatherings and picnics, and where young people can meet in groups or where couples can stroll. Why do you think Arturo was so reluctant to go there?

Intercambio

Paso 1

Imagine that you are going on a picnic and you are bringing fruit. List four fruits that you would pack to share in the picnic.

Paso 2

Now walk about the classroom and talk to your classmates to find out what they brought to the picnic.

> MODELO: Yo traje manzanas, un melón, uvas y bananas. ¿Qué trajiste tú?

Paso 3

Report back to the class who brought the same fruits as you.

> MODELO: Mark y yo tenemos el mismo gusto. Los dos trajimos las mismas frutas: manzanas, melón, uvas y bananas.

Más allá del episodio: Héctor Condotti

Héctor conoció a Ángel en el puerto de Buenos Aires. Ángel estaba pintando.[1] Héctor sintió curiosidad y fue a mirar el cuadro. ¡Era su pequeño barco! «¿Cómo puede un barco viejo y feo ser bonito en una pintura?» se preguntó Héctor. El cuadro le gustó mucho e[2] invitó a Ángel a tomar un café.

Los dos hablaron mucho aquel día. Ángel le habló de su viaje desde España que aún no había olvidado.[3] Desde entonces[4] los barcos siempre fueron algo muy especial para él. También le habló de la estancia de su padrastro. Héctor le preguntó: «¿Qué hace un niño rico[5] en este barrio?:» Y Ángel le contó con detalle los últimos problemas que tuvo con Martín y su decisión de no depender de nadie.

[1]estaba... *was painting*   [2]y   [3]aún... *he still hadn't forgotten*   [4] Desde... *From then on*   [5]*rich*

Pronto los dos se hicieron[6] buenos amigos. Héctor le ayudó a su joven amigo a encontrar trabajo. Lo recomendó al capitán de su barco. Ángel estaba encantado,[7] pero, como sospechó Héctor, Ángel no tenía ni idea sobre el trabajo a bordo.[8] ¡Tampoco nadaba muy bien![9] Pero era feliz.[10]

Ángel le dio a Héctor más de un dolor de cabeza.[11] Por ejemplo, nunca aprendió a hacer un buen nudo.[12] Y la disciplina... «Ángel, ¡que tienes que seguir el reglamento[13]!» ¡Cuántas veces le repitió Héctor lo mismo[14]! También pasaron ratos[15] estupendos y se divirtieron[16] mucho juntos. Pero Ángel nunca perdía ninguna ocasión para sacar sus lápices[17] y ponerse a dibujar. Después de unos años surgió[18] un viaje especial al Caribe y Ángel se embarcó sin su amigo.

¿Va a encontrar Héctor la carta de Ángel? ¿Por qué guardó Héctor la carta? ¿Vive Ángel todavía en la dirección que le dio a su amigo?

[6]se... *became* [7]estaba... *was in seventh heaven* [8]no... *he didn't have a clue about what you did on board* [9]¡Tampoco... *Nor was he a particularly good swimmer!* [10]contento [11]dolor... *headache* [12]knot [13]rules [14]lo... *the same thing* [15]periods of time [16]se... *they had a good time* [17]pencils [18]came up

Héctor Condotti, la persona que reconoció la foto de Ángel.

16

Caras

The interactive CD-ROM to accompany *Destinos* contains additional practice with the video story line and will help you improve your skills in Spanish.

reparación

VOCABULARIO

Los verbos		Los sustantivos		Los adjetivos
mostrar (ue)	to show	**la cara**	face	**pensativo/a** thoughtful, pensive
revelar (una foto)	to develop (a photo)	**la foto***	photo	
sacar una foto	to take a photo	**la verdura**	vegetable	

*Even though it ends in **-o**, the noun **foto** is feminine because it is derived from **la fotografía**.

Actividad A.

In the last video episode of *Destinos*, Raquel and Arturo spent a lot of time together while waiting for Héctor to find Ángel's letter. Complete this summary of the episode with the following words and phrases.

la atracción mutua
un mal presentimiento
está pensativo
pasan mucho tiempo juntos

ya murió
calmar
noticias de Héctor

Al principio del episodio previo, Raquel nota que Arturo _____.[1] Cuando ella le pregunta qué le pasa, Arturo le dice que tiene _____.[2]

—Arturo —dice Raquel— dime cuál es el mal presentimiento que tienes.

—Es que —contesta Arturo— algo me dice que Ángel _____.[3]

Raquel trata de _____[4] a Arturo. Y cuando están por salir para el hotel, se dan cuenta de _____[5] que sienten. Se besan y luego Arturo lleva a Raquel al hotel.

Al día siguiente los dos _____.[6] Van de compras en la calle Florida y más tarde van al Parque Rosedal. Lo pasan muy bien. Ahora, en este episodio, esperan tener _____.[7]

Para pensar...

Ahora Raquel y Arturo están conscientes de su atracción mutua. ¿Crees que esta atracción va a convertirse en una relación seria?

Parece que Raquel tendrá que hacer un viaje al Caribe para seguir con la búsqueda de Ángel. ¿Qué va a hacer Arturo?

Actividad B.

Read the following conversation. Then answer the questions.

ARTURO: ¿Sabés? Ángel es el único pariente que tengo. ¿Ya decidiste cuándo te vas a ir?
RAQUEL: Debería tomar el primer vuelo... don Fernando está muy mal. Y no puedo tardarme mucho.
ARTURO: Hace unos pocos días que te conozco... y parece como si hiciera muchos años.
RAQUEL: Yo siento lo mismo.
ARTURO: Te voy a extrañar.
RAQUEL: Yo también a ti.

1. Arturo says, "Hace unos pocos días que te conozco... y parece como si hiciera muchos años." What do you think he means?
    a. _____ I have known you for a few days, and I need more time to get acquainted.
    b. _____ I have known you for a few days, and it's as if I had known you for a long time.

2. A key word in this dialogue is the verb **extrañar**. Think about the context. Raquel has to travel to Puerto Rico to continue her search for Ángel. Given the mutual attraction that the two feel, when Arturo says to Raquel "Te voy a extrañar," and she responds "Yo también a ti," what do you think they are saying to each other?
    a. _____ I'm going to forget you.
    b. _____ I'm going to miss you.
    c. _____ I'm going to follow you.

. . . AFTER VIEWING

¿**T**ienes buena memoria?

¿QUÉ RECUERDAS?

Actividad A.   Preguntas
Briefly answer the following questions about **Episodio 16**.

1. ¿De qué es la foto cómica que miran Raquel y Arturo? _____

2. ¿Cuáles son cuatro de las verduras que hay en la foto? _____

3. ¿Quién está en la foto que saca Arturo en su casa? _____

4. ¿Adónde van a buscar a Héctor Raquel y Arturo? _____

5. ¿Qué información nueva hay en la carta que lee Arturo? _____

6. ¿A qué país tiene que ir Raquel ahora? _____

7. ¿Qué va a hacer Arturo cuando Raquel se vaya de (*leaves*) la Argentina? _____

8. ¿Por qué compra Raquel más verduras en el mercado? _____

Actividad B.   ¡Busca el intruso!
For each group of names, places, or items, underline the one that does not belong with the others.

1. las zanahorias, las fotos, las aceitunas, los chiles
2. el centro político, el centro económico, la producción del vino, el puerto importante
3. la foto, el mercado, la cara, las verduras
4. Carlos y Ramón, Héctor y Ángel, Miguel y Federico, Ángel y Arturo

Actividad C. ¿Cierto o falso?

Indicate whether the following statements are **Cierto (C)** or **Falso (F)**.

C F 1. A Arturo le gusta sacar fotos.
C F 2. Ángel vive ahora en Puerto Rico.
C F 3. Ángel es el único pariente de Arturo.
C F 4. Raquel va a salir de la Argentina al día siguiente.
C F 5. Arturo no tiene ningún interés en ir a Puerto Rico.

ACTIVIDADES

Actividad A. ¿Quién lo dijo?

Identify the character who makes the following statements in **Episodio 16**.

a. Raquel Rodríguez   c. Héctor Condotti
b. Arturo Iglesias   d. el ama de casa

1. _____ «Salgo mal en las fotos y la cámara lo sabe.»
2. _____ «Mira. Me gusta mucho esta foto. ¿La has visto? El fotógrafo debe ser muy imaginativo.»
3. _____ «Disculpe, doctor, lo llaman por teléfono. Un Sr. Héctor... »
4. _____ «Señorita, ¿está bien el señor?»
5. _____ «Otra vez... este presentimiento... algo me dice que Ángel ya murió.»
6. _____ «Yo también tengo una sorpresa para ti.... Pero me tienes que dar unos minutos para prepararla.»

Actividad B. ¿Qué pasó?

All of the following events happened in **Episodio 16**, but in what order did they occur? Put them in order, from 1 to 8.

a. _____ Héctor le da a Arturo la carta de Ángel.
b. _____ Raquel va al mercado para comprar legumbres y verduras.
c. _____ Arturo trata de tomar una foto con una cámara automática.
d. _____ Arturo lee la carta que Ángel le escribió a Héctor hace muchos años.
e. _____ Raquel encuentra una foto de una cara hecha de legumbres y verduras.
f. _____ Arturo le dice a Raquel que piensa viajar a Puerto Rico.
g. _____ Raquel le muestra dos caras de legumbres y verduras a Arturo.
h. _____ Arturo y Raquel van al puerto para buscar a Héctor.

Para pensar...

Arturo le dice a Raquel: «Tal vez yo podría ir a Puerto Rico y los dos continuar la búsqueda de Ángel.» ¿Por qué de repente quiere ir a Puerto Rico Arturo? ¿a causa de Ángel? ¿o a causa de Raquel?

Actividad C. La carta de Ángel

Raquel and Arturo have finally found out some specific information about what happened to Ángel. Indicate whether the following statements about Ángel are **Cierto (C)** or **Falso (F)**.

C F 1. La carta de Ángel es de Ponce, Puerto Rico.
C F 2. Ángel dice que ya no quiere ser marinero.
C F 3. Ya no pinta.
C F 4. Viajó a España.
C F 5. Piensa volver pronto a la Argentina.

Intercambio

Paso 1

Imagine that someone is cooking a stew with vegetables from the following list. When that person isn't looking, you remove the vegetable you like least and add more of the vegetable you like the most. Write out what you did.

tomate	ejotes/judías verdes	apio	guisantes
cebolla	papas	champiñones	maíz

MODELO: Al estofado le quité el apio y le puse más papas.

Paso 2

Your instructor will collect the statements and read half of them out loud. Based on what you know about your classmates, can you guess who did what? What do you think Raquel did to the stew?

Más allá del episodio: Ángel Castillo

Ángel Castillo, un joven en busca de su destino

Para Ángel, conocer a Héctor fue como encontrar a su «hada madrina».[1] En aquella época no tenía dinero y debía varios meses de alquiler.[2] No lo dudó[3] cuando el capitán del barco donde trabajaba Héctor Condotti le ofreció trabajo. No sabía nada de barcos pero era joven y pensaba que aprendería rápidamente.

El barco en que Héctor y Ángel trabajaban era bastante grande y realizaba viajes transatlánticos. Por fin Ángel podría admirar nuevos horizontes. Siempre tenía a mano[4] algo con que dibujar. Su vocación por la pintura aumentaba con el paso del tiempo. A la vez,[5] su trabajo como marinero le resultaba más pesado.[6] Era una vida muy dura y algo monótona. Le molestaba mucho tener que abandonar un dibujo para cumplir[7] con sus obligaciones a bordo.

En uno de los viajes el barco llegó a España. Cuando Ángel llegó al puerto de Bilbao, se sintió muy confundido. Era su país, pero le pareció estar en un lugar desconocido. Quiso visitar Guernica, la ciudad donde murió su padre. Allí caminó durante horas. Trató de imaginar cómo era todo cuando sus padres vivían allí. Inconscientemente creía ver a su padre entre la gente[8] de las calles. La ciudad terminó por deprimirle.[9] Decidió, entonces, viajar a Sevilla. Allí tampoco encontró lo que buscaba. Pero ¿qué buscaba Ángel en España?

Poco tiempo después el barco hizo un viaje al Caribe. Llevaban una carga[10] para Puerto Rico. Ángel supo inmediatamente que se quedaría[11] allí. Había algo en aquel sol[12] y en aquella tranquilidad que no había visto en otros lugares. Allí, de repente, se sintió completamente libre. Sin duda era el lugar ideal para pintar. Estaba decidido. Dejó el trabajo y le escribió una larga carta a Héctor. En la carta le hablaba de cuánto le gustó la isla, de su necesidad de dedicarse totalmente a la pintura. También le daba las gracias por su ayuda.

Pero, ¿encontró Ángel la felicidad en Puerto Rico? ¿Pudo vivir de su pintura? ¿Se hizo famoso?

---

[1]hada... *fairy godmother* [2]*rent* [3]*No... He didn't hesitate for a second* [4]*a... close by, at hand* [5]*A... At the same time* [6]aburrido [7]*to meet* [8]la... las personas [9]terminó... *ended up depressing him* [10]*load* [11]se... *he would stay* [12]Había... *There was something in that sun*

17

Inolvidable

The interactive CD-ROM to accompany *Destinos* contains additional practice with the video story line and will help you improve your skills in Spanish.

BEFORE VIEWING . . .

Preparación

VOCABULARIO

Los verbos	**Los sustantivos**		**Los adjetivos**	
pedir (i) to ask for	**el deseo**	wish	**conocido/a**	known, well-known
	el escritor/la escritora	writer	**inolvidable**	unforgettable
	la estrella	star		
	la obra	work (*written, dramatic, etc.*)		

Actividad A.

What happened in the last video episode of *Destinos?* Indicate whether the following brief narratives contain information that is **Cierto (C)** or **Falso (F)**. Can you correct the false information?

C   F   1.   Raquel y Arturo lo pasaron muy bien cuando Arturo trató de sacar una foto de los dos y tuvo problemas con la cámara.

C   F   2.   Héctor llamó a Arturo por teléfono. Quería pasar por su casa para darle la carta de Ángel.

C   F   3.   Cuando leyó la carta de Ángel, Arturo supo que Ángel decidió quedarse en Puerto Rico. Pensaba volver a la Argentina para sus vacaciones.

C   F   4.   Raquel y Arturo sienten una atracción mutua. Les gusta mucho estar juntos.

Para pensar...

Arturo dice que quiere ir a Puerto Rico con Raquel, para continuar la búsqueda de Ángel. ¿Crees que realmente va a poder acompañarla en su viaje? ¿Crees que esto es una buena idea? ¿No está pasando todo muy rápido?

Actividad B.

In this video episode Arturo and Raquel will each make a "wish upon a star," **una estrella**.

Paso 1

Pedir un deseo means *to ask for a wish*. Based on everything you know about Raquel and her personality, what do you think she will wish for?

_____ Pide a las estrellas que pueda encontrar a Ángel en Puerto Rico.

_____ Pide a las estrellas que Arturo pueda acompañarla a Puerto Rico.

Paso 2

Based on what you know about Arturo and on your observation of his behavior, what do you think he will wish for?

Paso 3

Now read the scene in its entirety.

ARTURO: Vení. Hay una tradición en mi familia que quiero compartir con vos.... ¿Qué ves?
RAQUEL: Veo la luna... las estrellas... y a ti.
ARTURO: ¿Alguna vez le pediste un deseo a una estrella?
RAQUEL: Sí. Cuando era una niña pequeña en California.
ARTURO: Bien. Pedí vos primero.
RAQUEL: ¿Yo?
ARTURO: Por supuesto.
RAQUEL: Les pido a las primeras cien estrellas que veo esta noche que podamos encontrar a Ángel en Puerto Rico... que esté bien y que por fin esta familia pueda reunirse definitivamente.
ARTURO: Yo también les pido lo mismo. Que podamos encontrar a mi hermano y que él pueda conocer a su padre, don Fernando. Y que esta persona, esta mujer, sea parte importante de mi vida... y que yo sea parte importante de su vida también.

Based on what you have read, which of the following do you think is the most appropriate title for this garden scene?

a. _____ La luna   b. _____ El jardín por la noche   c. _____ Declaración de amor

---

Para pensar...

¿Qué van a hacer Arturo y Raquel después de esta conversación? ¿darse la mano? ¿abrazarse? ¿besarse?

. . . AFTER VIEWING

¿Tienes buena memoria?

¿QUÉ RECUERDAS?

Actividad A.   Preguntas
Briefly answer the following questions about **Episodio 17**.

1. ¿Dónde bailan un tango Raquel y Arturo? _____

2. ¿Quién era (*was*) Carlos Gardel? _____

3. ¿A quiénes o a qué piden deseos Raquel y Arturo? _____

4. ¿De qué hablan Raquel y Arturo mientras cenan? _____

5. ¿Cuáles son dos de los sitios que visitan Raquel y Arturo? _____

6. ¿Qué protestan las madres de la Plaza de Mayo? _____

7. ¿Quién era Jorge Luis Borges? _____

8. ¿Qué opinión tiene Raquel de Buenos Aires? _____

Actividad B.   ¡Busca el intruso!
For each group of names, places, or items, underline the one that does not belong with the others.

1. el tango, la fotografía, Carlos Gardel, un baile típico
2. el Teatro Colón, la Plaza de Mayo, La Boca, el Museo Nacional de Bellas Artes
3. el baile, Jorge Luis Borges, el poeta, el escritor
4. la carne, Buenos Aires, el tango, Puerto Rico

Actividad C.   ¿Cierto o falso?
Indicate whether the following statements are **Cierto (C)** or **Falso (F)**.

C   F   1.   Arturo no sabe bailar el tango.
C   F   2.   Arturo le muestra a Raquel algunos sitios de interés cultural.
C   F   3.   En el Museo Nacional de Bellas Artes, es posible ver ópera y ballet.
C   F   4.   Jorge Luis Borges era un escritor argentino.
C   F   5.   El vuelo a Puerto Rico sale a las ocho de la noche.

ACTIVIDADES

Actividad A.   ¿Quién lo dijo?

Paso 1
Arturo and Raquel talk about a lot of things in this video episode. Indicate which of the two, Arturo (**A**) or Raquel (**R**), made each of the following statements.

A   R   1.   «Yo también les pido lo mismo. Que podamos encontrar a mi hermano y que él pueda conocer a su padre, don Fernando.»

A   R   2.   «Por favor, déjame terminar. Lo que quiero decir es que... no es fácil decir estas cosas. Todo ha sido tan... tan rápido... Necesito tiempo para pensar.»

A   R   3.   «Sabés, los argentinos somos más que la carne y el tango.»

A   R   4.   «Cuando volvamos con Ángel de Puerto Rico, los tres podremos venir a ver un espectáculo.»

A   R   5.   «¿Es posible que vuelvas entonces?»

Paso 2
Now indicate which of the preceding phrases expresses Raquel's answer to Arturo's declaration of his feelings. Is it an acceptance, a rejection, or something in between?

Actividad B.
In the last several video episodes you have learned information about Arturo and his half brother Ángel. In this episode you learned more about Raquel. Listen again to Raquel's answers to Arturo's dinner table questions, then complete this summary with these words and phrases.

se fue a vivir
en México
por un año entero
norteamericana
don Pedro, hermano de don Fernando
muy contenta
mucha gente interesante
un estudiante joven
pasó los veranos
en la Universidad de California
Los Ángeles
muy aburrida

Raquel nació en Los Ángeles, pero se siente tanto mexicana como _____.[1]

Ella siempre _____[2] en México con la familia mexicana de sus padres. Una

vez fue a México _____.[3] Le gustó mucho esa experiencia.

Raquel estudió _____.[4] Allí conoció a _____,[5] quien

llegó a ser su novio. Después de graduarse, él _____[6] a Nueva York y ella se

quedó en _____.[7] Ahora ella está _____[8] con su trabajo,

porque viaja mucho y conoce a _____.[9]

Actividad C. «¡Somos más que la carne y el tango!»

In **Episodio 17** you heard a great deal about the history and culture of Buenos Aires. Summarize some of that information by matching the numbered names below with the descriptions that follow them.

1. _____ el tango
2. _____ el Teatro Colón
3. _____ la Plaza de Mayo
4. _____ Domingo Faustino Sarmiento
5. _____ Jorge Luis Borges
6. _____ *Ficciones* y *El Aleph*

a. son colecciones de cuentos de Borges
b. es famosa por las madres que protestan allí cada semana
c. era la música de la gente de Buenos Aires
d. son cuadros del Museo Nacional
e. un autor argentino que ganó fama mundial por sus obras literarias
f. un dictador militar de la Argentina
g. es famoso por sus espectáculos: conciertos, teatro, ballet...
h. era la música de la clase alta
i. una gran figura política y literaria de la Argentina

Nota cultural: Premios Nobel

Varios argentinos han ganado (*have won*) un premio Nobel. ¿Reconoces el nombre de alguno de ellos?

Carlos Saavedra Lamas, premio Nobel de la Paz en 1936; Bernardo Houssay, premio Nobel de Medicina en 1947; Luis Federico Lenoir, premio Nobel de Química en 1970; Adolfo Pérez Esquivel, premio Nobel de la Paz en 1980; César Milstein, premio Nobel de Medicina en 1984

César Milstein, ganador del premio Nobel de Medicina.

¿Y el prestigioso premio Nobel de Literatura? No lo ha ganado todavía ningún argentino, aunque se sugirió con frecuencia el nombre de Jorge Luis Borges. Éstos son los escritores de lengua española que hasta la fecha (*until now*) han ganado este premio. ¿Los reconoces?

José Echegaray en 1904 (España); Jacinto Benavente en 1922 (España); Gabriela Mistral en 1945 (Chile); Juan Ramón Jiménez en 1956 (España); Miguel Ángel Asturias en 1967 (Guatemala); Pablo Neruda en 1971 (Chile); Vicente Aleixandre en 1977 (España); Gabriel García Márquez en 1982 (Colombia); Camilo José Cela en 1989 (España); Octavio Paz en 1990 (México)

Intercambio

Paso 1

This is a game to see which group can recall the most information in a short amount of time. Break up into groups of four and elect a secretary who will write down your ideas. You have ten minutes to jot down things that you remember have happened in **Episodios 12** to **17**. Your instructor will mark time.

Paso 2

Each group presents its ideas to the class. Your instructor will keep, or have a student keep, a tally of the ideas by category. Categories can include **lugares**, **comidas**, and so on.

Más allá del episodio: Luis, el ex novio de Raquel

Luis, el antiguo[1] novio de Raquel

Raquel conoció a su ex novio en casa de unos amigos. Los dos eran estudiantes en la Universidad de California en Los Ángeles. Ella estudiaba Derecho[2] y él Administración de Empresas.[3] Además tenían otra cosa en común. Ella era mexicoamericana y él, mexicano.

Raquel se fijó[4] inmediatamente en Luis. ¿Por qué le gustó tanto[5] aquel muchacho? Era un joven muy inteligente y muy ambicioso. Tenía grandes planes para el futuro. Era muy simpático y extrovertido. Raquel también admiraba su dinamismo. Siempre tenía algo que hacer.

Desde aquella tarde en casa de sus amigos se vieron con relativa frecuencia en la universidad. Eran encuentros aparentemente espontáneos, entre las clases o en el almuerzo. Un sábado Luis invitó a Raquel a ir al cine. Desde ese día fueron inseparables. Raquel lo pasaba muy bien con él. Además, él era un gran estímulo para su propia carrera, ya que[6] era muy buen estudiante.

Los problemas entre ellos comenzaron durante los últimos meses antes de graduarse. La idea de terminar los estudios con buenas notas[7] y conseguir un buen puesto[8] consumía todo el tiempo de Luis. Raquel trató de comprenderlo. Sabía que aquello era muy importante para él. Había semanas en las que él no tenía ni cinco minutos para tomar una Coca-Cola con ella.

Llegó la época de los exámenes y ¡los dos salieron bien[9]! Especialmente Luis. Obtuvo el segundo puesto entre los estudiantes de su clase. Muchas empresas lo entrevistaron.[10] Por fin, aceptó un puesto en una empresa en Nueva York. Estaba muy contento con la decisión y se mudó tan pronto como[11] terminó el semestre.

¿Y su novia? Raquel decidió quedarse en California. Luis se graduaba pero a Raquel le faltaba un año más.[12] ¿Crees que las relaciones entre Raquel y Luis fueron serias? ¿Por qué no se mudó ella a Nueva York? ¿Y por qué se fue Luis a Nueva York?

[1]*former* [2]*Law* [3]Administración... *Business Administration* (empresas = *corporations*) [4]*se... noticed* [5]*so much* [6]*ya... since* [7]*grades* [8]trabajo [9]salieron... *passed* [10]*interviewed* [11]tan... *as soon as* [12]a... *Raquel had another year to go*

Estimada
Sra. Suárez

The interactive CD-ROM to accompany *Destinos* contains additional practice with the video story line and will help you improve your skills in Spanish.

BEFORE VIEWING . . .

reparación

VOCABULARIO

Los verbos

reunirse (me reúno) (con) to be reunited (with), get back together (with)

Los sustantivos

la noticia piece of news

Los adjetivos

estimado/a dear (*often used in letters*)

triste sad

Actividad A.

Indicate whether the following events took place (**Sí, ocurrió**) or not (**No, no ocurrió**) in the previous video episode of *Destinos*.

¿Qué pasó en el episodio previo?

Sí No 1. Raquel y Arturo bailaron.
Sí No 2. Arturo le hizo a Raquel una declaración de amor.
Sí No 3. Decidieron salir a cenar.
Sí No 4. Raquel le dijo a Arturo que él era muy importante para ella.
Sí No 5. Arturo habló más de su ex esposa.
Sí No 6. Raquel le dijo a Arturo que lo amaba.

Al día siguiente, ¿qué hicieron Raquel y Arturo durante el día?

Sí No   7. Visitaron la casa de Jorge Luis Borges.
Sí No   8. Fueron a la ópera.
Sí No   9. Fueron a un parque.
Sí No 10. Comieron en un restaurante elegante.

Actividad B.

Look at the title of this lesson and at the photograph with which it begins. What do you think Raquel will do in this video episode?

a. _____ Llama por teléfono a la Sra. Suárez.
b. _____ Le escribe una carta a la Sra. Suárez.
c. _____ Le manda un telegrama a la Sra. Suárez.

If you selected *b*, you were correct. What might Raquel tell Sra. Suárez in her letter? Indicate all items that you think may be correct.

a. _____ las tristes noticias de Rosario
b. _____ de cómo pudo por fin encontrar a un hijo de Rosario
c. _____ de su relación con Arturo
d. _____ más noticias de don Fernando
e. _____ unos detalles de la búsqueda de Ángel en Buenos Aires
f. _____ la dirección de Ángel en Puerto Rico
g. _____ de sus compras en Buenos Aires
h. _____ de lo que comió

. . . AFTER VIEWING

¿Tienes buena memoria?

¿QUÉ RECUERDAS?

Actividad A.   Preguntas

Briefly answer the following questions about **Episodio 18**.

1. ¿Adónde va Raquel al principio del episodio? _____

2. ¿Cuándo van a verse (*see each other*) otra vez Raquel y Arturo? _____

3. ¿Qué hace Raquel mientras espera en el aeropuerto? _____

4. ¿Qué le escribe a esa persona? _____

Actividad B. ¡Busca el intruso!

For each group of names or items, underline the one that does not belong with the others.

1. una campera, una pulsera (*bracelet*), un beso (*kiss*), un billete de avión

2. Héctor, José, Ángel, Arturo

3. los mejillones, los calamares, los melones, los langostinos

4. el marinero, el puerto, el barco, la plaza

Actividad C. ¿Cierto o falso?

Indicate whether the following statements are **Cierto (C)** or **Falso (F)**.

C   F   1. Raquel tiene que viajar a México ahora.
C   F   2. Hay una demora en el vuelo de Raquel.
C   F   3. Rosario ya murió.
C   F   4. Arturo va a visitar a Raquel pronto.
C   F   5. Raquel quiere encontrar a Ángel cuanto antes (*as soon as possible*).

ACTIVIDADES

Actividad. Raquel se va

The following sentences describe what took place during Raquel's last hours in Argentina, but the words are out of order. Read all of the words in each group, then put them in the correct order to form complete sentences.

1. llevó / Raquel / a / aeropuerto / Arturo / al _____

2. se / los dos / entrada / en / despidieron / la _____

3. con / besaron / se / ternura _____

4. despedida / fue / triste / la _____

5. un / tuvo / poco / Raquel / esperar / que _____

6. carta / le / a / Sra. Suárez / escribió / una / la _____

Repaso de los Episodios 12–17

Actividad A. La búsqueda de Raquel

The following summary of the first part of Raquel's search in Buenos Aires is adapted from her letter to Sra. Suárez. Complete it with phrases from the following list. ¡OJO! Not all of the phrases will be used.

se mudó a Puerto Rico
murió hace algunos años
era el hijo de Rosario y don Fernando
no me sirvió para nada
había muerto

perdió contacto con su hermano
se fue de la casa
se quedó en casa
me sirvió bastante
ya no vivía allí

Estimada Sra. Suárez:

Ojalá que cuando reciba esta carta se encuentre bien de salud. Mi viaje a Buenos Aires ha resultado fructífero gracias a su bondad en ayudarme, pues la dirección de la estancia _____.[1] Sin embargo, me da mucha pena tener que decirle que su buena amiga Rosario _____.[2]

En la estancia averigüé que la familia Iglesias _____.[3] Un hombre me dio la dirección del hijo de Rosario. Fui a buscarlo, creyendo que _____.[4] Imagínese Ud. la sorpresa que tuve al encontrarme con otro hijo de Rosario.

Fue durante esa conversación que el hijo, Arturo Iglesias que así se llama, me contó que Rosario _____.[5] En el cementerio conseguí pruebas de la muerte de Rosario y allí Arturo me contó que Ángel Castillo _____[6] por una pelea que tuvo con su padrastro. A causa de ese doloroso episodio, Arturo _____.[7] Al día siguiente, comenzamos juntos la búsqueda del paradero de Ángel.

Actividad B.   La búsqueda de Arturo y Raquel

The following sentences from Raquel's letter describe her search with Arturo, but they are out of order. Put them in order, from 1 to 7.

a.   _____ Finalmente dimos con un hombre [Héctor].
b.   _____ En verdad, le estoy escribiendo esta carta desde el aeropuerto.
c.   _____ Sabiendo que Ángel se quedó a vivir en Puerto Rico y con la dirección de su casa en San Juan, hice los preparativos para salir de Buenos Aires.
d.   _____ Preguntamos por Ángel Castillo en varios lugares del barrio italiano, La Boca.
e.   _____ Después de varios días, Héctor llamó a Arturo para decirle que había encontrado la carta.
f.   _____ Pero nadie se acordaba de Ángel.
g.   _____ Ud. no tiene idea de lo difícil que nos fue conseguir la información que buscábamos.

Actividad C.   Las actividades de Raquel

As you know, Raquel's visit to Buenos Aires involved more than just the search for Ángel. Here are the last paragraphs of Raquel's letter to Sra. Suárez, but some of the information has been changed. Read through the letter and indicate the incorrect information.

Tendría que decirle que mi estancia en Buenos Aires no ha sido nada más que trabajo. En primer lugar, he tenido la oportunidad de conocer un poco el país. Pude hacer unas compras, pues como Ud. sabrá en la Argentina hay muchos artículos de oro muy bonitos. Y, claro, también comí y comí y comí y comí... pero no me gustó.

Si me permite la confianza, quisiera decirle que no seguí sus consejos. El hermano de Arturo, Ángel, se ha hecho buen amigo mío. Para decir la verdad, siento un amor muy especial por él. Resulta que Arturo me va a visitar en San Juan en un mes. Así concluye mi estancia en Buenos Aires.

Siento mucho la pelea que Ud. tuvo con su buena amiga tanto por Ud. como por don Fernando. Ojalá mi viaje a Puerto Rico tenga los resultados deseados, que encuentre a Rosario Castillo y que por fin se reúna con su madre.

Reciban Ud. y su familia un saludo cordial de
Raquel Rodríguez

Para escribir

In this activity you will write a short narrative in which you describe Raquel and Arturo's relationship to someone who has not seen the video episodes. You want to tell the reader as much as you can about them and about what happened to them in Buenos Aires, include some interesting information, and make some suggestions about what you think will happen to them in future episodes. Your narrative should be no fewer than 200 and not more than 300 words long.

Think About What You Will Write

In order to write this narrative the first thing you must do is think about what information you will include.

Review the sections called **Preparación** and **¿Tienes buena memoria?**—in particular those in **Lecciones 12–18**—and the review sections in this lesson. You may also want to scan other sections for information about Raquel and Arturo in particular. Be sure to reread the **Más allá del episodio** sections in **Lecciones 4** and **14** in particular, because they are about these two characters.

As you scan all of these sections, note the following useful or interesting information and key phrases. (It is a good idea to do this on a separate sheet of paper. Make one chart for Raquel and another for Arturo.)

> Personalidad
> Trabajo
> Familia
>
> Le gusta...
> No le gusta...

At the same time you should be making a list of only the most important events in **Episodios 12–18**, in order. For now, just jot them down as phrases (**conocer a Arturo, encontrar a Héctor, ...**) and don't be concerned about conjugating the verb forms.

You will not necessarily use all of the information or events in your narrative, but that's OK. For the moment you are just trying to create a bank of ideas upon which to draw.

Organizing Your Narrative

In the last **Para escribir** section you did not have to spend any time at all organizing your narrative because you were writing about a typical day in your life and the day itself was the organizing principle. For this narrative, however, you will need to spend some time thinking about the organization (order) of what you will write.

Begin by deciding which of the following questions you would like to answer in the narrative.

_____ What things did Raquel and Arturo do together in these video episodes?
_____ Who is Raquel?
_____ Who is Héctor Condotti?
_____ What is Raquel like as a person?

_____ What place is Raquel leaving for and why?
_____ Will Raquel and Arturo ever see each other again? If so, where and when?
_____ What is Arturo like as a person?
_____ Where and when do Raquel and Arturo meet doña Flora?
_____ How did Raquel and Arturo meet?
_____ Who is Arturo?
_____ What is their relationship like?
_____ Why is Raquel in Argentina?
_____ What does their search involve?
_____ Who is Ángel Castillo and why is he important?

There are several items that you probably did not indicate, because they are not important to the topic you are trying to address. Take the items you did select and think about whether any of them form a logical group; then consider the order in which you will present them. What sequence seems to make the most sense to you? Write a brief outline of that sequence.

Drafting

Paso 1
Now draft your narrative. At this stage you should not worry about grammar and spelling. Your goal is to get your ideas down on paper.

Paso 2
After you have completed your draft, look over what you have done. Are you still satisfied with the information you selected? Do you want to add some things and delete others, or go into more detail about certain details or events? Have you included at least one interesting detail about Raquel and one about Arturo? Keep in mind that you are writing for someone who doesn't know anything about them.

Finalizing Your Narrative
If you are satisfied with the information contained in your draft, it is time to look it over for language and style.

Paso 1
First, look at your narration for style. Does the narration flow, or is it disjointed and choppy? Does it contain words and phrases that connect events, or is it mostly an accumulation of sentences?

Here is a list of words and phrases that can help make your narration flow more smoothly.

también	also
pero	but
por eso	that's why, therefore
y	and

These words and phrases can help you express the sequence of events smoothly.

primero	first
luego	then, next
al día siguiente	the next day
pronto	soon
cuando	when
después	later (on)
por fin	finally
más tarde	later
de nuevo	again

Paso 2

Review your narrative for the following language elements or any others you have studied as well.

_____ gender of nouns
_____ adjective agreement
_____ subject-verb agreement
_____ correct tense (present, preterite, **ir** + **a** + *infinitive*)
_____ use of object pronouns

Paso 3

Prepare a clean copy of the final version of your narrative for your instructor.

Un viaje a Puerto Rico

El Morro, San Juan

Por fin...

The interactive CD-ROM to accompany *Destinos* contains additional practice with the video story line and will help you improve your skills in Spanish.

BEFORE VIEWING . . .

reparación

---

VOCABULARIO

Los verbos	
bajar	to go down
cruzar	to cross
seguir (i) derecho	to continue straight
virar	to turn (*Puerto Rico*)

Los sustantivos	
la bocacalle	intersection
las escaleras	steps
la esquina	corner
el/la pariente	relative, family member
la tumba	tomb, grave
el vecino/la vecina	neighbor

Los adjetivos	
enterrado/a	buried

Las palabras adicionales
a la derecha to the right
a la izquierda to the left

Actividad.

Paso 1

In this video episode Raquel has a conversation with a woman. In the conversation the woman will say the following: "Los dos están enterrados en el antiguo cementerio de San Juan." Read the line over a few times, so that you recognize it.

Paso 2

Now read the conversation. You should be able to obtain a lot of information from it.

LA VECINA: Señorita, ¿a quién busca?

RAQUEL: Buenos días, señora. Busco al señor Ángel Castillo.

LA VECINA: ¿No sabe Ud., señorita? El señor Castillo murió.

RAQUEL: ¿Cuándo murió?

LA VECINA: Hace poco. Es una pena, tan buenos vecinos que eran. Pero el pobre...

RAQUEL: ¿Ángel?

LA VECINA: Sí, Ángel Castillo. Nunca se repuso de la muerte de su esposa.

RAQUEL: ¿Entonces era casado?

LA VECINA: Sí. Su señora era una mujer muy linda. Era escritora. Pero murió ya hace varios años. Los dos están enterrados en el antiguo cementerio de San Juan.

Paso 3

Now answer the following questions about the conversation.

1. **Enterrados** means *buried*. Now that you know that, what two people do you think the woman is talking about? *Hint*: What two people would be of interest to Raquel at this moment?

2. The neighbor also says: "Nunca se repuso de la muerte de su esposa." The verb form **se repuso** comes from the infinitive **reponerse**, meaning *to get over* or *recover from* (*an illness*). Who is the woman describing in this sentence, a man or a woman? Do you think she is talking about Ángel or about someone who knew him well?

. . . AFTER VIEWING

¿Tienes buena memoria?

¿QUÉ RECUERDAS?

Actividad A. Preguntas

Briefly answer the following questions about **Episodio 19**.

1. ¿Cómo llega Raquel a la calle del Sol? _____

2. ¿Quién le da instrucciones para llegar allí? _____

3. ¿Qué le pregunta Raquel a la vecina? _____

4. ¿Dónde se puede encontrar a Ángel y a su esposa? _____

5. ¿A quién conoce Raquel en el cementerio? _____

6. ¿Qué importancia tiene esta persona en la búsqueda de Raquel? _____

7. ¿A quiénes llama Ángela al regresar a su casa? _____

8. ¿Qué lugar histórico visita Raquel mientras espera a la familia de Ángela? _____

Actividad B.   ¡Busca el intruso!

For each group of places, actions, or items, underline the one that does not belong with the others.

1.   virar, pagar, cruzar, seguir derecho
2.   el Viejo San Juan, la Casa Blanca, la Plaza de Mayo, el Parque de las Palomas
3.   visitar la tumba, sacar fotos, buscar la casa de Ángel, hablar con Arturo
4.   la tumba, la calle, la bocacalle, la esquina

Actividad C.   ¿Cierto o falso?

Indicate whether the following statements are **Cierto (C)** or **Falso (F)**.

C   F   1.   Raquel llega a Puerto Rico en barco.
C   F   2.   Raquel tiene que andar para llegar a la casa de Ángel.
C   F   3.   Al llegar a la casa de Ángel, Raquel se entera de (*finds out*) que él y su esposa se mudaron a otro apartamento.
C   F   4.   Ángela y Raquel se conocen en la tumba de los padres de Ángela.
C   F   5.   Ángela ya sabía que tenía parientes en México.

ACTIVIDADES

Actividad A.   Nuevos personajes

In this video episode of *Destinos* you have met some new characters. How much do you remember about them? Complete the following statements about the people shown in the photographs.

1.   Esta señora es la... esposa / vecina / viuda ...de Ángel Castillo.
2.   La señora le dice a Raquel que Ángel... se mudó a otro país / volvió a España / murió hace poco.
3.   Le dice también que la esposa de Ángel era... anciana / escritora / maestra de primaria.

4.   Raquel descubre que esta señorita es la... hija / novia / viuda ...de Ángel.
5.   Ángela llama a... unos parientes / unos amigos / sus hermanos ...para que vengan a conocer a Raquel.
6.   Hay otra sorpresa para Raquel al final del episodio. Ángela le dice que... ya sabe de don Fernando / tiene un hermano / ya conoce a Arturo.

Actividad B.   La primera tarde en San Juan

Raquel's investigation gets off to a quick start in Puerto Rico. She finds a member of Ángel's family quickly, and it appears that she will soon meet more family members. Complete this summary of part of her afternoon with Ángela with the following phrases. ¡OJO! Not all of the phrases will be used.

encontrar una foto de su padre
tomar una foto
llamar a sus tíos
mudarse
visitar un lugar de interés histórico
mostrarle otros lugares interesantes

está en Nueva York
van al cementerio
hablan más
debe ser muy triste para Ángela
regresan al apartamento
va a México

En el apartamento, Ángela le dice a Raquel que piensa _____.[1]
«No quiero vivir sola en este apartamento», dice. Raquel queda sorprendida, porque el apartamento es muy bonito. Pero también comprende que el recuerdo de sus padres _____.[2]

Ángela trata de _____,[3] pero no tiene suerte. Mientras sigue intentando, Raquel sale a _____,[4] la Casa Blanca. Luego Ángela se reúne con ella para visitar los jardines de la Casa Blanca y para _____.[5] Van al Parque de las Palomas y a la Capilla de Cristo y finalmente _____.[6]

Allí es donde Raquel descubre que Ángela tiene novio. Pero no lo va a conocer pronto porque _____.[7] Raquel también ve la foto de un joven atractivo. ¡Otro hijo de Ángel!

Nota cultural: La inmediatez puertorriqueña

You may have noticed that Raquel and Ángela have already developed a warm, comfortable relationship. This is partly because they are both women, not so far apart in age, and partly because Raquel has given Ángela some startling but potentially exciting news about her family.

There is another factor at work as well. Most visitors to the island of Puerto Rico comment on how friendly and open the people are and how quickly comfortable relationships are established. One phrase that describes this phenomenon is **la inmediatez de la gente**, related to the adjective **inmediato** (*immediate*).

Raquel responds warmly to this characteristic of the islanders. But even here, as in other parts of the Spanish-speaking world that Raquel has visited previously, another person—Ángela—initiates the use of **tú** with her.

Intercambio

Paso 1

Work with a partner to prepare a list in Spanish of important events from *Destinos*. For example, **Raquel viajó a Sevilla, Arturo y Raquel empezaron la búsqueda de Ángel en la Boca.** Your list should contain at least ten items and should not be limited to any one episode or country.

_____

_____

_____

_____

_____

_____

_____

_____

_____

Paso 2

Now pass your list to the group to your right. You will receive a list from the group to your left. Read the list you receive and try to add to the event. For example, **Raquel viajó a Sevilla pero la Sra. Suárez no vivía allí.** Return the list to the students who wrote it.

Paso 3

Take turns with other pairs of students to read some sentences to the class. After everyone has a turn, the class should decide on the ten most important events. When you have done this, you will have created a mini-synopsis of *Destinos*.

Más allá del episodio: Ángel Castillo, en Puerto Rico

Ángel estaba muy contento en Puerto Rico.

Para Ángel, los primeros meses en Puerto Rico fueron como un sueño.[1] Vivió plenamente[2] su nueva libertad. Con el poco dinero que tenía, alquiló[3] una pequeña habitación en el último[4] piso de una casa color claro[5] del Viejo San Juan. Era un lugar modesto pero cómodo,[6] y tenía una vista muy hermosa al mar.

Después de instalarse,[7] sacó de sus maletas sus pinturas y pinceles[8] y comenzó a pintar. Al principio fue como una obsesión. Pintaba día y noche, sobre todo escenas del barrio de La Boca que no podía borrar[9] de su memoria. Quiso vender sus pinturas pero, así como en la Argentina, no tuvo éxito.

Dentro de poco se quedó sin dinero... y la isla empezó a perder su encanto. La habitación le pareció muy pequeña. Empezó a extrañar el lujo[10] al que estaba acostumbrado en la estancia. La voz de su padrastro resonaba en su cabeza:[11] «Tienes que trabajar, Ángel. ¡La pintura no te llevará a nada[12]!». Solo, lejos de su familia y sin amigos, se sintió por primera vez desamparado.[13] De una cosa estaba seguro:[14] no podía admitir su fracaso y volver a la Argentina.

Una mañana Ángel salió a caminar. En una librería[15] de arte, vio un cartel[16] que decía: «Se necesita joven con conocimientos de arte». Al día siguiente empezó a trabajar en la tienda. Pronto volvió a sentirse feliz en este medio[17] intelectual. Y también volvió a sentir ganas de[18] pintar. Su estilo cambió. Ahora estaba pintando su realidad... el encanto de la isla. El mar le fascinaba y en él encontró su inspiración.

Ángel estaba muy contento, pero todavía le esperaba una sorpresa. Un día en la librería empezó a hablar con una clienta joven. Ángel se sintió inmediatamente atraído[19] por su inteligencia y belleza. La invitó a tomar un café en uno de los restaurantes del barrio. Poco después se enamoraron y decidieron casarse. La familia de María Luisa, que así se llamaba la joven, acogió[20] a Ángel en seguida.

[1]dream [2]fully [3]he rented [4]top [5]color... pastel-colored [6]comfortable [7]settling in [8]brushes [9]erase [10]luxury [11]resonaba... echoed in his mind [12]no... will never get you anywhere [13]abandoned [14]sure [15]bookstore [16]sign [17]environment [18]volvió... he felt like . . . again [19]attracted [20]welcomed, accepted

Relaciones estrechas

> The interactive CD-ROM to accompany *Destinos* contains additional practice with the video story line and will help you improve your skills in Spanish.

BEFORE VIEWING . . .

Preparación

VOCABULARIO

Los sustantivos

el gruñón/la gruñona	grouch
la suegra	mother-in-law
el yerno	son-in-law

Los adjetivos

atento/a	attentive
cariñoso/a	caring
estrecho/a	close-knit

Actividad A.
Complete the following statements about the previous video episode.

1. La hija de Ángel / Una vecina / Una amiga ...le dio a Raquel la triste noticia de la muerte de Ángel y de su esposa.
2. Ángela es... la hija / la esposa / la sobrina ...de Ángel.

3. Cuando Raquel le dijo a Ángela que tenía un abuelo en México, Ángela... estaba furiosa / estaba sorprendida / no lo creía.
4. Al final del episodio, Ángela y Raquel esperaban... a los tíos / a los hermanos / al novio ...de Ángela.
5. Mientras esperaban, Ángela le dijo a Raquel que... tenía un hermano también / no quería ir a México con ella / vendía su apartamento.

Para pensar...

¿Cómo va a reaccionar la familia de Ángela cuando todos sepan las noticias? ¿Van a creer la historia? ¿Va a poder Ángela ir a México con Raquel?

Actividad B.

Paso 1

In this video episode you will meet one of Ángela's aunts, **la tía Olga**. Ángela calls her **la gruñona de la familia**. Read a conversation from **Episodio 20** between Raquel, Olga, and Ángela.

RAQUEL: ...Y como don Fernando está gravemente enfermo en el hospital, es importante que Ángela vaya a México pronto.
OLGA: Creo que eso va a ser imposible.
ÁNGELA: ¿Por qué?
OLGA: Ángela, no conocemos a esa gente. Puede ser peligroso.
ÁNGELA: Titi Olga, por favor...

Paso 2

Now answer the following question.

Olga dice que un viaje a México «puede ser peligroso». ¿Qué significa **peligroso**?

a. _____ dangerous   b. _____ exciting   c. _____ inconvenient

---

Para pensar...

¿Crees que la reacción de la tía Olga es razonable? Escucha con atención las preguntas que Olga le hace a Raquel en este episodio. Nota también la reacción de Ángela a las preguntas de Olga. ¿Crees que su reacción es razonable?

Actividad C.

Paso 1

In this video episode you will hear Ángela read from a storybook that her father wrote for her when she was a child. Read the beginning of the story. You should also look carefully at this illustration from the storybook.

El coquí y la princesa

A nuestra hija Ángela, nuestra princesa...

Érase una vez un coquí. Le gustaba pintar. Su padre y su madre querían mandarlo a la escuela. Pero el pequeño coquí no quería estudiar. Sólo quería pintar.

Paso 2

1. Según el dibujo, ¿qué es un coquí?
   a. _____ un animal anfibio pequeño y verde
   b. _____ un animal grande y feroz
   c. _____ un animal grande pero dócil

2. El coquí representa a una persona de esta historia. ¿A quién representa? ¡OJO! ¿A quién le pasó lo mismo?
   a. _____ a Arturo
   b. _____ a Ángel
   c. _____ a don Fernando

3. ¿Qué significan las primeras palabras de la historia, «Érase una vez... »?
   a. _____ It was a cold and rainy night . . .
   b. _____ Call me . . .
   c. _____ Once upon a time . . .

. . . AFTER VIEWING

¿Tienes buena memoria?

¿QUÉ RECUERDAS?

Actividad A.   Preguntas

Briefly answer the following questions about **Episodio 20**.

1. ¿Por qué vienen los tíos de Ángela a su casa? _____

2. ¿Qué dice Ángela acerca de las relaciones entre su padre y su abuela? _____
   _____

3. ¿Cómo es la tía Olga? _____

4. ¿Por qué es importante que Ángela vaya a México inmediatamente? _____
   _____

5. ¿Por qué van Raquel y Ángela a San Germán? _____

6. ¿Qué lee Ángela por la noche? _____

7. ¿Por qué se pone triste al leer (*upon reading*) ese libro? _____

8. ¿Quién va a San Germán con Ángela y Raquel? _____

Actividad B.   ¡Busca el intruso!

For each group of names, places, actions, or items, underline the one that does not belong with the others.

1. amigo, yerno, suegra, tía

2. simpático, amable, gruñón, cariñoso

3. Elena, Carmen, Laura, Olga

4. ir a San Germán, conocer a la abuela de Ángela, pedir permiso, sacar fotos

Actividad C.   ¿Cierto o falso?

Indicate whether the following statements are **Cierto (C)** or **Falso (F)**.

C   F   1.   Las relaciones entre doña Carmen y Ángel fueron muy estrechas.
C   F   2.   Los tíos de Ángela tienen que aparcar muy lejos de la casa porque las
             calles están bloqueadas.
C   F   3.   La tía Olga es una mujer tranquila y razonable.
C   F   4.   La tía Olga no quiere que Ángela vaya a México porque no tiene confianza
             en los aviones.
C   F   5.   Doña Carmen quiere conocer a Raquel.

ACTIVIDADES

Actividad A.   ¿Quiénes son?

Complete the following activity about some of the characters you met in this video
episode.

1.   Esta señora es
     a.   _____ la tía de Raquel.
     b.   _____ la abuela de Ángela.
     c.   _____ la prima de Ángel.

2.   Se llama
     a.   _____ María Luisa de Castillo.
     b.   _____ Isabel Santana de Trujillo.
     c.   _____ Carmen Contreras de Soto.

3.   Vive en
     a.   _____ San Juan, Puerto Rico.
     b.   _____ San Germán, Puerto Rico.
     c.   _____ Nueva York.

4.   Ángela la llama porque
     a.   _____ quiere su permiso para ir a México.
     b.   _____ quiere pedirle dinero para viajar con Raquel.
     c.   _____ Raquel quiere conocerla.

a.   b.   c.   d.   e.   f.   g.

Now match Ángela's relatives with their names.

 5.   _____ la abuela de Ángela
 6.   _____ el tío Carlos
 7.   _____ el tío Jaime
 8.   _____ la tía Olga
 9.   _____ la tía Carmen
10.   _____ la madre de Ángela
11.   _____ Ángel Castillo, a los 50 años

Actividad B.   Yerno y suegra

Ángel era el yerno de doña Carmen. ¿Cuánto recuerdas acerca de su relación?

1. Según Ángela, los dos
   a. _____ tenían unas relaciones muy estrechas.
   b. _____ no se llevaban bien.
   c. _____ se toleraban el uno al otro.

2. Según el episodio, doña Carmen
   a. _____ no guarda nada de Ángel.
   b. _____ tiene algo que pertenecía a Ángel.
   c. _____ realmente no quería mucho a su yerno.

Actividad C.   Llamadas de larga distancia

En este episodio, dos personas llamaron a México. ¿Cuánto recuerdas de sus llamadas?

1. ¿Quiénes llamaron a México?
   a. _____ Raquel y doña Carmen
   b. _____ Raquel y el tío Jaime
   c. _____ Ángela y Raquel

2. ¿A quiénes llamaron? Y ¿pudieron hablar con ellos?

   _____ llamó a _____. Pudo / No pudo hablar con él/ella.

   _____ llamó a _____. Pudo / No pudo hablar con él/ella.

Para pensar...

¿Quién llamaba a la habitación de Raquel al final del Episodio 20? ¿Era una llamada de México... con malas noticias?

Nota cultural: Las familias hispanas

Ángela is a young professional who lives alone and who is, for all intents and purposes, in charge of her own life. Yet a major topic of the family conference that takes place in her apartment concerns whether or not she should go to Mexico with Raquel to meet her paternal grandfather and to find out more about this "new" branch of the family. As you have learned, Ángela and Raquel will have to travel to San Germán to discuss the topic with Ángela's maternal grandmother.

It is very difficult to generalize about family customs in any culture. Depending on your particular situation, you may find the family unity shown in this video episode to be "normal" or "strange." It is fair to suggest, however, that Hispanic families are thought to be more close-knit than the average non-Hispanic U.S. family. Hispanic young people often live at home longer than their typical non-Hispanic U.S. counterparts, and the family is more often regarded as an important source of emotional support. You can read more about Ángela's family situation in the **Más allá del episodio** section of this lesson.

In Hispanic families, just as in families throughout the world, the use of terms of endearment to refer to family members is common. Ángela calls her Aunt Olga **titi** instead of **tía**. The use of the endings **-ito** or **-ita**, as appropriate, is also quite common: **abuelito**, **hermanita**, and so on.

Intercambio

Paso 1

Select one of don Fernando's relatives from this lesson. Without saying who it is, describe the person in Spanish so your classmates might guess the character. They should respond by saying the name and the relationship to don Fernando.

_____

_____

Paso 2

Now imagine you are the person you described in **Paso 1**. Make up a series of four statements to talk about what you were doing when something else happened during one of the episodes of _Destinos_. Read your statements to the class and have the class decide whether what you say **Es posible** or **No es posible**.

_____

_____

_____

_____

Más allá del episodio: Ángela y su Titi Olga... y un poco de psicología

La tía Olga y Ángela son muy diferentes, pero se quieren mucho.

Ángela tiene 25 años, pero su familia todavía es muy importante para ella. ¿Por qué tiene tanta prisa por invitar a sus tíos a su casa? ¿Por qué vienen tan rápidamente? ¿Por qué parece que la tía Olga trata de controlarle la vida a Ángela?

Parte de la explicación de todo esto se encuentra en ciertos valores culturales del mundo de habla española. Más que en Norteamérica, la familia es parte importante de la vida diaria y emotiva[1] de una persona hispana. Aunque las generalizaciones siempre son peligrosas, muchos hispanos al llegar[2] a los Estados Unidos notan que las familias norteamericanas no son tan unidas como las familias hispanas.

Las relaciones entre Olga y Ángela también se explican al considerar[3] la personalidad de estas dos mujeres. Ángela siempre vacila entre el «soy independiente» y el «quiero que me necesites». Como muchas personas, ella a veces recurre a[4] la ayuda de su familia (o la de otras personas) sólo para llamar la atención, para asegurarse de que es importante para los otros. La conducta de Ángela no es patológica en este sentido; sus acciones son típicas de muchas personas y son parte de las mil maneras «normales» de adaptarse del ser humano.[5]

[1]diaria... _daily and emotional_   [2]al... _when they arrive_   [3]al... _by considering_   [4]_resorts to_   [5]ser... _human being_

Olga también necesita la atención de sus parientes y quiere ser «necesitada[6]». Desde pequeña, Olga ha creído[7] que es la menos querida entre los hijos de doña Carmen. No se creía tan inteligente como Jaime ni tan guapa como Carmen ni tan simpática como Carlos. Por eso Olga siempre ha tratado de dominar a los otros.

Desde que murió la madre de Ángela, Olga se ha visto a sí misma[8] como una madre sustituta para su sobrina. Así, ha tratado de ejercer más y más control sobre la vida de Ángela. Pero al mismo tiempo realmente ha ayudado a Ángela. Cuando Ángel murió, fue Olga quien ayudó con todos los arreglos funerarios. Cuando Roberto se fue a México, Olga le preguntó a Ángela si quería irse a vivir con ella, para que no estuviera[9] tan sola.

Sin embargo, es importante notar que Ángela y Olga se quieren mucho. La familia de doña Carmen Contreras de Soto sí es muy unida. Eso lo ve Raquel perfectamente bien. Cuando Ángela le saca la lengua[10] a Olga, Raquel le asegura que no es para tanto,[11] que la tía sólo está preocupada. Y seguramente la semana que viene —si Ángela no está en México— Olga y Ángela harán planes para ir de compras. Y lo pasarán muy bien juntas.

[6]*needed*　[7]ha... *has believed*　[8]se... *has seen herself*　[9]para... *so that she wouldn't be*　[10]le... *sticks her tongue out*　[11]no... *it isn't such a big deal*

21

El peaje

The interactive CD-ROM to accompany *Destinos* contains additional practice with the video story line and will help you improve your skills in Spanish.

BEFORE VIEWING . . .

Preparación

VOCABULARIO

Los verbos		**Los sustantivos**		**Las palabras adicionales**	
faltar	to be lacking	**el aceite**	oil	**Hace (muy) buen tiempo.**	The weather's (very) good.
funcionar	to work, function (*machines*)	**la autopista**	highway; toll road	**Hace (mucho) calor.**	It's (very) hot.
manejar	to drive	**el peaje**	tollbooth	**Hace (mucho) frío.**	It's (very) cold.
parar	to stop	**el taller**	repair shop (*automobiles*)	**Hace (muy) mal tiempo.**	The weather's (very) bad.
				¿Qué tiempo hace?	What's the weather like?

Actividad A.
Answer the following questions about the previous video episode.

1. ¿Cuál era la actitud de los tíos de Ángela mientras escuchaban la historia de la investigación de Raquel?
   a. _____ Escuchaban sin gran interés.
   b. _____ Escuchaban con mucha atención.

2. ¿Cuál de los tíos tenía mucho que decir acerca de la historia de Raquel?
   a. _____ el tío Carlos   b. _____ la tía Olga

3. En general, ¿cómo reaccionaban los tíos de Ángela ante las noticias?
   a. _____ Estaban preocupados.
   b. _____ Reaccionaban con indiferencia.

4. De los parientes de Ángela, ¿quién parecía ser el centro de la familia?
   a. _____ la tía Olga
   b. _____ el tío Jaime
   c. _____ la abuela

5. ¿Cómo eran las relaciones entre doña Carmen, la abuela y su yerno, Ángel?
   a. _____ Eran problemáticas.
   b. _____ Eran muy estrechas.

6. ¿Con quién tiene que hablar ahora Raquel?
   a. _____ con la tía Olga
   b. _____ con doña Carmen

Actividad B.

In this video episode Raquel has the following conversation with an employee at a tollbooth on the highway. Read it, keeping in mind that the word **taller** means *repair shop*.

RAQUEL: Perdone. Algo le pasó al carro. ¿Nos podría ayudar?

EMPLEADA: Me gustaría mucho, señorita, pero no puedo. ¿Por qué no llaman a un taller en Ponce?

Now answer the following questions.

1. ¿Qué problema tienen Raquel y Ángela en el camino a San Germán?
   a. _____ No funciona el carro.
   b. _____ Paran porque necesitan gasolina.

2. ¿Hay talleres en la autopista?
   a. _____ No, pero los hay en una ciudad que está cerca.
   b. _____ Sí, junto al peaje.

... AFTER VIEWING

¿Tienes buena memoria?

¿QUÉ RECUERDAS?

Actividad A.   Preguntas

Briefly answer the following questions about **Episodio 21**.

1. ¿Por qué van Ángela, Raquel y Laura a San Germán? _____

2. ¿Cómo se llega de San Juan a la ciudad de San Germán? _____

3. ¿Por qué no es necesario que Ángela tenga (*has*) pasaporte para entrar en México?

_____

4. ¿Qué le pasa al carro cerca del peaje? _____

5. ¿Qué tiempo hace cerca de Ponce? _____

6. ¿Por qué pasan las tres mujeres la noche en Ponce en vez de ir directamente a San Germán? _____

Actividad B. ¡Busca el intruso!

For each group of items, indicate the one that does not belong with the others.

1. la carretera, el peaje, la autopista, el taller

2. el tanque, el mapa, el radiador, el motor

3. el agua, la gasolina, el aceite, el jugo

4. el guineo, la naranja, el plátano, la banana

Actividad C. ¿Cierto o falso?

Indicate whether the following statements are **Cierto (C)** or **Falso (F)**.

C F 1. Raquel, Ángela y Laura van a San Germán para visitar a la madre de Ángela.
C F 2. En Puerto Rico se vende la gasolina por galones, como en los EE.UU.
C F 3. Según el primer mecánico, el coche de Ángela necesita un poco de aceite.
C F 4. En Ponce, el mecánico dijo que podría arreglar (*he could fix*) el coche en dos horas.
C F 5. Puerto Rico todavía es territorio de los EE.UU.

ACTIVIDADES

Actividad. La historia sigue

The following statements are taken from Raquel's summary at the end of **Episodio 21**. Indicate the phrase that completes the statement or answers the question.

1. Esta mañana Ángela, su prima Laura y yo salimos de San Juan para ir a
   a. _____ Ponce.   b. _____ San Germán.   c. _____ Caguas.

2. En ruta a San Germán aprendí muchas cosas interesantes. Por ejemplo, ¿es una peseta puertorriqueña igual a una peseta española?
   a. _____ No. Vale un dólar. Es una moneda norteamericana.
   b. _____ Sí. Son iguales. Una peseta puertorriqueña y una peseta española valen lo mismo.
   c. _____ No. Vale veinticinco centavos. Es una moneda norteamericana.

3. En Puerto Rico una banana es **un guineo**. En España se dice **plátano**. Otra fruta con un nombre diferente es
   a. _____ la manzana.   b. _____ la naranja.   c. _____ la pera.

4. En camino a San Germán, cerca del peaje, tuvimos problemas con
   a. _____ la comida.   b. _____ mi sombrero.   c. _____ el carro.

5. La mujer del peaje me dio un número de un taller para llamar. ¿En dónde estaba el taller?
   a. _____ En San Juan.   b. _____ En Caguas.   c. _____ En Ponce.

6. Luego vino el señor del taller y remolcó el carro a Ponce. En el taller, supimos que el carro
   a. _____ simplemente no tenía gasolina.
   b. _____ estaba en muy malas condiciones.
   c. _____ era imposible de reparar.

7. Y aquí estamos, cansadas y listas para dormir. Ahora tendré que esperar hasta
   mañana para conocer
   a. _____ al hermano de Ángela.
   b. _____ a Carmen Contreras.
   c. _____ al dueño del taller.

**Nota cultural: Los puertorriqueños, ciudadanos (*citizens*)
de los Estados Unidos**

When Raquel asks Ángela whether her passport is up to date, she has forgotten
something of which many people are not aware: Puerto Ricans are U.S. citizens.
They can travel back and forth freely from **la Isla** to the mainland, and, as U.S. citizens, they can go anywhere that other U.S. citizens are permitted to go without a
passport.

   Another result of Puerto Rico's relationship to the United States is the use of
U.S. currency . . . some with Spanish names! Can you remember the value in cents
(**centavos**) of the following coins?

   una peseta   un vellón de 10   un vellón de 5   un chavo (un chavito)

ntercambio

Paso 1
Create four statements about what you were doing and/or where you were at
8:00 A.M., 12:00 noon, 3:00 P.M., and 7:00 P.M. yesterday.

_____

_____

_____

_____

Paso 2
Find people in the class who were doing the same thing as you. Your goal is to find
at least two other people who were doing the same thing as you for any activity.

   MODELO: ¿Qué hacías ayer a las 3:00 de la tarde?

Paso 3
Report to the class what you and the other students from **Paso 2** were doing at a
particular time.

   MODELO: Ayer a las 3:00 Sheryl, Tom y yo estudiábamos en la biblioteca.

Paso 4
As a class, what do you think Raquel was doing yesterday at the times mentioned in
Paso 1?

Más allá del episodio: Mientras tanto... en la Argentina: Arturo Iglesias

Arturo espera hablar con Raquel con impaciencia.

Desde que se despidió de Raquel en el aeropuerto de Buenos Aires, Arturo no ha dejado de[1] pensar en dos personas. Primero, en Raquel. ¡La extraña muchísimo! Piensa en ella constantemente y desea ir a Puerto Rico para volver a verla[2] lo antes posible. Pero hay muchos obstáculos.

Primero, tiene que buscar a alguien que dé sus clases en la universidad. Y luego está el problema de sus pacientes. La ausencia inesperada[3] de su doctor podría ser traumático para muchos, sobre todo para los más delicados, y Arturo es más que nada un médico responsable, todo un profesional. La idea de causarle daño a alguno de sus pacientes le horroriza.

¿Y la segunda persona? Arturo tampoco puede dejar de pensar en Ángel y en su insistente mal presentimiento. Sus sentimientos hacia su hermano son todavía un poco confusos. Ya no lo considera responsable de la muerte de su padre. Pero a pesar de[4] eso no puede olvidar la terrible discusión entre Ángel y Martín... y el ataque cardíaco de su padre.

Y luego está la otra cara[5] de la moneda: su propio sentimiento de culpabilidad por no haber buscado a[6] su medio hermano a lo largo de[7] todos estos años.

Ni Ángel ni él son culpables. Esto es lo que le dice la razón.[8] Pero el corazón, los sentimientos le dicen... otra cosa. Claro, Arturo es psiquiatra. Pero eso no quiere decir que sea capaz de analizarse a sí mismo.

Y luego, volviendo al tema de Raquel... Arturo nunca imaginó que pudiera volver a enamorarse[9]... y mucho menos de una norteamericana. Otra vez, una extranjera. Ojalá que[10] la historia de su primera esposa no se repita...

[1]no... *hasn't stopped* [2]volver... *to see her again* [3]*unexpected* [4]a... *in spite of* [5]*side* (lit., *face*) [6]por... *about not having looked for* [7]a... *during* [8]*reason* [9]pudiera... *he could fall in love again* [10]Ojalá... *How he hopes that*

22

Recuerdos

Estas son mis amigos del puerto... los primeros en decirme que me dedicara a la pintura.

> The interactive CD-ROM to accompany *Destinos* contains additional practice with the video story line and will help you improve your skills in Spanish.

BEFORE VIEWING . . .

 **reparación**

VOCABULARIO

Los verbos		Los sustantivos	
confiar (confío) (en)	to trust (in)	la caña de azúcar	sugar cane
enfermarse	to get sick	el dueño/la dueña	owner
ocultar	to hide (*something*)	la finca	farm; ranch; hacienda
		el mar	sea
		el recuerdo	memory

Actividad.

In the previous video episode, Raquel and her traveling companions set off for San Germán, where Ángela's grandmother lives. Their trip was not uneventful, however. Complete the following summary of the previous episode. No words are given from which to choose, but you should be able to complete the paragraph easily. Read it through at least once before you fill in the blanks.

En camino a San Germán, Raquel, Ángela y Laura, la _____¹ de Ángela, tuvieron dificultades con el _____.² Llamaron a un _____³ de reparaciones. Vino un hombre y remolcó el carro a Ponce. El mecánico les dijo que el carro no iba a estar listo hasta el _____.⁴ Raquel y sus dos compañeras tuvieron que pasar la noche en _____.⁵

Para pensar...

Esto es un baúl. Contiene artículos personales de alguien. ¿De quién?

¿Qué hay en la caja que le está dando doña Carmen a Ángela? ¿Será algo relacionado con la historia de Ángel?

. . . AFTER VIEWING

¿**T**ienes buena memoria?

¿QUÉ RECUERDAS?

Actividad A.   Preguntas

Briefly answer the following questions about **Episodio 22**.

1. ¿Adónde van Raquel, Ángela y Laura por la mañana? ¿Por qué? _____

   _____

2. ¿Cuánto paga Ángela para el arreglo del carro? _____

3. ¿Dónde está doña Carmen cuando las tres llegan a San Germán? _____

4. ¿Cómo ganaron la vida (*earned a living*) doña Carmen y su esposo? _____

5. ¿Qué dice doña Carmen sobre el deseo de Ángela de conocer a su abuelo en

   México? _____

6. ¿Qué encontraron Raquel y Ángela en la antigua habitación de Ángel? _____

7. ¿Qué contenía? _____

8. ¿Qué le dio doña Carmen a Ángela al final del episodio? _____

9. ¿Qué importancia tiene este objeto? _____

Actividad B.   ¡Busca el intruso!

For each group of actions or items, select the one that does not belong with the others.

1. el efectivo, el remolque, el crédito, el cheque

2. el petróleo, el azúcar, el café, el tabaco

3. la finca, el baúl, el cultivo de la tierra, la caña de azúcar

4. sentir culpable, dejar su tierra natal, romper con la familia, no tener padre

Actividad C.   ¿Cierto o falso?

Indicate whether the following statements are **Cierto (C)** or **Falso (F)**.

C   F   1. Ángela pagó el arreglo del coche con tarjeta (*card*) de crédito.
C   F   2. Antes de morir, Ángel les reveló todo su pasado a sus hijos.
C   F   3. Doña Carmen le dio permiso a Ángela de viajar a México.
C   F   4. Mientras limpiaban la habitación de Ángel, Raquel y Ángela encontraron
          unas fotos de Rosario.
C   F   5. Doña Carmen le dio una copa de bodas a Ángela para que pudiera (*she
          could*) casarse con Jorge.

ACTIVIDADES

Actividad.   Las preguntas de Raquel

Paso 1

Here are the first questions that Raquel asks at the end of the video episode while she is waiting for the family to say good-bye. Read the questions and select the correct answer from the choices provided.

1. Esta mañana fuimos al taller a recoger el carro. ¿Estaba listo el carro cuando llegamos?
   a. _____ Sí.
   b. _____ No.

2. ¿Y cómo estaba Ángela?
   a. _____ Estaba muy contenta.
   b. _____ Estaba furiosa.

3. Cuando llegamos a San Germán, Dolores nos recibió en la casa. ¿Dónde estaba la abuela?
   a. _____ Estaba en la iglesia.
   b. _____ Estaba en el mercado.
   c. _____ Estaba en el patio.

Paso 2

Now read the following statements about Raquel's conversation with doña Carmen and indicate whether they are **Cierto (C)** or **Falso (F)**. Think both about what you have seen and heard in the video episode and what you know about the characters from other sources.

C   F   1.   Ángela estudió en la Universidad de Puerto Rico, en San Juan.
C   F   2.   Cuando la mamá de Ángela se enfermó, Ángela se quedó a vivir con la abuela.
C   F   3.   El padre de Ángela venía todos los fines de semana a San Germán.
C   F   4.   Pero en San Germán, Ángel no tenía interés en pintar.

Paso 3

Now continue to read and answer Raquel's questions.

1.   Después de la conversación, Ángela y yo fuimos al cuarto de Ángel. ¿Y qué encontramos allí? Encontramos unas hojas. ¿Y qué contenían las hojas?
     a.   _____ Poesías.   c.   _____ Fotografías.
     b.   _____ Recuerdos.

2.   Y estas hojas de recuerdos, ¿decían algo sobre la vida de Ángel en la Argentina?
     a.   _____ Sí.   b.   _____ No.

Nota cultural: La comida de Puerto Rico

Laura, Ángela's cousin, is still a growing girl who eats a lot. As her grandmother says, **¡Siempre tiene hambre esta chica!**

In this video episode, you saw the dessert course of a pleasant meal served in doña Carmen's house: **pasta de guayaba** (*guava paste*), which is served with cheese (**queso**). **La guayaba** is a tropical fruit from the West Indies, used in making preserves, jellies, and pastries of many kinds. Other fruits typical of Puerto Rican cuisine include **las piñas**, **los cocos**, **los mangos**, **los plátanos**, **la parcha** (*passion fruit*), and so on.

Bananas in particular appear in a number of dishes, including **el mofongo**, a type of fritter made with fried and baked bananas and served with a variety of sauces (shrimp or chicken, for example).

Intercambio

Paso 1

Using the phrases below, create statements about what your instructor used to do.

1.   Cuando era un/a niño/a de 5 años… _____

2.   Durante su adoloscencia… _____

3.   El semestre pasado… _____

_____

_____

Paso 2

Share your statements with two other classmates. Among the three of you, select the three statements most likely to be true.

Paso 3

Each group should read its statements out loud. Your instructor will say whether or not they are true. Which group was correct on all three?

Más allá del episodio: Doña Carmen, suegra de Ángel

Doña Carmen se llevaba muy bien con su hija y su yerno.

Doña Carmen es una mujer serena y comprensiva, el alma[1] de su familia. Al mismo tiempo, es una persona dinámica, jovial; da gusto[2] estar con ella... y todos los parientes lo reconocen. Al mismo tiempo que buscan sus consejos, también buscan su compañía. La respetan, pero también la quieren. Visitar a la abuela es un deber,[3] claro, pero en este caso es un deber ameno.

Doña Carmen adoraba a su hija María Luisa. Cuando ésta[4] se enamoró de repente de Ángel, pensaba que ella había encontrado[5] en ese ex marinero argentino al compañero ideal. Su hija y su yerno venían con frecuencia a San Germán a visitarla.

A Ángel le gustaba mucho pintar, pero sobre todo en el pueblo colonial donde vivía su suegra. Se sentaba en el jardín y pintaba todo el día; le gustaba sobre todo la luz de ese lugar, por la mañana o al anochecer.[6] A veces se quedaba en su cuarto y pintaba toda la noche. Doña Carmen perdonaba esa manía de su yerno porque le gustaban mucho sus pinturas; creía que realmente tenía talento. Y cuando María Luisa criticaba a su esposo en broma[7] por pasar tanto tiempo pintando, su madre la silenciaba. La suegra sí comprendía lo que era ser pintor. Así nació entre doña Carmen y Ángel una gran amistad.[8]

Doña Carmen observaba a Ángel y María Luisa y veía que eran muy felices. Pero su instinto de madre le decía que algo triste había ocurrido[9] en el pasado de Ángel. Un día lo encontró contemplando unos retratos que él había pintado. Vio emoción en su rostro[10] y lágrimas en sus ojos.[11] Le preguntó: «¿Quiénes son estas personas, Ángel?» Ángel no contestó inmediatamente. Doña Carmen no insistió, pero se quedó a su lado. Después de un largo silencio, Ángel la miró y murmuró: «Son mi madre y mi hermano.»

Doña Carmen no sabía qué decir. Se quedó sorprendida, esperando una explicación. Ángel, por su parte, sintió la necesidad de confiarle su secreto. Entonces le contó la historia de la muerte de su padrastro y cómo se sintió culpable... de cómo se fue de Buenos Aires y nunca quiso regresar. También le pidió que guardara[12] su secreto. No quería ni que María Luisa supiera[13] la verdad.

Doña Carmen le prometió no decirle nada a nadie. Ángel se sintió aliviado[14] y mucho más tranquilo. A los pocos días Ángel le confió a doña Carmen una pequeña caja. Le explicó el significado de su contenido y le pidió que se la entregara[15] a sus hijos cuando ella lo creyera[16] necesario.

---

[1]*soul* [2]*da... it is a pleasure* [3]*duty* [4]*the latter* [5]habían... *had found* [6]*al... at nightfall* [7]*en... jokingly* [8]*friendship* [9]había... *had happened* [10]*face* [11]lágrimas... *tears in his eyes* [12]*she keep* [13]*to know* [14]*relieved* [15]*she hand over* [16]*believed*

23

Vista al mar

The interactive CD-ROM to accompany *Destinos* contains additional practice with the video story line and will help you improve your skills in Spanish.

BEFORE VIEWING . . .

Preparación

VOCABULARIO

Los verbos

convencer	to convince
impresionar	to impress
proponer	to propose

Los sustantivos

el estacionamiento	parking
el jefe/la jefa	boss
la terraza	terrace
la ventana	window

Actividad A.

In the last video episode of *Destinos* Raquel and Ángela spent time with doña Carmen, Ángela's grandmother. Do you remember the most important things that happened? Select the best answer for the following questions.

1. ¿Cómo reaccionó la abuela cuando Ángela le dijo que quería ir a México a conocer a don Fernando?

   Estaba
   a. a favor.　　　　b. en contra.　　　　c. indiferente.

2. ¿Qué encontró Ángela entre las cosas de su padre?

   Encontró
   a. un álbum de fotografías.
   b. un libro de poesías.
   c. unas hojas con sus recuerdos.

3. ¿Qué le dio la abuela a Ángela?

   Le dio
   a. un retrato de Rosario.
   b. la copa de bodas de Rosario.
   c. una carta de Rosario.

Actividad B.

As you know, Ángela wants to sell her parents' apartment in **el Viejo San Juan**. What kind of house or apartment do you think she will want to move into?

Ángela va a querer
a. _____ una casa antigua, en el Viejo San Juan, similar a la casa de sus padres.
b. _____ un apartamento en un edificio muy moderno con una vista panorámica al mar.
c. _____ un apartamento pequeño pero cómodo, cerca de la universidad (donde trabaja su novio).

Para pensar...

¿Ha hablado Ángela con su hermano, Roberto, sobre la venta de la casa de sus padres? ¿Debe vender la casa sin consultar con él?

...AFTER VIEWING

¿Tienes buena memoria?

¿QUÉ RECUERDAS?

Actividad A.   Preguntas
Briefly answer the following questions about **Episodio 23**.

1. Cuando Raquel llamó a Arturo, ¿qué le dijo? _____

2. ¿Por qué hablaron Raquel y Ángela con la Sra. Santiago? _____

3. ¿Qué profesiones tiene Jorge, el novio de Ángela? (Hay dos.) _____

4. ¿Por qué estuvo Jorge en Nueva York? _____

5. ¿Qué apartamento le gustó más a Ángela, el con vista al mar o el *town house*? _____
    _____

6. ¿Qué le propone Jorge a Ángela al final del episodio? _____

Actividad B.   ¡Busca el intruso!

For each group of names or items, choose the one that does not belong with the others.

1. los años cuarenta, la persecución política, la emigración a Nueva York, la situación económica
2. la terraza, el balcón, la cocina, el radio
3. el actor, el profesor, el marinero, el novio
4. estacionamiento, estufa, nevera, lavadora

Actividad C.   ¿Cierto o falso?

Indicate whether the following statements are **Cierto (C)** or **Falso (F)**.

C   F   1. Al regresar a San Juan, Raquel llamó a su madre para decirle que llegó sin problemas.
C   F   2. Arturo le dijo a Raquel que la quería.
C   F   3. Jorge enseña clases de teatro en la Universidad de Río Piedras.
C   F   4. A Ángela no le gustó mucho el apartamento con vista al mar.
C   F   5. A Ángela le dio su jefa dos semanas de vacaciones para que pudiera (*she could*) conocer a sus parientes en México.

ACTIVIDADES

Actividad A.   ¿Relaciones serias?

Part of the video episode you have just seen focused on Raquel's activities. Can you complete this summary of the episode without consulting the choices that follow?

Esta tarde Raquel está en la facultad de la Universidad de Puerto Rico. Está esperando a Ángela, y ella _____[1] su novio Jorge.

Ángela y Raquel regresaron de San Germán _____.[2] Tan pronto como Raquel llegó a su habitación, hizo una llamada de larga distancia _____.[3] Afortunadamente Arturo estaba en casa y los dos pudieron hablar un rato. Arturo le sorprendió a Raquel cuando le dijo que _____.[4]

Ahora Raquel está un poco perpleja. Arturo le gusta mucho, eso sí. Pero Raquel _____[5] quiere tener relaciones serias en estos momentos.

1. está hablando afuera con / está tratando de llamar a
2. ayer por la mañana / ayer por la noche
3. a Buenos Aires para hablar con Arturo / a México para hablar con Pedro
4. la quería mucho / ya no la quería como antes
5. no sabe si / está segura que

Actividad B.   La vida de Ángela

The rest of **Episodio 23** focused on events and decisions in Ángela's life. Can you answer these questions about Ángela without referring to the list of **Frases útiles** that follows?

1. ¿Dónde trabaja Ángela? _____
2. ¿Con quién tenía que hablar allí? _____
3. ¿Con quién quería hablar en la universidad? _____
4. ¿Qué hacía esta persona cuando Raquel y Ángela llegaron? _____
5. ¿Qué le mostró Ángela a esta persona? _____

Frases útiles: en una tienda / un banco, con una amiga / su jefa / su profesor / su novio, tomar/dar una clase, una copa / unas hojas

Nota cultural: Vivo en el segundo piso

Just as in the United States, a wide range of types of housing is available in the Spanish-speaking world. In large cities the most common type of housing is an apartment or condominium, often in a high-rise building. An option available depending on the country is a separate house (generally called **una casa** but also called **un chalet** in Spain). Of the dwellings you have seen so far, Teresa Suárez's apartment best typifies middle-class housing. Héctor's apartment (seen only from the outside) is typical of people of more modest means.

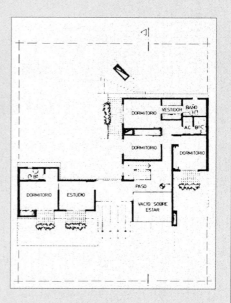

The apartments Ángela looks at in this video episode, while luxurious by some standards, are relatively typical of modern apartments in most parts of the world. Note that Ángela and the agent use the term *town house*; in other parts of the Spanish-speaking world **el condominio** or **la casa adosada** would probably be used.

Something that is quite different about Hispanic buildings is the way the floors are numbered. The ground floor is generally **la planta baja**. The next floor up (the second floor in the United States) is **el primer piso**; the next floor (the third floor in this country) is **el segundo piso**; and so on. (This usage does not occur in Puerto Rico.)

Look at this floor plan. Is it for the first floor (**la planta baja**) or the second floor (**el primer piso**)? How do you know?

Intercambio

Paso 1

The class should divide itself into four groups and complete the tasks below.

Group 1: Select six of the places in/around a house and number them 1–6 on a separate sheet of paper.

Group 2: Select six characters from the Puerto Rico episodes and number them 1–6 on a separate sheet of paper.

Group 3: Select six activities (e.g., **tomar un cerveza**) and number them 1–6 on a separate sheet of paper.

Group 4: Sit quietly and read something from your book.

Paso 2

Group 4 will now ask a series of questions. A member from each group must answer the question adhering to the numerical order in which the group selected places, characters, or activities. You may come up with some zany scenarios!

MODELO:

GROUP 4: ¿Qué lugar tienen para el número 1?
GROUP 1: la terraza
GROUP 4: ¿Quién estaba en la terraza anoche?
GROUP 2: (*referring to item 1 on their list*) Olga estaba en la terraza.
GROUP 4: ¿Qué estaba haciendo Olga en la terraza?
GROUP 3: (*referring to item 1 on their list*) Estaba mirando la televisión.

Paso 3

Without looking at your notes or lists, which group can remember all six scenarios?

Más allá del episodio: Ángela y el apartamento

Raquel no comprende por qué Ángela quiere dejar su apartamento en el Viejo San Juan. ¿Por qué quiere mudarse Ángela de este bonito e histórico apartamento de la calle del Sol? ¿Qué le está motivando para querer venderlo?

¿Debe vender el apartamento Ángela?

Después de la muerte de su padre, Ángela pasó por una larga depresión. Su hermano Roberto no lo pasó tan mal. Él se fue a México a estudiar dos semanas después de los servicios funerarios. Pero Ángela tenía que quedarse... y se encontró muy sola en el apartamento de la calle del Sol. Tenía el apoyo[1] de su tía Olga, que la ayudaba mucho en aquel trance, pero siguió sintiendo una gran tristeza.

Ahora Ángela está mucho mejor. Ya no está tan triste como antes y además está muy contenta con su relación con Jorge, su novio. Jorge tiene varias ambiciones, y una de ellas es abrir un nuevo teatro. Pero no tiene mucho dinero. Se le ocurre a Ángela que podría ayudarlo. Si vende el apartamento y compra uno más barato, entonces puede darle a Jorge parte de su dinero. Si vende el apartamento, también puede dejar atrás el triste recuerdo de la muerte de sus padres y empezar otra vida.

¿Sabe todo esto Roberto? ¿Comprende la tristeza de su hermana? ¿su deseo de ayudar a su novio? ¿Y tú? ¿Crees que es buena idea que Ángela le dé dinero a Jorge?

[1]*support*

24

El don Juan

The interactive CD-ROM to accompany *Destinos* contains additional practice with the video story line and will help you improve your skills in Spanish.

Preparación

VOCABULARIO		
Los verbos	**Los sustantivos**	**Los adjetivos**
enfadarse to get mad	**el mujeriego** womanizer	**incómodo/a** uncomfortable
irritar to irritate		

Actividad A.

Here is the text of the summary of **Episodio 23**, which you will hear at the beginning of this video episode. But some of the details have been changed. Read through the text and correct as many details as you can. *Hint*: There are three incorrect details in each paragraph.

Al final de su estancia en San Germán, la abuela doña Carmen le da a Ángela un objeto muy especial... un regalo de su madre. Desde el hotel, Raquel manda un telegrama a Buenos Aires. Le cuenta a Arturo que Ángel ya murió... y que Ángel tenía dos hijas.

Ángela y Raquel hablan con la supervisora de la tienda donde Ángela trabaja. Le pide dos meses libres para ir a México a visitar a su abuelo, don Fernando. Don Fernando está muy enfermo y Ángela le explica a la supervisora que don Fernando va a enfadarse.

Raquel y Ángela hacen los preparativos para salir mañana para Los Ángeles. Luego van a la universidad para ver a Jorge, el hermano de Ángela. En un patio de la universidad, Ángela y Jorge hablan del viaje.

Para pensar...

Piensa en el título de este episodio. ¿Qué es un «don Juan»? ¿A quién se podría referir este nombre en este episodio?

Una palabra importante que vas a oír en este episodio es **mujeriego**. ¿Hay un hombre mujeriego en este episodio?

Actividad B.

Read the following conversation between Ángela, Raquel, and Jorge. Then answer the question about it.

JORGE: ¿Por qué no nos vamos a vivir a Nueva York?

ÁNGELA: No, gracias. Me gusta visitar esa ciudad, pero ¿vivir? No. Además, ¿no vas a formar una compañía de teatro acá en San Juan?

JORGE: Hay en San Juan un cine que puede funcionar como teatro.

RAQUEL: Tiene que ser caro.

JORGE: Sí, lo es. Pero es el mejor sitio. Perdónenme. Voy a cambiarme.

Piensa bien en lo que Jorge quiere hacer, porque esto va a provocar un conflicto. ¿Cuál podría ser el conflicto?

a. _____ Ángela cree que la idea de Jorge no es buena. Por eso pelean.

b. _____ Jorge le pide consejos sobre asuntos legales a Raquel, pero ella se niega a dárselos.

c. _____ Ángela quiere ayudarle a Jorge, pero Raquel cree que no es una buena idea.

. . . AFTER VIEWING

¿**T**ienes buena memoria?

¿QUÉ RECUERDAS?

Actividad A.   Preguntas

Briefly answer the following questions about **Episodio 24**.

1. ¿Cómo es Jorge? _____

2. ¿Por qué no pudo ir Jorge con las mujeres a ver la colección de pinturas de Oller?

_____

3. ¿A quién le confiesa Raquel de sus dudas sobre Jorge? _____

4. ¿Qué recomienda esta persona que haga Raquel? _____

5. ¿Qué quiere hacer Ángela con una parte del dinero que va a recibir de la venta de
    la casa de sus padres? ¿Por qué? _____

6. ¿Por qué se puso tan defensiva Ángela cuando Raquel le aconsejó que no le diera
    (*she advised her not to give*) el dinero a Jorge? _____

7. ¿Por qué no se podían comunicar Raquel y Ángela con Roberto?
    _____

Actividad B.   ¡Busca el intruso!

For each group of names or items, underline the one that does not belong with the
others.

1. alegrarse, enfadarse, oponerse a, irritarse

2. las reservaciones, las maletas, el piragua, los boletos

3. la playa, el mar, la isla, el coro

4. un funeral, un teatro, un velorio, un cumpleaños

Actividad C.   ¿Cierto o falso?

Indicate whether the following statements are **Cierto (C)** or **Falso (F)**.

C   F   1. Raquel no quería que Jorge la tratara (*treat*) con tanta confianza.
C   F   2. Ángela ya sabía que su novio era mujeriego.
C   F   3. Raquel llamó a Pedro en México para decirle que iba a salir pronto.
C   F   4. La madre de Raquel le dijo a su hija que no debía meterse en los asuntos
            de Ángela y Jorge.
C   F   5. Ángela no entiende por qué todo el mundo se opone a sus relaciones con
            Jorge.

ACTIVIDADES

Actividad.   Las preguntas de Raquel

As usual, Raquel recapped the most important moments of the video episode in her
review at the end of the show. Here is a series of statements based on her review. Can
you complete them with phrases from the following list?

a. viajar a México en unos días   f. el novio de Ángela
b. tutearla   g. un don Juan
c. Jorge las esperaba   h. nadaban
d. estaba muy contento   i. hacía llamadas
e. lo esperaba un estudiante   j. se enojó con Raquel

1. Raquel fue con Ángela a la universidad para conocer a Jorge, el novio de Ángela.
    Para Raquel, fue una sorpresa cuando Jorge empezó a _____.
2. Por sus acciones, Raquel creía que Jorge era _____.
3. Cuando Ángela quería llevar a Raquel al museo de Oller, Jorge no quería acom-
    pañarlas porque _____.
4. Las dos mujeres vieron la colección de obras de Oller. _____ cuando salieron del
    museo. Todos fueron a unas tiendas cerca de la universidad, donde Raquel compró
    unos cassettes.

5. En el hotel, Jorge y Ángela _____ mientras Raquel _____. Habló con su madre y con Arturo.

6. Con su madre, Raquel habló sobre _____. Según su madre, Raquel no debe meterse en la vida personal de otras personas. Efectivamente, cuando Raquel trató de hablar con Ángela, ésta _____.

7. Con Arturo Raquel tuvo una conversación agradable porque Arturo _____. Raquel también se alegra, porque Arturo va a _____.

Nota cultural: Más sobre la comida

In **Episodio 21**, on the road to San Germán, Ángela stopped the car to buy snacks at a small roadside store. Laura wanted **un pilón** (also called **un pirulí**), a fruit-based lollipop with seeds. Another popular Puerto Rican snack purchased by the characters in this video episode is **una piragua** (called a snow cone in parts of the United States), a small cone filled with chipped ice that is then flavored with a fruit syrup. Raquel and Ángela preferred **una piragua de frambuesa** (*raspberry*), while Jorge asked for **una piragua de tamarindo**, a tropical fruit popular in the Caribbean. Although snow cones are machine-made in the continental United States, in Puerto Rico **piragüeros** make them by hand and sell them from carts on the street.

Snack foods and treats are consumed all over the Spanish-speaking world and some places are famous for a particular food. Influenced by Italian culture, **heladerías** (*ice cream shops*) can be found on any street in Argentina, especially in Buenos Aires. In Spain **helados** of many kinds are also quite popular as a snack food, as are **patatas fritas** (*potato chips*). In Mexico street vendors routinely sell **chicle** (*chewing gum*) and **dulces** (*candy*) as well as **tacos**.

Intercambio

Paso 1

Prepare four to five statements about yourself. The statements should describe activities you have done or liked to do that reveal something about your personality. For example, saying that you once parachuted out of an airplane might suggest that you are daring and adventurous. The statements should address the following:

*   at least three things you've done in the past that reflect something about you
*   something that you used to do that you no longer do

_____

_____

_____

_____

_____

Paso 2

In groups of four, take turns reading your statements. After hearing the statements, the others should discuss what personality traits the statements reveal.

Más allá del episodio: Jorge Alonso

Ángela conoció a Jorge a través de[1] un amigo común, quien los presentó en una fiesta. Simpatizaron[2] en seguida y comenzaron a salir juntos.

Jorge, ¿un hombre oportunista o un novio cariñoso?

Desde el principio doña Carmen no vio con buenos ojos las relaciones de Jorge con su nieta. Piensa que Jorge es un hombre oportunista y cree que va a hacerle daño a Ángela. Doña Carmen estaba tan preocupada por esta situación que hasta llamó a México hace unas semanas para hablar con Roberto, el hermano de Ángela. Quería saber si Roberto sabía algo de Jorge. Roberto le dijo que, en la Universidad de Puerto Rico, Jorge tiene gran fama de ser mujeriego y que, en su opinión, no era el hombre para Ángela.

Doña Carmen le ha dicho varias veces a Ángela que se opone a sus relaciones con Jorge, pero su nieta no la escucha. «Abuela», le dice, «sólo has visto a Jorge un par de veces. No lo conoces bien.» Doña Carmen espera que, cuando Ángela se dé cuenta de la realidad, no sea demasiado tarde. Desgraciadamente, hasta ahora nadie se atreve a[3] decirle a Ángela toda la verdad sobre su novio.

¿Y cuál es esta verdad? Para empezar, Jorge es muy vanidoso. Para él, la vida es un juego. Es actor y su papel favorito es el de seductor, papel que interpreta con frecuencia dentro y fuera de la escena. Ángela está muy enamorada de él y no está consciente de la situación. Le encanta cuando Jorge le declara su amor... pero no sabe que también les declara su amor a muchas otras mujeres.

Es cierto que Jorge siente una gran debilidad por las mujeres, a tal punto que flirtea con Raquel. En el fondo es un simple don Juan sin escrúpulos. Siempre tiene grandes proyectos que nunca realiza, como el teatro que quiere establecer.

Jorge va a menudo a Nueva York. Para sus salidas usa como pretexto el trabajo. En realidad pasa la mayor parte de su tiempo con sus conquistas o con gente no muy recomendable. En Nueva York hay una mujer en particular que está locamente enamorada de él. Es una mujer dulce, inocente, ingenua... como Ángela.

¿Debe decirle Raquel a Ángela cómo es Jorge? ¿Qué le va a decir Roberto cuando sepa del plan de Ángela? ¿Y tú? ¿Crees que Ángela debe ayudarle a Jorge, dándole dinero?

[1]a... *through*   [2]*They hit it off*   [3]se... *dares*

25

Reflexiones I

The interactive CD-ROM to accompany *Destinos* contains additional practice with the video story line and will help you improve your skills in Spanish.

BEFORE VIEWING . . .

Preparación

Para pensar...

Las noticias sobre Roberto dejan a Raquel en *shock*. En ese trance, comienza a recordar y reflexionar sobre su difícil investigación. ¿Qué acontecimientos de su investigación recuerda? ¿Cuáles son los acontecimientos más importantes desde su salida de México hasta su llegada a Puerto Rico?

¿Tienes buena memoria?

¿QUÉ RECUERDAS?

Actividad A. Preguntas

Briefly answer the following questions about **Episodio 25**.

1. ¿Por qué viajó Raquel a España? _____

2. ¿Cuáles son las dos ciudades que Raquel visita en España? _____

3. ¿Quién es la Sra. Teresa Suárez? _____

4. Después de España, ¿a qué país va Raquel? _____

5. ¿Dónde está Rosario ahora? _____

6. ¿Cómo se llama el segundo hijo de Rosario? _____

7. ¿Quién es Héctor? _____

8. ¿Qué información tiene Héctor sobre Ángel? _____

9. ¿Cuál es el presentimiento que tiene Arturo? _____

10. ¿A qué país tiene que ir Raquel ahora? _____

Actividad B. ¡Busca el intruso!

For each group of names, places, or items, underline the one that does not belong with the others.

1. el cupón, el ciego, la cartera, la lotería

2. Guernica, Madrid, Sevilla, Buenos Aires

3. La Gavia, Ángel, el certificado de nacimiento, Sevilla

4. el matrimonio, la brocheta, el divorcio, la esposa

5. la carne, Buenos Aires, el tango, el Viejo San Juan

Actividad C. ¿Cierto o falso?

Indicate whether the following statements are **Cierto (C)** or **Falso (F)**.

C F 1. Don Fernando Castillo vive en México y está muy enfermo.
C F 2. Teresa Suárez vive ahora en Sevilla.
C F 3. Rosario tiene tres hijos que viven en la Argentina.
C F 4. Arturo se sentía culpable porque no trató de volver a comunicarse con Ángel.
C F 5. Raquel necesita ir a una isla del Caribe.

ACTIVIDADES

Actividad.   ¿Lo recuerda o no?

All of the following events have happened so far during Raquel's investigation, but did Raquel remember them as she thought back over the last few weeks? Indicate whether the following events were part of the review in **Episodio 25** (**Sí**) or not (**No**).

Sí   No   1.   Raquel conoció a la familia de la persona que le escribió la carta a don Fernando.

Sí   No   2.   Jaime y su perro se perdieron en las calles de Sevilla.

Sí   No   3.   Raquel viajó a Madrid en tren.

Sí   No   4.   Conoció a Teresa Suárez y habló con ella sobre Rosario.

Sí   No   5.   En la Argentina, visitó una hacienda y conoció a un gaucho.

Sí   No   6.   Supo que Rosario ya murió pero conoció a otro hijo de ella.

Sí   No   7.   Pasó mucho tiempo con Arturo buscando a Ángel, el hijo de Rosario y don Fernando.

Sí   No   8.   Raquel y Arturo se besaron por primera vez.

Sí   No   9.   Héctor les dijo que Ángel se fue a vivir a Puerto Rico.

Sí   No   10.   Arturo prometió ir a Puerto Rico para seguir la búsqueda.

Repaso de los Episodios 1–18

Actividad A.   Raquel habla con Teresa Suárez

You have now seen and heard several times the important conversation that takes place between Raquel and Teresa Suárez. It should be easier for you to understand most of it now. Here is part of the conversation, with all but the first of Teresa Suárez's lines missing. Complete the conversation with the appropriate lines from the list of possibilities on the next page.

RAQUEL: En su carta Ud. le dice que Rosario no murió en la guerra.

TERESA: Es verdad. Rosario no murió. _____.[1]

RAQUEL: Ay...

TERESA: _____.[2]

RAQUEL: También en su carta Ud. le dice que Rosario tuvo un hijo.

TERESA: _____.[3]

RAQUEL: ¿Y qué nombre le puso?

TERESA: _____.[4]

RAQUEL: ¿Y dónde nació Ángel?

TERESA: _____.[5]

RAQUEL: ¿Y dónde vive Rosario ahora?

TERESA: _____.[6]

RAQUEL: ¿A la Argentina?

TERESA: _____.[7]

RAQUEL: ¿Y sabe dónde se estableció Rosario?

TERESA: _____.[8]

RAQUEL: ¿Se casó de nuevo?

TERESA: _____.[9]

RAQUEL: Sí, sí. Lo comprendo. ¿Y con quién se casó?

TERESA: _____.[10]

a. Después de la guerra se fue a vivir a la Argentina.
b. Sí. Todo este asunto es muy triste.
c. Ángel... Ángel Castillo.
d. Sí, sí. Como Ud. sabe, muchos españoles salieron del país después de la guerra.
e. Pues sí. Rosario era muy atractiva... muy simpática. Y como ella creía que Fernando había muerto...
f. Gracias a Dios, escapó de esa tragedia... pero ella creía que Fernando había muerto.
g. Muy cerca de Buenos Aires. La última carta que recibí de ella fue cuando se casó de nuevo.
h. Con un hacendado... un argentino llamado Martín Iglesias.
i. Sí.
j. En Sevilla, claro. Es allí donde conocí a Rosario.

Actividad B.   La búsqueda en la Argentina

In Argentina Raquel meets Arturo and the two search for Ángel, Arturo's half brother and the son of Rosario and don Fernando. Together they find Héctor Condotti, who once knew Ángel and who has some important information about him. The following narration about their meeting with Héctor contains some false information. Indicate the information you think is incorrect. *Hint:* There are one or two incorrect details in each paragraph.

Después de conocer a Héctor en el Piccolo Navio, Raquel y Arturo lo acompañaron a su casa. En la calle le mostraron a Héctor un cuadro de Ángel y le preguntaron si conocía al artista. «Ángel», respondió Héctor. «Claro que lo recuerdo bien. Era mi amigo.»

En el camino, empezaron a hablar de Ángel. Cuando llegaron a la casa de Héctor, él los invitó a entrar. Héctor les dijo que creía que Ángel consiguió trabajo en un barco. En ese momento, su esposa lo llamó y Héctor subió a su apartamento.

Arturo y Raquel ya se iban, pero Héctor volvió con una foto de Ángel que le dio a Arturo. Muy conmovido, Arturo le dio las gracias. Héctor también les dijo que creía que Ángel se quedó a vivir en el extranjero. No estaba seguro, pero creía que era en España.

Luego recordó una tarjeta postal que había recibido de Ángel. Ésta debería indicar la dirección de Ángel. Entonces Raquel y Arturo se fueron. Esa noche, los dos estaban muy pensativos, especialmente Arturo.

Actividad C.   «Hay que dedicarle tiempo al corazón.»

During Raquel's stay in Argentina, she and Arturo begin to feel a strong attraction for each other. But Raquel must leave Buenos Aires to continue the search for Ángel. They begin to say their good-byes on a pier, after receiving Ángel's letter from Héctor. Complete their conversation with items from the lists.

Verbos: decir, dejar, estar, extrañar, me gustaría, recordar, te gustaría

Sustantivos: la búsqueda, el extranjero, el tiempo, el trabajo, el primer vuelo

Adjetivos: muy bien, muy mal, regular

El tiempo: muchos años, unas semanas, unos pocos días

ARTURO: ¿Ya decidiste cuándo te vas a ir?

RAQUEL: Debería tomar _____.[1] Don Fernando está

_____.[2] Y no puedo tardarme mucho.

ARTURO: Hace _____[3] que te conozco... y parece como si hiciera

_____.[4]

RAQUEL: Yo siento lo mismo.

ARTURO: Te voy a _____[5]

RAQUEL: Yo también a ti.

ARTURO: Aunque... tal vez...

RAQUEL: ¿Tal vez?

ARTURO: Tal vez... yo podría ir a Puerto Rico, y los dos continuar

_____[6] de Ángel.

RAQUEL: ¿Quieres decir que irías a Puerto Rico?

ARTURO: ¿ _____[7]?

RAQUEL: ¡Claro que sí! Mucho. Pero, ¿tú puedes?

ARTURO: Creo que sí.

RAQUEL: ¿Y tu _____[8]? ¿tus pacientes?

ARTURO: Bueno, no sería fácil _____[9] todo. Pero... yo
quiero ir.

Para escribir

In this activity you will write a short letter that Raquel might send to a friend named
Susan Winters, who lives in Los Angeles. Susan is a colleague at Raquel's law firm, and
she is also interested in learning Spanish. Susan is currently taking a second-year
Spanish course at a local college. Raquel will write to her in Spanish.

This is the first letter that Raquel has sent to Susan since leaving the United States,
and, although Raquel and Susan are good friends as well as colleagues, she was not
able to talk to Susan before she left. So Susan knows nothing about the case nor about
Raquel's trip so far, and she has never traveled either to Spain or Argentina.

As you write from Raquel's point of view, tell Susan as much as you can about the
important events that have happened, and include interesting information whenever you
can. Your letter should be no fewer than 200 and no more than 300 words long.

Thinking About What You Will Write

In order to write this letter, you must first of all think about what information you will
include.

Look over the section called **Repaso de los Episodios 12–17** in the Handbook
Lección 18. The activities in that section are based on Raquel's letter to Sra. Suárez,
written from the airport in Buenos Aires. That letter was written to someone who has a
very different relationship to Raquel than Susan—and very different interests in Raquel's

trip—but still the information in it may be useful. You may also want to look back at what you wrote in the **Para escribir** section in **Lección 18**, because it was about Raquel and Arturo.

As you scan these sections, note the following useful or interesting information and key phrases. (It is a good idea to do this on a separate sheet of paper.)

Background information	Important people
Major events	Things enjoyed
Major problems	Arturo

For now, just jot down information in the six categories as phrases (**perder mi cartera**, **conocer a la mujer que escribió la carta**, and so on), and don't be concerned about conjugating the verb forms.

You will not necessarily use all of the information or events in your letter, but that is OK. For the moment, you are just trying to create a "bank" of ideas upon which to draw.

Organizing Your Letter

In order to begin to write this letter, you must decide how you will address Susan. Because this is a letter, you will address Susan directly, but will you use **tú** or **Ud.**? And how do letters start in Spanish? Look back at the letter that Raquel wrote to Sra. Suárez in **Episodio 18**. Will Raquel address Susan in the way in which she addressed Teresa Suárez? Or will she use a more relaxed greeting such as **Querida...** (*Dear . . .*)? Note also for the heading of your letter that the date in Spanish should be written in the following manner: **(15) de (octubre) de (200–)**.

The next thing you need to do is to spend some time thinking about the organization (order) of what you will write. Begin by deciding in which of the six categories of information Susan is most likely to be interested. Because this will not be a long letter, you cannot give her lots of details or develop all of the categories. Here they are again.

_____ Background information	_____ Important people
_____ Major events	_____ Things enjoyed
_____ Major problems	_____ Arturo

Look at the categories you selected and think about whether any of them group together logically, then consider the order in which you will present them. What sequence seems to make the most sense to you? Write a brief outline of that sequence.

Now look at the categories you didn't select and see whether there is an important piece of information or two that can fit into the categories you have outlined.

Finally, note that one common way to end a letter between friends is to use the Spanish phrase **Abrazos** (*Hugs*) **de tu amiga** _____.

Drafting

Paso 1

Now draft your letter. At this stage you should not worry about grammar and spelling. Your goal is to get your ideas down on paper.

Write the date and the greeting you have chosen. Then begin to write the letter. If you wish, you may select one of the following as your opening sentence. Doing so may help you get started.

¡Te va a parecer imposible el viaje que estoy haciendo!

Saludos desde la Argentina. Aquí te mando unos detalles interesantes de este viaje de sorpresa.

Te extraño mucho, pero lo estoy pasando muy bien. Te estoy escribiendo hoy desde...

Paso 2

After you have completed your draft, look over what you have done. Are you still satisfied with the information you selected? Do you want to add some things and delete others or go into more detail about certain events? Have you included at least one interesting detail in each of the major topics about which you have written? Keep in mind that you are writing for someone who knows nothing about your trip and who has not visited the places that Raquel has visited.

Finalizing Your Letter

If you are satisfied with the information contained in your draft, it is time to look it over for style and language.

Paso 1

First, look at your letter for style. Have you been consistent throughout in the way in which you have addressed Susan? Does the letter flow, or is it disjointed and choppy? Does it contain words and phrases that connect events, or is it mostly an accumulation of sentences? Remember to use words and phrases that can smooth out the flow of a composition and help express the sequence of events clearly.

Paso 2

Review your letter for the following language elements.

_____ gender of nouns

_____ adjective agreement

_____ subject-verb agreements

_____ correct tense (present, **ir** + **a** + *infinitive*, preterite, imperfect, progressive forms)

_____ use of object pronouns

_____ use of **por** and **para**

_____ comparisons

Paso 3

Prepare a clean copy of the final version of your letter for your instructor.

26

Reflexiones II

> The interactive CD-ROM to accompany *Destinos* contains additional practice with the video story line and will help you improve your skills in Spanish.

Preparación

Actividad.

On the next page are photographs of people Raquel met or heard about in Puerto Rico. Match the photos with the names given below. Then read the statements that accompany them and indicate which is correct. Then add one true statement of your own about the character. Your statement can be factual or it can be your own opinion about the character.

a   Jorge Alonso
b.   los tíos de Ángela y Roberto
c.   doña Carmen
d.   Ángel, con su esposa y suegra
e.   Ángela Castillo
f.   Roberto Castillo

1.

1. Es _____.
   a. Es una joven tranquila que sigue siempre lo que le dice la razón.
   b. Es una joven impaciente e ingenua... y muy enamorada.

   _____

2. Es _____.
   a. Su opinión es muy importante para Ángela... y para los otros parientes también.
   b. Nadie en la familia le hace mucho caso.

   _____

2.

3. Es _____.
   a. Como en el estereotipo, este yerno no se llevó muy bien con su suegra.
   b. Este yerno era el hijo favorito de su suegra.

   _____

3.

4. Son _____.
   a. Están ayudando a Ángela en esta época importante y difícil de su vida.
   b. No les importa la vida de Ángela en este momento.

   _____

4.

5. Es _____.
   a. Estudia comercio y trabaja en un banco en México.
   b. Estudia arqueología y trabaja en una excavación en México.

   _____

5.

6. Es _____.
   a. Este hombre le gusta mucho a Raquel... tanto que casi no piensa más en Arturo.
   b. Raquel le gusta mucho a él, pero él no le cae muy bien a ella.

   _____

6.

. . . AFTER VIEWING

¿Tienes buena memoria?

¿QUÉ RECUERDAS?

Actividad A.   Preguntas
Briefly answer the following questions about **Episodio 26**.

1. ¿Quién es Ángela? _____

2. ¿Dónde se conocen Raquel y Ángela? _____

3. ¿Por qué la tía Olga no quiere que Ángela vaya a México? _____

4. ¿Por qué van Raquel y Ángela a San Germán? _____

5. ¿Qué problema tienen en la carretera cerca de Ponce? _____

6. ¿Qué encontraron Raquel y Ángela en la antigua habitación de Ángel? _____

_____

7. ¿Qué le dio doña Carmen a Ángela antes de que ella regresara a San Juan? ¿Qué

importancia tiene este objeto? _____

8. ¿Cómo es Jorge, el novio de Ángela? _____

9. ¿Qué quiere hacer Ángela con una parte del dinero de la venta de la casa de sus

padres? ¿Por qué? _____

10. ¿Cuáles son las malas noticias que Raquel y Ángela recibieron antes de salir para

México? _____

Actividad B.   ¡Busca el intruso!

For each group of names, places, or items, underline the one that does not belong with the others.

1. simpático, amable, gruñón, cariñoso
2. el agua, la gasolina, el aceite, el jugo
3. el baúl, «Recuerdos», la copa de bodas, Ponce
4. el tío Jaime, Jorge, el novio, un don Juan

Actividad C.   ¿Cierto o falso?

Indicate whether the following statements are **Cierto (C)** or **Falso (F)**.

C   F   1. Ángela estaba sorprendida cuando vio que Raquel sacaba fotos de la
              tumba de sus padres.
C   F   2. La esposa de Ángel murió después de él.
C   F   3. La tía Olga no tiene mucha confianza en otras personas.
C   F   4. Es importante que Ángela vaya a México porque va a recibir mucho
              dinero.
C   F   5. La abuela de Ángela vive con su esposo en una finca de guineos.
C   F   6. A doña Carmen no le gusta mucho Jorge.

ACTIVIDADES

Actividad.   ¿A quiénes conoció Raquel?

Complete the following paragraphs with the names of people Raquel met or heard about while in Puerto Rico.

Raquel conoció a _____[1] en el cementerio donde estaban enterrados Ángel y su

esposa. Más tarde conoció a los cuñados de Ángel, incluyendo a la tía _____[2] Ésta

no reaccionó bien al oír que su sobrina tenía otro abuelo en México.

Raquel fue con Ángela y su prima _____[3] a San Germán a ver a su abuela, doña

_____[4] Al volver a San Juan, Ángela le presentó a Raquel a su novio,

_____[5] quien acababa de regresar de Nueva York.

Cuando estaban por salir para el aeropuerto Ángela y Raquel, el tío _____[6] vino a

darle a su sobrina unas malas noticias. Su hermano _____[7] había tenido un accidente

en México.

Repaso de los Episodios 19–24

Actividad A.   ¿En qué orden?

All of the following events took place in **Episodios 19–24**, but in what order did they occur? Put them in order, from 1 to 13.

a. _____ En San Germán, doña Carmen le dio a Ángela una idea.

b. _____ Una vecina le dijo a Raquel: «Ángel Castillo murió hace poco.»

c. _____ Raquel y Ángela tenían que ir a San Germán.

d. _____ Doña Carmen también le dio a Ángela algo muy especial.

e. _____ Raquel conoció a los tíos de Ángela.

f. _____ Allí Ángela encontró unas hojas de su padre.

g. _____ Raquel trató de aconsejar a Ángela sobre sus relaciones con Jorge.

h. _____ Raquel tomaba una foto de la tumba de Ángel cuando Ángela apareció.

i. _____ Llegó el tío Jaime con unas malas noticias.

j. _____ Los tíos no sabían si Ángela debía hacer el viaje a México.

k. _____ ¿Por qué no revisaba lo que había entre las cosas de su padre?

l. _____ De regreso en San Juan, Raquel conoció al novio de Ángela.

m. _____ En San Juan, Raquel buscó una casa en la calle del Sol.

Actividad B.   ¿Y qué más?

The following sentences expand on the information given in the statements in **Actividad A**. Can you match these continuations with those statements? The first item is done for you.

a. _____ Era la copa de bodas de su abuela Rosario.

b. _____ Hubo un accidente en la excavación donde trabajaba Roberto.

c. _____ Pero Ángela se enfadó.

d. _____ También dijo que estaba enterrado en el cementerio del Viejo San Juan.

e. _____ Las hojas tenían sus recuerdos de la Argentina y de su vida en Puerto Rico.

f. __1__ Creía que Ángel Castillo vivía allí.

g. _____ Salieron en el carro de Ángela, con Laura, su prima.

h. _____ Fue al cuarto con Raquel y las dos encontraron un baúl.

i. _____ Raquel le contó la historia de su abuelo.

j. _____ No le gustó mucho.

k. _____ Debía ir al cuarto de su padre.

l. _____ Les contó la historia de Ángel Castillo.

m. _____ Creían que Ángela debía consultar con la abuela.

SPANISH—ENGLISH VOCABULARY

The Spanish-English Vocabulary contains all the words that appear in the Student Viewer's Handbook with the following exceptions: (1) most close or identical cognates; (2) most conjugated verb forms; (3) diminutives ending in **-ito/a**; (4) absolute superlatives ending in **-ísimo/a**; (5) most adverbs ending in **-mente** (if the corresponding adjective is listed); and (6) most vocabulary that is glossed in the Handbook. Only meanings that are used in the Handbook are given. In addition, some vocabulary useful for discussing the story has been included even though it does not appear in the Handbook.

The gender of nouns is indicated, except for masculine nouns ending in **-o** and feminine nouns ending in **-a**. Stem changes and spelling changes are indicated for verbs: **dormir (ue, u)**; **llegar (gu)**; **seguir (i, i) (g)**.

The letter **ñ** within words follows **n**. For example, **añadir** follows **anuncio**.

The following abbreviations are used:

adj.	adjective		*m.*	masculine
adv.	adverb		*Mex.*	Mexico
approx.	approximately		*n.*	noun
Arg.	Argentina		*obj. (of prep.)*	object (of a preposition)
C. Am.	Central America		*pers.*	personal
conj.	conjunction		*pl.*	plural
def. art.	definite article		*poss.*	possessive
d.o.	direct object		*p.p.*	past participle
f.	feminine		*P.R.*	Puerto Rico
fam.	familiar		*prep.*	preposition
form.	formal		*pron.*	pronoun
gram.	grammatical term		*refl. pron.*	reflexive pronoun
inf.	infinitive		*s.*	singular
interj.	interjection		*Sp.*	Spain
inv.	invariable form		*sub. pron.*	subject pronoun
i.o.	indirect object		*U.S.*	United States
irreg.	irregular		*v.*	verb
L.A.	Latin America			

A

a to; at (*with time*); **a bordo** aboard, on board; **a cargo (de)** in charge (of); **a causa de** because of, on account of; **a continuación** following, below, immediately after; **a favor** in favor; **a la(s) ...** at (*hour*); **a menos que** unless; **a menudo** often; **a nombre de** in the name of; **a pesar de** in spite of; **a punto de** at the point of; about to; **¿a quién?** to whom?; **a veces** at times, sometimes; **a ver** let's see, let's have a look

abandonar to abandon

abierto/a (*p.p. of* **abrir**) open(ed)

abogado/a lawyer

abrazarse (c) to embrace

abrazo embrace, hug

abrir (*p.p.* **abierto/a**) to open

absoluto/a absolute; **en absoluto** (not) at all

abuelo/a grandfather, grandmother; *m. pl.* grandparents

aburrido/a: ser (*irreg.*), **aburrido/a** to be boring; **estar** (*irreg.*) **aburrido/a** to be bored

aburrirse to become bored

acá here

acabar to finish; **acabar de** + *inf.* to have just (*done something*)

accidente *m.* accident

acción *f.* action

aceite *m.* oil

aceituna olive

acento accent

aceptar to accept

acerca de *prep.* about, concerning

acercarse (qu) (a) to approach, draw near

acoger (j) to receive, welcome

acompañar to accompany

aconsejar to advise

acontecimiento event

acordarse (ue) (de) to remember

acostar (ue) to put to bed; **acostarse** to go to bed

acostumbrarse (a) to get accustomed to

actitud *f.* attitude

actividad *f.* activity

actor *m.* actor

actriz *f.* (*pl.* **actrices**) actress

actualidad present time; **en la actualidad** at this time, nowadays

actuar to act, perform; **actuarse** to behave

acuerdo agreement; **de acuerdo** OK, I agree; **estar** (*irreg.*) **de acuerdo (con)** to agree, be in agreement (with)

acusar to accuse

adaptar(se) to adapt

además (de) besides, in addition (to)

adicción *f.* addiction

adicto/a addict

adiós good-bye

adjetivo *n.* adjective

administración *f.* administration; **administración de empresas** business administration

administrador(a) administrator

admirar to admire

admitir to admit

adolescente *m., f.* adolescent

adonde where

¿adónde? (to) where?

adorar to adore

adosado/a: casa adosada condominium

aeropuerto airport

afectar to affect

afecto affection

afectuoso/a affectionate

afirmación *f.* affirmation

afortunadamente fortunately

afuera *adv.* outside

agencia agency; **agencia de viajes** travel agency

agente *m., f.* agent; **agente de bienes raíces** real estate agent; **agente de viajes** travel agent

agitado/a upset, worried; shaky; excited

agradable agreeable, pleasant

agradar to be pleasing

agradecer (zc) to thank

agradecido/a grateful, thankful

agua *f.* (*but* **el agua**) water; **agua mineral** mineral water

águila *f.* (*but* **el águila**) eagle

ahí there

ahora now; **ahora mismo** right now; **justo ahora** right now, just now

aire *m.* air

al (*contraction of* **a** + **el**) to the; **al** + *inf.* upon, while, when + *verb form;* **al anochecer** at nightfall, dusk; **al comienzo** at the beginning; **al día siguiente** the next day; **al final** in the end; **al final de** at the end of; **al menos** at least; **al (mes, año, ...)** per (month, year, . . .); **al mismo tiempo** at the same time; **al poco tiempo** shortly after; **al principio** at first, at the beginning; **al terminar...** when . . . is/was over
alarmado/a alarmed
alcázar *m.* fortress; castle
alegrarse (de) to be glad, happy (about)
alegre happy
alegría happiness; happy nature
alejarse (de) to go far away (from); to separate (from); to draw away, grow apart (from)
algo something, anything
alguien someone; **caerle** (*irreg.*) **bien/mal a alguien** to like (not like), make a good/bad impression on someone; **darle** (*irreg.*) **de alta a alguien** to release someone (*from an institution*); **poner** (*irreg.*) **a alguien a cargo (de)** to put someone in charge (of)
algún, alguno/a some; any; **alguna vez** ever
aliviar to alleviate, relieve
allá there
allí there
alma *f.* (*but* **el alma**) soul
almacén *m.* department store; storehouse
almorzar (ue) (c) to have lunch
almuerzo lunch
alojado/a *adj.* staying, lodged (*at a hotel*)
alojarse to stay, lodge
alquilado/a rented
alquilar to rent
alquiler *m.* rent
alta: darle (*irreg.*) **de alta a (alguien)** to release (someone) (*from an institution*)
alternar to alternate
alternativa *n.* alternative
altiplano high plateau
altitud *f.* altitude
alto *n.* height; **de alto** in height
alto/a *adj.* tall; high; loud; **clase** (*f.*) **alta** upper class
altura height
alumno/a student
ama (*f.* [*but* **el ama**]) **de casa** homemaker; housekeeper
amable nice, kind
amar to love
amarillo/a yellow
ambición *f.* ambition
ambicioso/a ambitious
ambiente *m.* atmosphere
ambos/as both
ambulancia ambulance
amenaza threat
ameno/a pleasant, agreeable
América Latina Latin America
amigablemente amicably, in a friendly way
amigo/a friend
amistad *f.* friendship
amor *m.* love; **amor a primera vista** love at first sight
analizarse (c) to analyze oneself
anciano/a elderly person
¡anda! *interj.* move it!; go on!
Andalucía Andalusia
andaluz, andaluza (*pl.* **andaluces**) Andalusian

andar (*irreg.*) to walk; to go; **andar bien/mal** to be going well/badly; **andar buscando** to be looking for; **andar en barco** to take a boat ride; **andar en bicicleta** to go for a bicycle ride; **andar en bote** to take a rowboat ride; **andar en mateo** to take a carriage ride
anfibio: animal (*m.*) **anfibio** amphibian
angustia anguish
angustiado/a anguished
animado/a lively, animated, spirited
animal *m.* animal; **animal anfibio** amphibian
anoche last night
anochecer: al anochecer at nightfall, dusk
anónimo/a anonymous; **sociedad** (*f.*) **anónima** incorporated; stock company
ante before, in the presence of; with regard to
anterior previous, preceding
antes *adv.* before, formerly; **antes de** *prep.* before (*in time*); **antes (de) que** *conj.* before; **lo antes posible** as soon as possible
antigüedad *n. f.* antique; **tienda de antigüedades** antique store
antiguo/a former; old, ancient
antropología anthropology
anuncio announcement, advertisement
añadir to add
año year; **hace muchos años** many years ago; **tener** (*irreg.*) **... años** to be . . . years old
aparato system, apparatus; **aparato circulatorio** circulatory system
aparcar (qu) to park
aparecer (zc) to appear
aparente apparent
apartamento apartment
apasionado/a passionate
apellido surname, last name
apenado/a grieved
apéndice *m.* appendix
apetito appetite
apoyar to support
apoyo support
apreciar to appreciate, esteem
aprender to learn; **aprender a** + *inf.* to learn to (*do something*)
apropiado/a appropriate
aprovechar to take advantage of
aproximadamente approximately
aquel, aquella *adj.* that (*over there*); **en aquel entonces** back then, in those days; **aquél, aquélla** *pron.* that one (*over there*)
aquello that, that thing, that fact
aquellos/as *adj.* those (*over there*); **aquéllos/as** *pron.* those (ones) (*over there*)
aquí here
árbol *m.* tree
área *f.* (*but* **el área**) area
argentino/a *n., adj.* Argentine
armario closet
arqueología archeology
arqueólogo/a archeologist
arreglar to arrange; to fix
arreglo arrangement; repair
arrojar to indicate, show
arruinado/a ruined
arte *m.* (*but* **las artes**) art; **bellas artes** (*f.*) fine arts
artículo article
artista *m., f.* artist
artístico/a artistic
ascender (ie) to advance
ascenso promotion

ascensor *m.* elevator
asegurar to assure
asentir (ie, i) to assent, agree
así *adv.* so, thus; that way; therefore, consequently; **así que** *conj.* so, then
asiento seat; breeding ground; site; **asiento de atrás** back seat
asignatura subject (*school*)
asistente/a assistant
asistir (a) to attend
asumir to assume (*responsibilities; command*)
asunto issue, matter
asustar to frighten
ataque *m.* attack; **ataque cardíaco** heart attack
atención *f.* attention; **llamar la atención** to attract attention
atender (ie) to attend to, take care of
atento/a attentive
atlántico/a Atlantic; **Océano Atlántico** Atlantic Ocean
atleta *m., f.* athlete
atracción *f.* attraction; **atracción turística** tourist attraction
atractivo/a *adj.* attractive
atraído/a attracted
atrapado/a trapped
atrás behind
atrasado/a *adj.* late, arriving late
atreverse (a) to dare (to)
auditor(a) auditor
aumentar to increase
aun *adv.* even
aún *adv.* still, yet
aunque although
ausencia absence
austral *n. monetary unit of Argentina; adj.* southern
autobús *m.* bus
automático/a automatic
automóvil *m.* automobile, car
autopista highway; toll road
autor(a) author
autoridad *f.* authority
autorizar (c) to authorize
avanzar (c) to advance
aventura adventure
avergonzado/a embarrassed
avería breakdown
averiguar (gü) to find out, ascertain
avión *m.* airplane
¡ay! *interj.* oh!
ayer yesterday
ayuda help, assistance
ayudante *m., f.* assistant
ayudar to help, assist
ayuntamiento city hall
azteca *n. m., f., adj.* Aztec
azúcar *m.* sugar; **caña de azúcar** sugar cane
azul blue

B
bachillerato baccalaureate, bachelor's degree
bailar to dance
baile *n. m.* dance; **baile de gala** formal dance
bajar to go down(stairs); to bring down (*a fever*)
bajo *prep.* under
bajo/a *adj.* short (*in height*); low; **clase** (*f.*) **baja** lower class; **planta baja** ground floor
ballet *m.* ballet
banco bank; bench
bañarse to bathe, take a bath

bar *m.* bar
barato/a inexpensive, cheap
barba beard
barbacoa barbecue
barbería barber shop
barca boat, barge
barco boat; **andar** (*irreg.*) **en barco** to take a boat ride; **navegar (gu) en barco** to sail
barrera barrier
barrio district; neighborhood
basarse to be based; **basarse en** to base one's ideas or opinions on
bastante enough; a great deal; rather, quite
batalla battle
baúl *m.* trunk
béisbol *m.* baseball
belleza beauty
bello/a beautiful; **bellas artes** *f.* fine arts
besar to kiss
beso kiss
bien *adv.* well; **andar** (*irreg.*) **bien** to be going well; **caerle** (*irreg.*) **bien a (alguien)** to like, make a good impression on (someone); **llevarse bien (con)** to get along well (with); **manejar bien** to manage well; **muy bien** very well; **pasarlo bien** to have a good time; **por bien o por mal** for better or worse; **sentirse (i, i) bien** to feel well
bien *n. m.* good; *pl.* goods; **agente** (*m., f.*) **de bienes raíces** real estate agent; **bienes raíces** *pl.* real estate
bienestar *m.* well-being
bienvenido/a welcome
billete *m.* ticket (*Sp.*); **billete de ida y vuelta** round-trip ticket
blanco/a white
bloqueado/a blocked, closed off
blusa blouse
boca mouth
bocacalle *f.* intersection
bocadillo sandwich (*Sp.*)
boda wedding
boleto ticket (*L.A.*)
bolsa purse, handbag
bombardeo bombing
bondad *f.* goodness; kindness
bonito/a pretty, attractive
bordo: a bordo aboard, on board
borrar to erase
bota boot
bote *m.* rowboat; **andar** (*irreg.*) **en bote** to take a rowboat ride
botones *m. s.* bellhop
breve brief
brindis *m. s.* toast (*drink*)
brocheta brochette, skewer
broma joke; **en broma** as a joke, jokingly
buen, bueno/a *adj.* good; **buen día** good day (*greeting*) (*Arg.*); **buena suerte** good luck; **buenas noches** good evening/night; **buenas tardes** good afternoon; **buenos, buenas** good day, good afternoon/evening; **buenos días** good morning; **hace (muy) buen tiempo** the weather's (very) good; **bueno** (*when answering the telephone*) hello (*Mex.*); **bueno** *adv.* all right
bufete *m.* lawyer's office
busca search; **en busca de** in search of
buscar (qu) to look for, seek; **andar** (*irreg.*) **buscando** to be looking for; **en busca de** in search of
búsqueda search, quest

C

cabaña cabin
cabeza head
cabezón, cabezona stubborn, hard-headed
cabo end
cacahuete *m.* peanut
cada *inv.* each, every; **cada vez más** more and more
caer (*irreg.*) to fall; **caerle bien/mal a (alguien)** to like (not like), make a good/bad impression on (someone)
café *m.* (cup of) coffee; café, coffee shop; **café con leche** strong coffee served with warm or hot milk; **café solo** black coffee
caja box, case, chest
calamares *m. pl.* squid
calificación *f.* grade
callado/a silent, quiet
calle *f.* street
calmado/a quiet, calm
calmante *m.* sedative
calmar to calm
calor *m.* heat; **hace (mucho) calor** it's (very) hot
cama bed; **guardar cama** to stay in bed
cámara camera
cambiar (de) to change; **cambiarse de ropa** to change one's clothes
cambio change; exchange; **en cambio** on the other hand
caminar to walk
camino street, road; way; **camino a** on the way to
camión *m.* truck; bus (*Mex.*)
campana bell
campera short jacket (*Arg.*)
canasta basket
cancelar to cancel
cansado/a tired
cansar to tire; **cansarse** to get tired
cantante *m., f.* singer
cantar to sing
cantidad *f.* quantity, amount
cantina bar
caña cane; **caña de azúcar** sugar cane
capaz capable
capilla chapel
capital *f.* capital (city); *m.* capital (*money*)
capitán *m.* captain
captar to grasp; to depict; to pick up (*sound*)
capturar to capture
cara face; side
carácter *m.* character
caramelo caramel; candy
cardíaco/a *adj.* cardiac, heart; **ataque** (*m.*) **cardíaco** heart attack
carga cargo, freight
cargo position; **poner** (*irreg.*) **a alguien a cargo (de)** to put (someone) in charge (of)
Caribe *n. m.* Caribbean
caribeño/a *n., adj.* Caribbean
cariño affection; **tomarle cariño a (alguien)** to start to have affection for (someone)
cariñoso/a affectionate
carne *f.* meat
caro/a expensive
carrera career, profession; course of study
carretera highway
carro car
carta letter; **jugar (ue) (gu) a las cartas por dinero** to gamble on cards
cartel *m.* poster
cartera wallet

casa house; home; **casa adosada** condominium; **ama** (*f.* [*but* el ama]) **de casa** homemaker; **en casa** at home
casado/a married; **recién casado/a** recently married, newly wed
casar(se) (con) to marry (someone); to get married (to)
casi almost
casino casino
caso case; **hacer** (*irreg.*) **caso a** to pay attention to; **no hacer caso (de)** to pay no attention (*to an issue*)
casualidad: dar (*irreg.*) **la casualidad** to just happen; **por casualidad** by chance
catedral *f.* cathedral
causa cause; **a causa de** because of, on account of
causar to cause, be the cause of; **causar una buena impresión** to make a good impression
celebración *f.* celebration
celebrar to celebrate
celos jealousy; **tener** (*irreg.*) **celos (de)** to be jealous (of)
celoso/a jealous; **estar** (*irreg.*) **celoso/a (de)** to be jealous (of)
cementerio cemetery
cena dinner, supper
cenar to have dinner
censura censorship
centavo cent
centro center; downtown; **centro comercial** shopping center
cerca *adv.* near, nearby, close; **cerca de** *prep.* near (to)
cercano/a *adj.* close
cerdo pig; **carne** (*f.*) **de cerdo** pork
ceremonia ceremony
cerrado/a closed
cerrar (ie) to close
certeza *f.* certainty
certificado certificate; **certificado de nacimiento** birth certificate
cervecería beer tavern, pub
cerveza beer
cesar to stop
chaqueta jacket
chavo money, "dough" (*P.R.*)
cheque *m.* check
chicle *m.* chewing gum
chico/a *adj.* little, small; *n.* boy, girl; *pl.* boys, girls; children
chocar (qu) (con) to run into, collide (with)
chofer *m.* chauffeur, driver
choque *m.* accident, collision
chorizo spicy sausage
ciego/a *n.* visually impaired person, blind person; *adj.* visually impaired, blind
cien, ciento (one) hundred
ciencia science; **ciencias económicas** economics; **ciencias naturales** natural sciences
cierto/a true; certain; **es cierto** it's certain, true; **por cierto** by the way, certainly
cinco five
cine *m.* cinema, movie theater; **ir** (*irreg.*) **al cine** to go to the movies
circulatorio/a circulatory; **aparato circulatorio** circulatory system
circunstancia circumstance
ciudad *f.* city; **Ciudad de México** Mexico City
civil: guerra civil civil war
civilización *f.* civilization
claro/a clear; light (*colors*); **¡claro!** *interj.* of course!; **claro que sí** of course

clase *f.* class; kind; **clase alta** upper class; **clase baja** lower class; **dar** (*irreg.*) **una clase** to teach a class
clásico/a *adj.* classic(al)
cliente/a client
clínica clinic
coche *m.* car
coche-comedor *m.* dining car (*on a train*)
cocina kitchen
cocinero/a *n.* cook, chef
coco coconut
colaboración *f.* collaboration
colección *f.* collection
coleccionar to collect
colega *m., f.* colleague
colegio grade/high school
colmo last straw
colonia colony; neighborhood (*Mex.*)
colonial colonial
color *m.* color
columna column
comedor *m.* dining room; **coche-comedor** *m.* dining car (*on a train*)
comentar to comment (on); to discuss
comentario comment; commentary
comenzar (ie) (c) to begin
comer to eat; **comerse** to eat up
comercial *adj.* commercial; **centro comercial** shopping center
comercio commerce, business
comestible *n. m.* food; *adj.* edible; **tienda de comestibles** food store
cómico/a comical, funny
comida food; meal
comienzo *n.* beginning; **al comienzo** at the beginning
comino: me importa un comino I couldn't care less
como as (a); like; since; **tan ... como** as . . . as; **tan pronto como** as soon as; **tanto/a/os/as ... como** as much/many . . . as
¿cómo? how?, how's that?, what?, I didn't catch that
cómodo/a comfortable
compañero/a companion; mate, "significant other"
compañía company (*business*)
comparación *f.* comparison
comparar to compare
compartimento compartment
compartir to share
completar to complete
completo/a complete, full; **por completo** completely
complicado/a complicated
comportarse to behave oneself
composición *f.* composition
compra purchase; **hacer** (*irreg.*) **las compras** to shop; **ir** (*irreg.*) **de compras** to go shopping
comprar to buy
comprender to understand
comprensivo/a understanding
computación *f.* computer science
computadora computer (*L.A.*); **programación** (*f.*) **de computadoras** computer programming; **programador(a) de computadoras** computer programmer (*L.A.*)
común common; **en común** in common; **sentido común** common sense
comunicación *f.* communication
comunicarse (qu) (con) to communicate (with); to get in touch (with), contact
comunidad *f.* community
con with; **con destino a** bound for; **con frecuencia** frequently; **¿con quién?** with whom?; **con razón** understandably so

concentrar(se) to concentrate
concepto concept
concierto concert
conciliador(a) conciliatory
concluir (y) to conclude
conclusión *f.* conclusion
condición *f.* condition; **buenas/malas condiciones** *pl.* good/bad shape, condition
conducir (zc) to transport
conducta conduct
conductor(a) conductor
conferencia lecture
confesar (ie) to confess
confesión *f.* confession
confianza confidence; **de confianza** trustworthy, reliable
confiar (en) to trust (in); to confide (in)
confirmar to confirm
conflicto conflict; **conflicto armado** armed conflict; **en conflicto** in conflict
confundir to confuse
confusión *f.* confusion
congreso convention; congress
conmemorar to commemorate
conmigo with me
conmovido/a moved (*emotionally*)
conocer (zc) to know, be acquainted with; to meet
conocimiento knowledge
consciente conscious
consecuencia consequence; **como consecuencia** as a result
conseguir (i, i) (g) to get, obtain, attain; to succeed in
consejo(s) advice
conservador(a) *adj.* conservative
considerar to consider
consigo with himself, with herself; with it; with them
consistir (en) to consist (of)
consulta *s.* consulting hours
consultar to consult
consumir to consume, use
contacto contact
contar (ue) to tell (about); to count; **contar con** to have; to rely on; to have available
contemplar to contemplate; to look at, study
contener (*like* **tener**) to contain
contenido *n. s.* contents
contento/a happy, content
contestar to answer
contigo with you (*fam.*)
continuación *f.* continuation; **a continuación** below, immediately after, following
continuar to continue, go on; to follow
contra against; **en contra (de)** against
contratar to hire
contrato contract
controlar to control
controversia controversy
convencer (z) to convince
convencido/a convinced
conversación *f.* conversation
conversar to converse
convertirse (ie, i) (en) to become; to change (into); to convert
copa goblet, wineglass; drink (*slang*)
copia copy
coquí *small tree frog indigenous to Puerto Rico that makes a characteristic musical sound*
corazón *m.* heart
corbata necktie
coro chorus, choir

correcto/a correct, right
corregir (i, i) (j) to correct
correo mail; post office; **(por) correo aéreo** (by) airmail
correr to run; **correr riesgo** to run a risk
corresponder to correspond, match
corriente common, ordinary; **cuenta corriente** checking account
cortés, cortesa courteous, polite
corto/a brief, short (*in length*)
cosa thing
coser to sew
cosmopolita *m., f.* cosmopolitan
costa coast
costar (ue) to cost; **costarle trabajo (a alguien)** to be hard, take a lot of effort (for someone)
costumbre *f.* custom, habit
crédito: tarjeta de crédito credit card; **dar** (*irreg.*) **crédito** to believe
creer (y) (en) to think, believe (in); **creer que sí/no** to think (not think) so
criar to raise
criollo/a creole
crisis *f.* crisis
Cristo Christ
crítica criticism
criticar (qu) to criticize
cronológico: en orden cronológico in chronological order
cruz *f.* (*pl.* **cruces**) cross
cruzar (c) to cross
cuaderno notebook
cuadra city block
cuadro painting; picture
cual *relative pron.* whom, which; **lo cual** which
¿cuál? what?, which?; **¿cuál (es)?** which one(s)?
cualidad *f.* quality
cualquier(a) whatever, whichever; any; **cualquier cosa** anything
cuando when
¿cuándo? when?
cuanto: en cuanto as soon as; **en cuanto a ...** as for, as far as . . . is concerned
¿cuánto/a? how much?; **¿cuántos/as?** how many?
cuarenta forty
cuarto *n.* fourth; quarter (*hour*); (bed)room
cuatro four
cubano/a *n., adj.* Cuban
cubierto/a (*p.p. of* **cubrir**) **(de)** covered (with)
cuenta account; bill, check; calculation; **cuenta corriente** checking account; **cuenta de ahorros** savings account; **darse** (*irreg.*) **cuenta (de)** to realize, become aware (of); **hacer** (*irreg.*) **cuentas** to do the accounts; **llevar (las) cuentas** to keep the books; **revisar las cuentas** to audit the accounts; **tener** (*irreg.*) **en cuenta** to keep in mind
cuento short story
cuero leather
cuerpo body
cuestión *f.* question; problem; matter
cuidado care; **con cuidado** carefully; **tener** (*irreg.*) **cuidado** to be careful
cuidar to take care of
culpa fault; blame; **tener** (*irreg.*) **la culpa (de)** to be to blame (for), to be guilty (of)
culpabilidad *f.* guilt; **sentido de culpabilidad** sense of guilt or responsibility
culpable *n. m., f.* guilty person; responsible person; *adj.* guilty, responsible

cultura culture
cumpleaños *m. s.* birthday
cumplir to perform; to keep (a promise); **cumplir años** to have a birthday; **cumplir con** to live up to; to meet, fulfill
cuna birthplace
cuñado/a brother/sister-in-law
cupón *m.* ticket
cura *m.* priest; *f.* cure
curar to heal, cure
curioso/a curious
curso course, class
cuyo/a whose

D

daño harm, injury; **hacerle** (*irreg.*) **daño (a alguien)** to hurt (someone)
dar (*irreg.*) to give; **dar una clase** to teach a class; **dar con** to meet up with; **dar un paseo** to take a walk; **darle de alta (a alguien)** to release (someone) (*from an institution*); **darse cuenta (de)** to realize, become aware (of); **darse la mano** to shake hands
dato fact
de *prep.* of; from; **de acuerdo** OK, I agree; **de confianza** trustworthy, reliable; **de moda** fashionable; **de momento** for the moment; **de nacimiento** by birth; **de nada** you're welcome; **de nuevo** again; **¿de quién?** whose?; **de regreso** *adj.* return (*flight*); **de regreso a** on returning to; **de repente** suddenly; **de una vez** now, right away; **de vez en cuando** sometimes; **estar** (*irreg.*) **de acuerdo (con)** to agree, be in agreement (with); **más allá de** *prep.* beyond; **más de** more than; **vivir de** to live off of, support oneself by
deber *v.* should, ought to; to owe; **deber + inf.** should, must, ought to (*do something*); **deberse a** to be due to
deber *n. m.* duty
debilidad *f.* weakness
decidir to decide; **decidirse** to make up one's mind
decir (*irreg.*) to say, tell; **decir la verdad** to tell the truth; **es decir** that is to say
decisión *f.* decision; **tomar decisiones** to make decisions
declaración *f.* declaration
declarar to declare
dedicar (qu) to dedicate; **dedicarse** to dedicate oneself
defender (ie) to defend; **defenderse** to defend oneself; to get along/by
definitivo/a final, definitive
dejar to leave (behind); to let, allow; to quit
del (*contraction of* **de** + **el**) of the; from the
delante *adv.* ahead; **por delante** ahead (of one); **delante de** *prep.* in front of
delgado/a thin, slender
delicado/a delicate
demanda demand
demás: los/las demás the rest, the others, others, other people
demasiado *adv.* too, too much
demócrata *m., f.* democrat
demora delay
demostrar (ue) to show, demonstrate
dentista *m., f.* dentist
dentro de inside, within; **dentro de poco** very soon
depender (de) to depend (on)
dependiente *adj.* dependent

dependiente/a *n.* clerk
deportivo/a *adj.* sports
depresión *f.* depression
deprimir to depress
derecha: a la derecha to the right
derecho *n.* law; right
derrumbarse to collapse, cave in
derrumbe *m.* collapse; caving in
desamparado/a abandoned
desaparecer (zc) to disappear
desarrollar to develop
desastroso/a disastrous
desayunar to have breakfast
desayuno breakfast
descansar to rest; **que en paz descanse** may he/she rest in peace
descanso rest; relaxation
descendiente *m., f.* descendant
desconocido/a unknown
describir (*p.p.* **descrito/a**) to describe
descripción *f.* description
descrito/a (*p.p. of* **describir**) described
descubierto/a (*p.p. of* **descubrir**) discovered
descubrir (*p.p.* **descubierto/a**) to discover
desde *prep.* from; **desde hace años** for a number of years; **desde pequeño/a** since he/she was small; **desde que** *conj.* since
deseado/a desired
desear to want, wish; **desear + inf.** to wish, want to (*do something*)
desembarcarse (qu) to land; to disembark
desempeñar to play, fulfill (*a role*)
deseo desire, wish
desesperado/a desperate
desgraciadamente unfortunately
despedida *n.* farewell, leave-taking, good-bye; **regalo de despedida** going-away present
despedir (i, i) to fire (*an employee*); **despedirse (de)** to say good-bye (to), take leave (of)
despegarse (gu) to take off (*airplane*)
despertar (ie) (*p.p.* **despierto/a**) to wake (*someone up*); **despertarse** to awaken, wake up
despierto/a awake; alert
despreciar to hold in low esteem
después *adv.* later, afterwards; **después de** *prep.* after; **después de que** *conj.* after
destino destiny; destination; **con destino a** bound for
destruido/a destroyed
detalle *m.* detail
deteriorar to deteriorate
determinar to determine
detrás de *prep.* behind
deuda debt
día *m.* day; **al día siguiente** the next day; **buenos días** good morning; **Día del Trabajo** Labor Day; **hoy día** today, nowadays; **todos los días** every day; **un par de días** a few days
dialecto dialect
diario *n.* daily newspaper
diario/a *adj.* daily; **vida diaria** daily life
dibujar to draw
dibujo drawing; sketch
dicho/a (*p.p. of* **decir**) said
diciembre *m.* December
dictador *m.* dictator
diez ten
diferencia difference
diferente different
difícil difficult, hard
dificultad *f.* difficulty
dinamismo dynamism
dinámico/a dynamic

dinero money
Dios *m. s.* God **¡gracias a Dios!** *interj.* thank God!
dirección *f.* address; direction
directamente directly
director(a) director; head, leader
dirigir (j) to direct, run
discreto/a discreet
disculpar to excuse, make excuses for; **disculparse** to apologize; **disculpe** pardon me, excuse me
discusión *f.* discussion; argument, (*verbal*) fight
discutir to discuss; to argue; to fight (*verbally*)
disfrutar to enjoy
disgustar to dislike
disiparse to disappear
dispuesto/a (a) ready, willing (to)
distancia distance; **llamada de larga distancia** long-distance call
distinto/a distinct, different
distrito district; **distrito federal** federal district
divertido/a fun
divertirse (ie, i) to have a good time
dividirse to be divided
divorciarse (de) to divorce, get divorced (from)
doble double; **habitación** (*f.*) **doble** double room
dócil docile
doctor(a) doctor
documento document, paper
dólar *m.* dollar
dolor *m.* pain
doloroso/a painful
dominante dominant
dominar to dominate; to master
domingo Sunday
don *title of respect used with a man's first name*
donde where
¿dónde? where?; **¿de dónde?** from where?
doña *title of respect used with a woman's first name*
dormido/a asleep
dormir (ue, u) to sleep
drástico/a drastic
duda doubt
dudar to doubt; to hesitate
dudoso: es dudoso que it's doubtful that
dueño/a owner; **dueño/a de negocios** shop owner
dulce *adj.* sweet
dulces *m. pl.* candy
durante during; for (*period of time*)
durar to last
duro/a hard; harsh

E

e and (*used instead of* **y** *before words beginning with* **i** *or* **hi**)
echar to throw out
económico/a economic; economical; **ciencias económicas** economics
edad *f.* age
edificio building
educación *f.* education; **educación física** physical education
educado/a educated
efectivamente actually, in fact
efectivo cash
efecto effect
egocéntrico/a egocentric, self-centered
egoísta *m., f.* egotistical, selfish
¿eh? *tag phrase with approximate English equivalent of* **OK?**

ejecutivo/a executive
ejemplo example; **por ejemplo** for example
ejercer (z) to exert; to practice (*a profession*)
ejército army
el the (*m. def. art.*)
él *sub. pron.* he; *obj. of prep.* him
elegante elegant
elegir (i, i) (j) to select, choose
ella *sub. pron.* she; *obj. of prep.* her
ello *pron. neut.* it
ellos/as *sub. pron.* they; *obj. of prep.* them
elogio praise
embarazada pregnant
embarcarse (qu) to embark, board ship
embargo: sin embargo nevertheless
emigración *f.* emigration
emoción *f.* emotion
emocionado/a moved, emotional
emocionante exciting
emotivo/a emotional
empanada turnover, pie
emperador *m.* emperor
empezar (ie) (c) to begin; **empezar a + inf.** to begin to (*do something*)
empleado/a employee
empresa firm, company, business; **administración** (*f.*) **de empresas** business administration
en in, on, at; **en la actualidad** at this time, nowadays; **en aquel entonces** back then, at that time, in those days; **en broma** as a joke, jokingly; **en busca de** in search of; **en cambio** on the other hand; **en casa** at home; **en común** in common; **en conflicto** in conflict; **en contra (de)** against; **en cuanto a …** as far as . . . is concerned; **en este momento, en estos momentos** right now, currently; **en el fondo** deep down, at heart; **en forma** in good shape; **en general** generally, in general; **en realidad** actually, really; **en seguida** right away, immediately; **en venta** for sale; **pensar (ie) en** to think about
enamorado/a *n.* sweetheart; **estar** (*irreg.*) **enamorado/a (de)** to be in love (with)
enamorarse (de) to fall in love (with)
encantado/a charmed, delighted
encantar to enchant, charm; to love, like
encanto *n.* charm, enchantment; delight
encarcelado/a imprisoned
encima *adv.* above; over; overhead; moreover; **encima de** *prep.* on top of
encontrar (ue) to meet; to find; **encontrarse** to find (*oneself*); **encontrarse con** to meet with
encuentro meeting, encounter
energía energy
enero January
enfadarse (con) to get angry (at, with)
enfermarse to get sick
enfermedad *f.* illness
enfermo/a *n.* sick person; *adj.* sick, ill
enfrentar to face, confront; **enfrentarse (con)** to deal with, face (*a problem*)
engañar to deceive
enojado/a angry
enojarse (con) to get angry (at)
ensayar to rehearse
enseñar to teach; to show
entender (ie) to understand
enterarse (de) to find out (about)
entero/a entire, whole
enterrado/a buried, interred
entonces then, at that time; **en aquel entonces** back then, in those days

entrada entrance; price of admission
entrar (en/a) to enter, go (in)
entre between, among; **entre la espada y la pared** between a rock and a hard place
entregar (gu) to surrender; to hand over
entrevista interview
entrevistar to interview
envidia envy; **tenerle** (*irreg.*) **envidia (a alguien)** to envy (*someone*)
episodio episode
época epoch, period, era
equipado/a equipped
equis: sacar (qu) rayos equis to take X rays
equivocado/a mistaken
equivocarse (qu) to make a mistake
érase una vez once upon a time
error *m.* error
escalera step, stair; stairway; ladder; *pl.* stairs, steps
escándalo scandal
escapar(se) to escape
escena scene; stage
escribir (*p.p.* **escrito/a**) to write
escrito/a (*p.p. of* **escribir**) written
escritor(a) writer
escrúpulo scruple
escuchar to listen (to)
escuela school; **escuela secundaria** high school
escultor(a) sculptor
ese, esa *adj.* that; **ése, ésa** *pron.* that one
esencial essential
esfuerzo effort
eso that, that thing, that fact; **por eso** for that reason, that's why
esos/as *adj.* those; **ésos/as** *pron.* those (ones)
espada: entre la espada y la pared between a rock and a hard place
España Spain
español *m.* Spanish (*language*)
español(a) *n.* Spaniard; *adj.* Spanish; **mundo de habla española** Spanish-speaking world
especial special
especialista *m., f.* specialist
especialización *f.* specialization
especializarse (c) (en) to specialize (in); to major (in)
especialmente especially
espectacular spectacular
espectáculo spectacle, show
esperanza(s) hope
esperar to wait (for); to hope; to expect
espíritu *m.* spirit; **espíritu de hierro** iron will
espontáneo/a spontaneous
esposo/a husband/wife; spouse; *m. pl.* husband and wife, spouses
esquiar to ski
esquina corner
estable *adj.* stable
establecer (zc) to establish; **establecerse** to establish oneself, get settled
estación *f.* station; season; resort; **estación de gasolina** gas station; **estación del metro** subway station; **estación del tren** train station
estacionamiento parking
estado state
Estados Unidos *pl.* United States
estadounidense *of or from the United States*
estancia ranch; stay, visit
estar (*irreg.*) to be; to be located; **está a** it's at (it's worth); **estar a punto de** to

be about to; **estar al tanto** to be informed, up to date; **estar de acuerdo (con)** to agree, be in agreement (with); **estar enamorado/a de** to be in love with; **estar envidioso/a (celoso/a) (de)** to be envious (jealous) (of); **estar harto/a (de/con)** to be fed up (with); **estar listo/a** to be ready; **estar mal** to be ill; **estar por + inf.** to be about to (*do something*); to be ready to (*do something*); **(no) estar seguro/a** (not) to be sure
este/a *adj.* this; **éste/a** *pron.* this one; **en este momento** right now, currently; **esta noche** tonight
estereotipo stereotype
estilo style
estimado/a dear (*correspondence salutation*)
estímulo stimulus
esto this, this thing, this matter
estos/as *adj.* these; **éstos/as** *pron.* these (ones); **en estos momentos** right now, currently
estrecho/a *adj.* narrow; close-knit; **relación** (*f.*) **estrecha** close, intimate relationship
estrella star
estrenar to debut, perform for the first time
estricto/a strict
estudiante *m., f.* student
estudiar to study
estudio study; **estudios agrícolas** agricultural studies
estudioso/a studious
estufa stove
estupendo/a wonderful, fantastic
etiqueta: de etiqueta formal (*dress*)
Europa Europe
europeo/a *n., adj.* European
ex esposo/a ex-husband/wife
exagerar to exaggerate
examen *m.* exam; examination
examinar to examine
excavación *f.* excavation
excavar to excavate
exclamar to exclaim
excluido/a excluded
excusa excuse
exhausto/a exhausted
existir to exist
éxito success; **tener** (*irreg.*) **éxito** to be successful
exótico/a exotic
experiencia experience; experiment
experimentar to experience
explicación *f.* explanation
explicar (qu) to explain
expresivo/a expressive
exquisito/a exquisite
extranjero *n.* abroad; **en el extranjero** abroad
extranjero/a *n.* foreigner; *adj.* foreign; **lengua extranjera** foreign language
extrañar to miss, long for
extraño/a *n.* stranger; *adj.* strange
extravagancia folly
extrovertido/a extrovert

F

fabricar (qu) to manufacture, make
fácil easy
fácilmente easily
facultad *f.* faculty, school
falda skirt
falso/a false
falta lack; **hacer** (*irreg.*) **falta** to be lacking, needed; **hacerle** (*irreg.*) **falta a**

alguien to need (*something*)
faltar to be missing, lacking; to be absent
fama fame, reputation
familia family
familiar *n. m.* relation, member of the family; *adj.* family, related to the family
familiarizarse (c) to familiarize oneself
famoso/a famous
farmacia pharmacy
fascinante fascinating
fascinar to fascinate
fastidiar to "drive up a wall"
favor *m.* favor; **a favor** in favor; **por favor** please
favorito/a favorite
fe *f.* faith
febrero February
fecha date
fechado/a dated
federal: distrito federal federal district
felicidad *f.* happiness
feliz (*pl.* **felices**) happy
feo/a ugly
feroz (*pl.* **feroces**) ferocious
ficción *f.* fiction
fiebre *f.* fever; **bajar la fiebre** to bring down one's fever; **tienes una fiebre alta** you (*fam.*) have a high fever; **tener** (*irreg.*) **una fiebre** to have a fever
fiesta party; holiday; festival; **dar** (*irreg.*) **una fiesta** to give a party
figura figure
figurar (en) to be important (in)
fijarse en to pay attention to, take notice of, concentrate on
fijo/a fixed
fin *m.* end; **fin de semana** weekend; **por fin** at last, finally
final *n. m.* end; *adj.* final; **al final** in the end; **al final de** at the end of
financiero/a financial
finanzas finances
finca farm, ranch, hacienda
fineza class, good taste
fino sherry
firmar to sign
físico/a *adj.* physical; **educación** (*f.*) **física** physical education
flirtear to flirt
flor *f.* flower
folklórico/a *adj.* folk
fondo background; *pl.* funds; **en el fondo** deep down, at heart
forma form; **en forma** in good shape
formación *f.* (professional) training; education
formar to form; to make; to shape; **formar parte de** to be or form a part of
foto(grafía) *f.* photo(graph); **tomar/sacar (qu) una foto** to take a picture, photograph
fotográfico/a photographic
fracaso failure
frambuesa raspberry
francés, francesa *n.* Frenchman, Frenchwoman; *adj.* French
Francia France
frase *f.* phrase; sentence
frecuencia frequency; **con frecuencia** often; frequently
frecuentar to frequent, go regularly to
frecuente frequent
frente a opposite, facing
fresco/a fresh; **hace fresco** it's cool (*weather*)
fríamente coolly, coldly
frío *n.* cold; **hace (mucho) frío** it's (very) cold (*weather*)

frío/a *adj.* cold; **tener** (*irreg.*) **(mucho) frío** to be (very) cold
frito/a fried
frontera border
fructífero/a fruitful
frustrado/a frustrated
fruta fruit
frutería fruit store
frutilla strawberry (*Arg.*)
fue: se fue he/she went away
fuera *adv.* out, outside; **fuera de** *prep.* out(side)
fuerte strong; nasty; hard
fuerza strength; *pl.* strength; forces
fumar: sección de (no) fumar (non)smoking section
funcionar to function, work (*machines*)
fundación *f.* foundation
fundador(a) founder
fundar to found
funerario/a *adj.* funeral
furioso/a furious
fusilar to shoot
futuro *n.* future

G

gala: baile (*m.*) **de gala** formal dance
galería gallery
galón *m.* gallon
ganador(a) winner
ganar to win; to earn; to gain
ganas: tener (*irreg.*) **ganas de + *inf.*** to feel like (*doing something*)
garganta throat
gasolina gasoline; **estación** (*f.*) **de gasolina** gas station
gato cat
gemelo/a twin
generación *f.* generation
general *n. m., adj.* general; **en general** generally, in general
generalización *f.* generalization
generoso/a generous
gente *f. s.* people
geografía geography
gerente *m., f.* manager
gobernar (ie) to govern, rule
gobierno government
golfo gulf
golpe *m.* blow (*injury*)
gordito/a plump, fat
gordo/a fat
gorra cap
gracias thank you; **dar** (*irreg.*) **las gracias** to thank; **¡gracias a Dios!** *interj.* thank God!; **muchas gracias** thank you very much
grado grade; degree (*temperature*)
graduación *f.* graduation
graduarse (en) to graduate (from)
gran, grande large, big; great
grave grave, serious
gripe *f.* influenza, flu
gritar to shout
grito shout; cry
grosero/a crude, brutish
gruñón, gruñona *n.* grouch; *adj.* grouchy, irritable
grupo group
guantes *m.* gloves
guapo/a handsome; pretty
guardar to save, keep (*things, a secret*); to have; **guardar cama** to stay in bed
guayaba guava; **pasta de guayaba** guava paste
guerra war; **guerra civil** civil war
guía *m., f.* guide; **guía turístico/a** tour guide
guineo banana (*P.R.*)
guitarra guitar

gustar to like; to be pleasing to; **me gustaría + *inf.*** I would really like to (*do something*); **(no) gustarle + *inf.*** to (dis)like to (*do something*)
gusto pleasure; like, preference; taste; **mucho gusto** pleased to meet you

H

haber (*irreg.*) *inf.* form of **hay**; to have (*auxiliary*); to be; **va a haber** there's going to be
había there was, there were (*imperfect of* **hay**)
habitación *f.* room; **habitación doble** double room; **habitación individual** single room
habitante *m., f.* inhabitant
hablar to talk; to speak
hacendado/a wealthy rancher
hacer (*irreg.*) to do; to make; **desde hace años** for a number of years; **hace muchos años** many years ago; **hacer caso a** to pay attention to; **hacer las cuentas** to do the accounts; **hacer la maleta** to pack one's suitcase; **hacer una oferta** to make an offer; **hacer un picnic** to have a picnic; **hacer planes** to make plans; **hacer una reservación** to make a reservation; **hacer un viaje** to take a trip; **hacerle daño (a alguien)** to hurt (someone); **hacerle preguntas (a alguien)** to ask (someone) questions; **hacerse tarde** to be getting late; **no hacer caso (de)** to pay no attention (*to an issue*); **no hacerle caso (a alguien)** to ignore (someone); **¿qué tiempo hace?** what's the weather like?; **se me hace tarde** it's getting late
hacia toward
hacienda estate, hacienda
hada madrina fairy godmother
hambre *f.* (*but* **el hambre**) hunger; **tener** (*irreg.*) **hambre** to be hungry
harto/a: estar (*irreg.*) **harto/a (de/con)** to be fed up (with)
hasta *prep.* until; **hasta finales de** until the end of; **hasta luego** until later, see you later; **hasta mañana** until tomorrow, see you tomorrow; **hasta pronto** see you soon; **hasta** *conj.* even; **hasta que** *conj.* until; **¿hasta qué punto?** up to what point?
hay there is, there are; **no hay** there is not/are not; **no hay de qué** you're welcome (*form.*)
hecho fact, **de hecho** in fact
hecho/a (*p.p.* of **hacer**) made, done
heladería ice cream shop
helado ice cream
helicóptero helicopter
herido/a wounded
hermanastro/a stepbrother, stepsister
hermano/a brother, sister (*family; religious vocation*); *m. pl.* brothers and sisters; **medio/a hermano/a** half brother, half sister
hermoso/a beautiful
héroe *m.* hero
hierro iron; **espíritu de hierro** iron will
hijastro/a stepson, stepdaughter
hijo/a son, daughter; child; *m. pl.* children; **hijo/a único/a** only child
hispánico/a *adj.* Hispanic
hispano/a *adj.* Hispanic
histérico/a hysterical
historia history; story
histórico/a historic(al)
hoja leaf; sheet of paper

hojear to leaf through, glance through; to scan
hola hello, hi
hombre *m.* man; **hombre de negocios** businessman; **tienda de ropa para hombres** men's clothing store
honestidad *f.* honesty
honesto/a honest
honrar to honor
hora hour; time; **¿a qué hora?** at what time?
horizonte *m.* horizon
horrorizar (c) to horrify
hospital *m.* hospital
hotel *m.* hotel
hoy today
huérfano/a *n., adj.* orphan
humano/a human; **ser** (*m.*) **humano** human being

I

ida *n.* departure; **billete** (*m.*) **de ida** one-way ticket; **pasaje** (*m.*) **de ida y vuelta** round-trip ticket (fare)
identidad *f.* identity
identificar (qu) to identify
idioma *m.* language
iglesia church
igual equal; the same
imaginación *f.* imagination
imaginar(se) to imagine
imaginativo/a imaginative
impaciencia impatience
impaciente impatient
impacto impact
imperio empire
importancia importance
importante important
importar to be important, matter; **me importa un comino** I couldn't care less
imposible impossible
impresión *f.* impression; **causar una buena impresión** to make a good impression
impresionado/a impressed
impresionante impressive
impresionar to impress
improbable improbable
incidente *m.* incident
incierto/a uncertain
incluir (y) to include
incómodo/a uncomfortable
inconsciente unconscious
incorrecto/a incorrect
increíble incredible
independencia independence
independiente independent
indicar (qu) to indicate, point out
indiferencia indifference
indiferente indifferent
indígena *n. m., f.* native; *adj.* indigenous, native
individual: habitación (*f.*) **individual** single room
industria industry
industrial *n. m.* industrialist, manufacturer
inesperado/a unexpected
inestable unstable
infancia childhood
influencia influence
influir (y) to influence
información *f.* information
informar to inform; **informarse** to inquire, find out
ingenuo/a naive, ingenuous
inglés *m.* English (*language*)
iniciar to initiate; to start
inmediatamente immediately, right away
inmediatez *f.* immediacy

inocente innocent
inolvidable unforgettable
inquieto/a anxious
insinuar to insinuate, hint at; **insinuarse** to ingratiate oneself
insistir (en) to insist (on)
inspiración *f.* inspiration
instalarse to establish oneself, settle in
instante *m.* instant
instinto instinct
insultar to insult
inteligencia intelligence
inteligente intelligent
intención *f.* intention
intenso/a intense
intentar to try, attempt
intento intention; attempt
interacción *f.* interaction
interés *m.* interest
interesante *adj.* interesting
interesar to interest, be of interest; **interesarse (en)** to be interested (in)
interior *n. m.* interior
internacional international
interno/a internal
interpretar un papel to play a role
interrumpido/a interrupted
intervenir (*like* **venir**) to intervene; to interfere
intriga intrigue
intruso/a intruder
invadir to invade
inventar to invent
inversión *f.* investment
investigación *f.* investigation
investigar (gu) to investigate
invierno winter
invitar to invite (*with the intention of paying*)
involucrar to involve, implicate
inyección *f.* shot, injection; **ponerle** (*irreg.*) **una inyección** to give (someone) a shot, injection
ir (*irreg.*) to go; **ir a** + *inf.* to be going to (*do something*); **ir a un parque** to go to a park; **ir de compras** to go shopping; **irse** to go away, leave (*for a place*); **va a haber** there's going to be; **¿vamos?** shall we go?; **¡vamos!** *interj.* let's go!
irónico/a ironic
irritar to irritate
isla island
Italia Italy
italiano/a *n., adj.* Italian
izquierda: a la izquierda to the left

J

jamás never
jamón *m.* ham; **jamón serrano** *cured Spanish ham similar to prosciutto*
jardín *m.* garden
jefe/a boss
jerez *m.* sherry
joven *n. m., f.* young person; *adj.* young
jubilado/a *n.* retired person; *adj.* retired
judío/a *n.* Jew; *adj.* Jewish
juego game; gambling
jugador(a) player; gambler
jugar (ue) (gu) (a) to play (*a game or sport*); **jugar (por dinero)** to gamble; **jugar al póquer** to play poker
jugo juice
julio July
junto a next to; **junto con** together with
juntos/as together
justificar (qu) to justify
justo *adv.* just, exactly; **justo ahora** right now, just now
juventud *f.* youth

L

la the (*f. def. art.*); **a la(s) ...** at (*hour*)
la *d.o.* you (*form. s.*), her, it (*f.*)
lado side; **al lado de** beside, next to; **de al lado** next door; **por un/otro lado** on the one (other) hand
lágrima tear
langostino prawn
lápiz *m.* (*pl.* **lápices**) pencil
largamente at length, for a long time
largo/a long; **llamada de larga distancia** long-distance call; **a lo largo de** during
las the (*pl. f. def. art.*); you (*pl. f. form. pers. pron.*), them (*pl. f. pers. pron.*); *pron.* those; **las demás** the rest, the others, others, other people
le *i.o.* to/for you (*form. s.*), him, her, it
lástima *n.* pity; **es (una) lástima** it's a shame
lastimado/a hurt
latino/a *n., adj.* Latin; **América Latina** Latin America
Latinoamérica Latin America
latinoamericano/a *n., adj.* Latin American
lavadora washing machine
le *i.o.* to/for you (*form. s.*), him, her, it
leche *f.* milk
leer (y) to read
legal legal
legitimidad *f.* legitimacy
legítimo/a legitimate
legumbre *f.* vegetable
lejos far away; **lejos de** *prep.* far from
lengua language; tongue; **lengua extranjera** foreign language; **sacar (qu) la lengua** to stick out one's tongue
les *i.o.* to/for you (*form. pl.*), them
lesión *f.* injury, wound, lesion
letra letter (*of alphabet*); lyrics; *pl.* liberal arts
levantar to lift, raise; **levantarse** to get up; to rise up, rebel
libertad *f.* liberty
libre free; **ratos libres** free time, spare time
librería bookstore
libro book
ligar (gu) con to pick (*someone*) up
limitado/a limited
limpiar to clean
lindo/a pretty
línea line
lista list
listo/a: estar (*irreg.*) **listo/a** to be ready, prepared; **ser** (*irreg.*) **listo/a** to be bright, smart
literario/a literary; **obras literarias** literary works
literatura literature
llama: se llama (he/she) is called, named
llamada *n.* call; **llamada de larga distancia** long-distance call; **llamada telefónica** telephone call
llamado/a named; so-called
llamar to call (out); to call (*by phone*); **llamar la atención** to attract attention; **llamarse** to be called, named
llave *f.* key
llegada arrival
llegar (gu) to arrive; **llegar a ser** to become
lleno/a full, filled
llevar to take; to carry; to wear; to have spent (time); **llevar (las) cuentas** to keep the books; **llevarse bien/mal (con)** to get along well/badly (with)

llorar to cry, weep

lo *d.o.* you (*form. s.*), him, it (*m.*); **lo antes posible** as soon as possible; **lo cual** which; **lo más posible** as much as possible; **lo más pronto posible** as soon as possible; **lo que** what, that which; **lo siento** I'm sorry

loco/a crazy

lograr to manage to, be able

los the (*pl. m. def. art.*); *d.o.* you (*form. pl.*), them (*m.*); *pron.* those; **los demás** the rest, the others, others, other people

lotería lottery

lucha fight

luchar to fight

luego then, next; later; **desde luego** of course; **hasta luego** until later, see you later

lugar *n. m.* place; **en primer lugar** in the first place, firstly; **tener** (*irreg.*) **lugar** to take place

lujo luxury

luna moon; **luna de miel** honeymoon

lunes *m. s., pl.* Monday

luz *f.* (*pl.* **luces**) light

M

macho male, manly, macho

madrastra stepmother

madre *f.* mother

madrileño/a native of Madrid

madrina: hada madrina fairy godmother

madrugada *f.* dawn

maestro/a teacher; master

majestuoso/a majestic

mal, malo/a *adj.* bad; **hace (muy) mal tiempo** the weather's (very) bad; *adv.* badly; **andar** (*irreg.*) **mal** to be going badly; **caerle** (*irreg.*) **mal (a alguien)** to not like, make a bad impression on (someone); **estar** (*irreg.*) **mal** to be ill; **llevarse mal (con)** to get along badly (with); **manejar mal** to manage (*something*) badly; **pasarlo mal** to have a bad time; **sentirse (ie, i) mal** to feel bad, ill

maleta suitcase; **hacer** (*irreg.*) **la maleta** to pack one's suitcase

mandar to send; to order

mandón, mandona bossy

manejar to drive; **manejar (bien/mal)** to manage (*something*) (well/badly)

manera manner, way

manía mania

mano *f.* hand; **darse** (*irreg.*) **la mano** to shake hands

mantener (*like* **tener**) to maintain, keep up; to support (*a family*)

manzana apple; city block (*Sp.*)

mañana *adj.* morning; *adv.* tomorrow

mapa *m.* map

máquina tragamonedas slot machine

mar *m., f.* sea

marcar (qu) to mark

marco frame

margarita daisy; drink made with tequila

marinero/a sailor

marisco shellfish; *pl.* seafood

marítimo/a maritime

más more; most; plus; **a más tardar** at the latest; **cada vez más** more and more; **lo más posible** as much as possible; **lo más pronto posible** as soon as possible; **más allá de** *prep.* beyond; **más de** more than; **más o menos** more or less; **más tarde** later

matemáticas mathematics

mateo carriage; **andar** (*irreg.*) **en mateo** to take a carriage ride

materia subject, *pl.* courses

matricularse to matriculate; enroll

matrimonial marital

matrimonio marriage; married couple

maya *n. m., f.* Maya; *adj.* Mayan

mayo May

mayor bigger; biggest; older; oldest; greater; main

mayoría majority

mayoritario/a pertaining to the majority

me *d.o.* me; *i.o.* to/for me; *refl. pron.* myself; **¿me permite... ?** could you give me . . . ?

mecánico mechanic

media thirty (*half past*) (*with time*)

médico/a *n.* doctor; *adj.* medical

medida measure, step

medio *n.* middle; means; medium; environment; culture

medio/a *adj.* half; average; **medio/a hermano/a** half brother, half sister

Mediterráneo Mediterranean

mejillón *m.* mussel

mejor better; best

mejorar to improve; to raise

melón *m.* melon

memoria memory; **de memoria** by heart

mencionar to mention

menino/a *young page of the royal family; young lady-in-waiting*

menor younger

menos less; least; minus; except; **a menos que** unless; **al menos** at least; **echar de menos** to miss, long for; **más o menos** more or less; **por lo menos** at least

mensaje *m.* message

menudo: a menudo often

mercadillo market

mercado market

mes *m.* month

meseta plain, plateau

mestizo/a *n., adj.* mestizo

meta goal

meterse (en) to get involved (with, in); to meddle (in)

metro: estación (*f.*) **del metro** subway station

México Mexico; **Ciudad** (*f.*) **de México** Mexico City

mexicano/a *n., adj.* Mexican

mexicoamericano/a *n., adj.* Mexican American

mi(s) *poss.* my

mí *obj. of prep.* me; myself

miedo: tener (*irreg.*) **miedo (de)** to be afraid (of)

miel *f.* honey; **luna de miel** honeymoon

miembro member

mientras *conj.* while; *adv.* meanwhile; **mientras tanto** meanwhile

mil (one) thousand

milagro miracle

militar *n.* soldier, military man; *adj.* military

mimado/a spoiled, overindulged

mínimo/a minimal

minuto minute

mío/a(s) *poss.* my; mine; of mine

mirar to look (at); to watch

mismo/a same; **ahora mismo** right now; **al mismo tiempo** at the same time; **sí mismo/a** himself, herself, itself

misterioso/a mysterious

moda fashion, mode; **de moda** fashionable

modelo *n.* model

modelo *adj. m., f.* model

moderar to moderate

moderno/a modern

modificar (qu) to modify

moldear to mold

molestar to bother, annoy; **molestarse** to get irritated

molestia bother; **siento la molestia** I'm sorry to bother you

momento moment; **de momento** for the moment; **en este momento, en estos momentos** right now, currently; **por el momento** for the time being

monarca *m., f.* monarch

moneda coin

montaje *m.* production

monumento monument

morado/a purple

morir(se) (ue, u) (*p.p.* **muerto/a**) to die

mostrar (ue) to show

motivo motif; motive; **el motivo por el cual** the reason why

motor *m.* motor

muchacho/a young boy/girl

mucho *adv.* much, a lot of

mucho/a *adj.* a lot of; *pl.* many; **muchas gracias** thank you very much; **muchas veces** often; **mucho gusto** pleased to meet you

mudarse to move (*from one residence or city to another*)

muerte *f.* death

muerto/a (*p. p.* of **morir**) dead

muestra proof

mujer *f.* woman; wife; **mujer de negocios** businesswoman; **tienda de ropa para mujeres** women's clothing store

mujeriego womanizer

mundial world(wide)

mundo world; **Nuevo Mundo** New World; **todo el mundo** the whole world; everybody

muralista *m., f.* muralist

murmurar to murmur, whisper

museo museum; **visitar un museo** to visit a museum

música music

mutuo/a mutual

muy very; **muy bien** very well

N

nacer (zc) to be born

nacimiento birth; **certificado de nacimiento** birth certificate; **de nacimiento** by birth

nación *f.* nation

nacional national

nada *pron.* nothing, not anything; *adv.* not at all

nadar to swim

nadie no one

naranja *n.* orange (*fruit*)

narración *f.* narration

narrador(a) narrator

natal natal, native

natural: ciencias (*f.*) **naturales** natural sciences

necesario/a necessary

necesidad *f.* necessity, need

necesitar to need

negativa *n.* refusal

negativo/a *adj.* negative

negocio(s) business; shop; **dueño/a de negocios** shop owner; **hombre** (*m.*) **de negocios** businessman; **mujer** (*f.*) **de negocios** businesswoman

negro/a black

nevera refrigerator

ni neither, nor

nieto/a grandson, granddaughter; *m. pl.* grandchildren

ningún, ninguno/a *adj.* no, none, not any; **en ninguna parte** not anywhere, nowhere

ninguno/a *pron.* not one, not any

niño/a young boy, young girl; young child; *m. pl.* young children

no no; not; **¿no?** right?, don't they (you, etc.)?; **no hay** there is not/are not; **ya no** no longer

noche *f.* night, evening; **buenas noches** good evening/night; **esta noche** tonight; **por la noche** in the evening

nombre *m.* (first) name; **a nombre de** in the name of

norte *m.* north

Norteamérica North America

norteamericano/a *n., adj.* North American; *adj.* from the United States; **fútbol** (*m.*) **norteamericano** football

nos *d.o.* us; *i.o.* to/for us; *refl. pron.* ourselves

nosotros/as *sub. pron.* we; *obj. of prep.* us

nota note; grade, mark (*in schoolwork*); **sacar (qu) buenas/malas notas** to get good/bad grades

notar to note, notice; **notarse** to be noted

noticia piece of news; *pl.* news

novela novel; **leer (y) novelas** to read novels

noviembre *m.* November

novio/a boyfriend, girlfriend; fiancé(e)

nudo knot

nuera daughter-in-law

nuestro/a(s) *poss.* our

nuevo/a new; **de nuevo** again

número number

nunca never, not ever

O

o or

obelisco obelisk

objeto object

obligación *f.* obligation

obra work (*of art, literature, etc.*); play; **obra de teatro** play, dramatic work; **obra literaria** literary work

observar to observe; watch

obsesión *f.* obsession

obsesionarse to be(come) obsessed

obstáculo obstacle

obtener (*like* **tener**) to obtain, get

obvio/a obvious

ocasión *f.* occasion

océano ocean; **Océano Atlántico** Atlantic Ocean; **Océano Pacífico** Pacific Ocean

ocho eight

octavo/a eighth

octubre *m.* October

ocultar to hide

ocupado/a busy

ocupar to occupy; **ocuparse** to occupy oneself

ocurrir to happen, occur; **ocurrirse** to come to mind

ofensa offense, affront

ofensivo/a offensive

oferta offer; **aceptar la oferta** to accept the offer; **hacer** (*irreg.*) **una oferta** to make an offer; **oferta de trabajo** job offer

oficial *adj.* official

oficina office

ofrecer (zc) to offer

oír to hear; to listen

ojalá (que) God willing; I hope

ojo eye; **¡ojo!** *interj.* watch out!, be careful!, pay close attention!; **ojos expresivos** expressive eyes

olvidar(se) (de) to forget (about)

omitir to omit, leave out

once eleven

ópera opera

opinar to think, have an opinion

opinión *f.* opinion

oponer(se) (*like* **poner**) to oppose; to be opposed

oportunidad *f.* opportunity

oportuno/a opportune

optimista *m., f.* optimist; *adj.* optimistic

oración *f.* sentence

orden *m.* order (*chronological*); *f.* order (*command*); **en orden** (*m.*) **cronológico** in chronological order

ordenado/a orderly, tidy

ordinario/a ordinary

orfanato orphanage

organización *f.* organization

organizar (c) to organize

órgano organ

orgulloso/a proud

oro gold

os *d.o.* you (*fam. pl. Sp.*); *i.o.* to/for you (*fam. pl. Sp.*); *refl. pron.* yourselves (*fam. pl. Sp.*)

oscuro/a dark

otoño autumn

otro/a other, another

P

paciente *n. m., f.* patient; *adj.* patient

pacífico/a peaceful; **Océano Pacífico** Pacific Ocean

padrastro stepfather

padre *m.* father; priest; *pl.* parents

paella *Spanish dish of rice, shellfish, chicken, and meat*

pagar (gu) to pay (for)

página page

país *m.* country, nation

pájaro bird

palabra word

palacio palace

paloma pigeon

panceta bacon (*Arg.*)

panorámico/a panoramic

pantalón, pantalones *m.* pants

papá *m.* dad, father

papel *m.* paper; role

par *m.* pair; **un par de** a pair of; **un par de (días)** a few (days)

para *prep.* for, in order to; **no es para tanto** it's not that big a deal; **para que** *conj.* so that, in order that (for)

paradero whereabouts, location

parar to stop

parcha passion fruit

parecer (zc) *v.* to seem, appear; **parecerse a** to be similar to; to resemble

parecer *n. m.* appearance

parecido *n.* resemblance

parecido/a *adj.* similar

pared *f.* wall; **entre la espada y la pared** between a rock and a hard place

pareja couple

parentesco relationship

pariente *m.* relative, family member

parque *m.* park

párrafo paragraph

parrilla grill

parrillada barbecue

parte *f.* part; **por otra parte** on the other hand; **por parte (de alguien)** on behalf of (someone)

participar to participate

particular *n.* matter; *adj.* particular; private

partido game, match; (political) party; side

pasado *n.* past

pasaje *m.* passage, fare; ticket; **pasaje de ida y vuelta** round-trip fare

pasajero/a *n.* passenger; *adj.* passing

pasaporte *m.* passport

pasar to happen; to pass (*someone*); to come by; to pass, spend (*time*); **pasar por** to come by to pick up (*someone, something*); **pasarlo bien/mal** to have a good/bad time; **para saber qué pasó** to find out what happened

pasatiempo hobby

pasear to stroll, take a walk

paseo walk; drive; avenue; **dar** (*irreg.*) **un paseo** to take a walk

pasión *f.* passion

paso step; float (*in parade*); passing, passage

pasta de guayaba guava paste

pastelería pastry shop; bakery

patata potato (*Sp.*); **tortilla de patatas** potato omelette

paterno/a paternal

patio patio; yard

patológico/a pathological

patriarca *m.* patriarch (*male head of the family*)

patrocinador(a) sponsor; backer

paz *f.* peace; **que en paz descanse** may he/she rest in peace

peaje *m.* toll; tollbooth

pedir (i, i) to ask for, order

pelea fight

pelear(se) (con) to fight (with)

película movie, film

peligro danger

peligroso/a dangerous

pelo hair

peluquero/a barber; hairdresser

pena punishment; sorrow; **es una pena** it's a pity; **me da pena** I'm sorry; **(no) vale la pena** it's (not) worth the trouble; **¡qué pena!** *interj.* what a pity!

pensar (ie) to think; **pensar + inf.** to intend to (*do something*); **para pensar** something to think about; **pensar en** to think about

pensativo/a thoughtful, pensive

peor *adv.* worse; worst

pequeño/a small; **desde pequeño/a** since he/she was small

pera pear

percusión *f.* percussion

perder (ie) to lose; to miss; **perderse** to get lost

pérdida loss

perdón *m.* pardon; *interj.* pardon me, excuse me

perdonar to pardon; **perdone** *interj.* pardon me, excuse me

perfecto/a perfect

periódico newspaper

periodismo journalism

período period

permanente permanent

permiso permission

permitir to permit, allow; **¿me permite...?** could you give me . . . ?

pero *conj.* but

perplejo/a perplexed

perro/a dog

persecución *f.* persecution

persistente persistent

persona person

personaje *m.* character

personal *n. m.* personnel; *adj.* personal

personalidad *f.* personality

pertenecer (zc) to belong

pesadilla nightmare

pesado/a heavy; tiresome

pesar to weigh

pesar: a pesar de in spite of
pescadería fish market
pescadero/a fishmonger; fishwife
pescado (*caught*) fish
peseta *monetary unit of Spain;* **peseta puertorriqueña** quarter (*U.S. coin used as monetary unit of Puerto Rico*)
pesimismo pessimism
pesimista *n. m., f.* pessimist; *adj.* pessimistic
peso *monetary unit of Mexico;* weight; **bajar de peso** to lose weight
petróleo petroleum
pez *m.* (*pl.* **peces**) fish
picnic *m.* picnic; **hacer** (*irreg.*) **un** *picnic* to have a picnic
pijama *m. s.* pajamas
pilón *m. frozen dessert similar to a popsicle* (*P.R.*)
pincel *m.* brush (*for painting*)
pintar to paint
pintor(a) painter
pintoresco/a picturesque
pintura painting
piña pineapple
piragua snow cone (*P.R.*)
piragüero/a person who makes snow cones (*P.R.*)
pirulí *another word for* **pilón** (*P.R.*)
piso floor
plan *m.* plan; **hacer** (*irreg.*) **planes** to make plans
planchado/a ironed, pressed
planear to plan
plano (turístico) map (*of a city*)
planta baja ground floor
plátano banana
playa beach
plaza plaza, square; place
plenamente fully
pobre *n. m., f.* poor person; *adj.* poor
poco *n.:* **un poco de** a little
poco *adv.* little; **poco a poco** little by little; **por poco** almost, nearly
poco/a *adj.* little; *pl.* few, a few; **al poco tiempo** shortly after
poder *v.* (*irreg.*) to be able, can; *n. m.* power
poderoso/a powerful
¿podría + *inf.?* could I (*do something*)?; is it possible for me to (*do something*)?
poema *m.* poem
poesía poetry
poeta *m., f.* poet
policía police
poliéster *m.* polyester
político/a *n.* politician; *adj.* political
poner (*irreg.*) to put, place; to put on; **poner (a alguien) a cargo (de)** to put (someone) in charge (of); **ponerle una inyección (a alguien)** to give (*someone*) a shot, injection; **ponerse** + *adj.* to become + *adj.;* **ponerse a mando** to take command
por *prep.* by; in (*the morning, evening, etc.*); through; along; for; because of; per; **estar** (*irreg.*) **por** + *inf.* to be about to (*do something*); to be ready to (*do something*); **pasar por** to come by to pick up (*someone, something*); **por bien o por mal** for better or worse; **por casualidad** by chance; **por cierto** by the way; certainly; **por completo** completely; **por delante** ahead of one; **por desgracia** unfortunately; **por Dios** *interj.* for heaven's sake; **por ejemplo** for example; **por eso** for that reason, that's why; **por excelencia** par excellence; **por favor** please; **por fin** at last, finally; **por un**

lado on the one hand; **por lo general** generally, in general; **por la mañana** in the morning; **por lo menos** at least; **por el momento** for the time being; **por otra parte** on the other hand; **por otro lado** on the other hand; **por parte (de alguien)** on behalf of (*someone*); **por poco** almost, nearly; **por primera vez** for the first time; **por su propia cuenta** on his/her/its/your/their own account; **por supuesto** of course; **por la tarde/noche** in the afternoon/evening; **por teléfono** by telephone; **por todas partes** all over; everywhere; **por última vez** for the last time
¿por qué? why?
porque because
portarse to behave; **portarse +** *adv.* to act + *adj.,* to behave + *adv.*
poseer (**y**) to possess
posibilidad *f.* possibility
posible possible; **lo antes posible** as soon as possible; **lo más pronto posible** as soon as possible
posición *f.* position
postal *f.* postcard; **tarjeta postal** postcard
práctica practice
pragmático/a pragmatic
precio price
precisamente precisely, exactly
preferencia preference
preferir (ie, i) to prefer
pregunta question; **hacerle** (*irreg.*) **preguntas (a alguien)** to ask (*someone*) questions
preguntar to ask (*a question*); **preguntarse** to wonder; to ask oneself
prehispánico/a *n., adj.* pre-Hispanic
premio prize
preocupación *f.* preoccupation, worry
preocupado/a worried
preocupar(se) to worry
preparación *f.* preparation
preparar to prepare
preparativos preparations
presentar to present; to introduce; **presentarse** to appear
presente *n. m.; adj. m., f.* present
presentimiento presentiment, premonition
presentir (ie, i) to have a presentiment of
presidencial presidential
presidente *m., f.* president
prestigio prestige
prestigioso/a prestigious
pretexto pretext
previo/a previous
primaria: (escuela) primaria elementary school
primavera spring
primer, primero/a first; **amor** (*m.*) **a primera vista** love at first sight; **en primer lugar** in the first place, firstly; **(por) primera vez** (for the) first time
primo/a *adj.:* **materia prima** raw material; *n.* cousin
princesa princess
principal main, principal
príncipe *m.* prince
principio beginning; **al principio** at first; at the beginning
prisa haste; **tener** (*irreg.*) **prisa (por +** *inf.*) to be in a hurry (*to do something*)
privado/a private, personal; **vida privada** personal life
probable probable
probar (ue) to try (on); to taste (*food*); to prove
problema *m.* problem
problemático/a problematic

producción *f.* production
producir (zc) to produce
producto product
productor(a) producer
profesión *f.* profession
profesional *adj.* professional; **secreto profesional** confidentiality
profesor(a) teacher, professor
profundo/a profound
programación (*f.*) **de computadoras** computer programming
programador(a) programmer; **programador(a) de computadoras** computer programmer (*L.A.*)
promesa promise
prometer to promise
pronto soon; **lo más pronto posible** as soon as possible; **tan pronto como** as soon as
propietario/a proprietor, owner
propio/a *adj.* own, one's own; **por su propia cuenta** on his/her/its/your/their own account
proponer (*like* **poner**) to propose
prosperar to prosper
próspero/a prosperous
proteger (j) to protect
protestar (por) to protest (about)
provocar (qu) to provoke
próximo/a next
proyecto project
prueba(s) proof; test
psicología psychology
psicológico/a psychological
psiquiatra *m., f.* psychiatrist
psiquiatría psychiatry
pueblo people; town
puente *m.* bridge
puerta door; **tocar (qu) la puerta** to knock on the door
puerto port
puertorriqueño/a *n., adj.* Puerto Rican
pues *interj.* well
puesto *n.* position, job
puesto/a (*p.p. of* **poner**) put, placed
pulsera bracelet
punto point; (**estar** [*irreg.*]) **a punto de** (to be) at the point of; about to

Q

que that, who; **lo que** what, that which; **para que** so that, in order that/for; **que en paz descanse** may he/she rest in peace; **el mes/año... que viene** the coming, next month/year . . .; **ya que** since
¿qué? what?; which?; **¡qué +** *n./adj./adv!* *interj.* what a . . . !; how . . .!; **¡qué barbaridad!** how awful!; **¿qué diablos?** what the devil?; **¡qué pena!** what a pity!; **¿qué tal?** how are you (doing)?; how about . . . ?; **¿qué tal si ... ?** what if . . .? **¡qué va!** don't put me on!; **¡qué vergüenza!** how embarrassing!; **¿y qué?** so what?; what do you want me to do?
quedar to be situated; **quedar +** *adj.* to be + *adj.;* **quedarse** to stay, remain; to be left; **quedarse +** *adj.* to become + *adj.*
quejarse (de) to complain (about)
querer (*irreg.*) to wish, want; to love
querido/a (de) *adj.* dear; loved (by)
queso cheese
quien who
¿quién(es)? who?, whom?; **¿a quién?** to whom?; **¿con quién?** with whom?; **¿de quién?** whose?; **¿para quién?** for whom?
química chemistry
quinto/a fifth

quisiera + *inf.* I would like to (*do something*)
quizá(s) maybe, perhaps

R

radiador *m.* radiator
radicar (qu) to live; to be located
radio *m.* radio (set)
raíz (*pl.* **raíces**) root; (**agente** [*m., f.*] **de**) **bienes** (*m. pl.*) **raíces** real estate (agent)
rápido/a rapid, fast; express, fast (*train*)
raro/a rare, uncommon; odd, peculiar
rato while, short time; period of time; **ratos libres** *pl.* spare time, free time
rayo ray; **rayos X** X rays; **sacar (qu) rayos X** to take X rays
razón *f.* reason, cause; reason, faculty of reasoning; **con razón** understandably so; **tener** (*irreg.*) **razón** to be right
razonable reasonable
reacción *f.* reaction
reaccionar to react
real royal
realidad *f.* reality; **en realidad** actually, really
realista *n. m., f.* realist; *adj.* realistic
realizar (c) to carry out; to fulfill, accomplish
realmente really, truly; actually
recepción *f.* front desk (*in a hotel*); reception
recepcionista *m., f.* receptionist
rechazar (c) to reject; **rechazar la oferta** to reject the offer
rechazo rejection
recibir to get, receive; to receive (*visitors*)
recibo receipt
recién casado/a recently married, newly wed
reciente recent; fresh
recoger (j) to pick up; to go for
recomendable commendable, reputable
recomendación *f.* recommendation
recomendar (ie) to recommend
reconciliarse (con) to be reconciled, come together; to make up (with)
reconocer (zc) to recognize; to acknowledge
recordar (ue) to remember, recall; to recollect; **recordarle (algo) (a alguien)** to remind (someone) of (something)
recuerdo memory; memento, souvenir
recuperar to recover, retrieve
recurrir(a) to resort (to)
recurso natural natural resource
referirse (ie, i) (a) to refer (to)
reflexión *f.* reflection
reflexionar (sobre) to reflect (on)
reflexivo/a reflective, thoughtful
refrescarse (qu) to refresh oneself
regalo gift, present
región *f.* region
reglamento regulation; rules
regresar to return, come or go back
regreso *n.* return; **de regreso a** on returning to
regular fair, average; common, ordinary
rehacer (*like* **hacer**) to remake, make over
reino kingdom
relación *f.* relation, relationship; **relación estrecha** close, intimate relationship
relacionar to relate; to associate
relativo/a *adj.* relative
religioso/a religious
remar to row
remolcar (qu) to tow
remolque *m.* tow, towing

renunciar to renounce, give up (*right, claim*); to resign (*post, position*)
reparaciones *f.* repairs; **taller** (*m.*) **de reparaciones** repair shop
reparar to repair
repaso *n.* review
repente: de repente suddenly
repetir (i, i) to repeat
reponerse (*like* **poner**) to recover (*from an illness*); to get better
reportaje *m.* article; report; special feature
reporte *m.* report
reportero/a reporter
representación *f.* performance; representation
representar to represent; to act, perform; to show, express
reprochar to reproach
requerir (ie, i) to require
rescatar to save, rescue
rescate *m.* rescue
reserva reservation (*Sp.*)
reservación *f.* reservation (*L.A.*); **hacer** (*irreg.*) **una reservación** to make a reservation
reservado/a reserved
resfriado *n.* cold
residencia residence
resolver (ue) (*p.p.* **resuelto/a**) to resolve; to solve
resonar (ue) to ring, resound
respectivo/a respective
respetar to respect
responder to respond
responsabilidad *f.* responsibility
respuesta answer
restaurante *m.* restaurant
restaurar to restore
resto *n.* rest
resultado result
resultar to turn out to be
resumen *m.* summary
resumir to sum up, summarize
retrato portrait
reunión *f.* meeting, gathering
reunirse (con) to get (back) together (with); to be reunited (with)
revelación *f.* revelation; unveiling
revelar to reveal
revisar to check, inspect; **revisar las cuentas** to audit accounts
revista magazine
revolución *f.* revolution
rey *m.* king
rezongón, rezongona *n.* grouch, grumbler; *adj.* grouchy
rico/a *n.* rich person; *adj.* rich; wealthy; tasty, delicious (*food*); abundant (*crops*)
rivalidad *f.* rivalry
rojo/a red
romántico/a romantic
romper (con) to break off relations with (*someone*)
ropa clothing; **cambiarse de ropa** to change one's clothes; **tienda de ropa para hombres/mujeres** men's/women's clothing store
rosa rose; rose color
rosado/a pink
rubio/a blond(e)
ruina: en ruinas in ruins
ruta route, way
rutina routine

S

S.A. (sociedad anónima) Inc. (incorporated; stock company)
sábado Saturday

saber (*irreg.*) to know (*information*); **saber** + *inf.* to know how (*to do something*)
sabroso/a delicious, tasty
sacar (qu) to get out; to take out; to take out, withdraw (*from an account*); to get, receive (*grades*); **sacar buenas/malas notas** to get good/bad grades; **sacar una foto** to take a picture, photograph; **sacar la lengua** to stick out one's tongue; **sacar rayos X (equis)** to take X rays
sacrificar (qu) to sacrifice
sala living room; **sala de cine/teatro** theater
salida departure
salir (*irreg.*) to leave (*a place*), go out; to turn out
salmón *m.* salmon
salud *f.* health; **¡salud!** *interj.* to your health!
saludar to greet
saludo greeting
salvar to save; to rescue
san, santo/a *n.* saint; *adj.* holy
sangre *f.* blood
sanguíneo/a: vasos sanguíneos blood vessels
sano/a healthy; wholesome; sound
satisfacer (*like* **hacer**) (*p.p.* **satisfecho/a**) to satisfy
se (*impersonal*) one; *refl. pron.* yourself (*form.*), himself, herself, yourselves (*form.*), themselves
secadora clothes dryer
sección *f.* section
secretario/a secretary
secreto secret; **secreto profesional** confidentiality
secundaria secondary; **(escuela) secundaria** high school
seda silk
seductor(a) seducer
seguida: en seguida right away, immediately
seguir (i, i) (g) to follow; to continue; to keep on
según according to
segundo *n.* second (*time*)
seguro/a *adj.* sure, certain; safe; **(no) estar** (*irreg.*) **seguro/a** (not) to be sure; **seguro que** of course, certainly
semana week; **fin** (*m.*) **de semana** weekend
semestre *m.* semester
senador(a) *m., f.* senator
sencillo/a simple
sensible sensitive
sentar (ie) to seat, lead to a seat; **sentarse** to sit, sit down
sentido sense; **sentido común** common sense; **sentido de culpabilidad** sense of guilt or responsibility
sentimiento feeling
sentir (ie, i) to feel; to regret; to feel sorry about; **lo siento** I'm sorry; **sentirse** to feel; **sentirse bien/mal** to feel well/bad (*ill*)
señal *f.* signal; sign
señor (Sr.) *m.* Mr., sir; gentleman, man
señora (Sra.) *f.* Mrs., lady, woman
señores (Sres.) *m. pl.* Mr. and Mrs.; gentlemen
señorita (Srta.) Miss; young lady, woman
separar(se) to separate
septiembre *m.* September
ser (*irreg.*) to be; **es cierto** it's certain; **es decir** that is to say; **es una pena** it's a pity; **llegar (gu) a ser** to become; **ser listo/a** to be bright, smart; **ser unido/a** to be united, close-knit, close

ser *n. m.* being; life; **ser humano** human being

serenidad *f.* serenity

sereno/a calm, serene

serie *f.* series; (TV) series

serio/a serious; **tomar en serio** to take seriously

serrano/a: jamón (*m.*) **serrano** *cured Spanish ham similar to prosciutto*

servicio service

servir (i, i) to serve; to be suitable, useful; **servir de** to serve as, act as

sesenta sixty

severo/a strict

sexto/a sixth

si if

sí yes; **¡claro que sí!** *interj.* of course!

sí mismo/a himself, herself, oneself, itself

siempre always

siesta siesta, nap; **dormir (ue, u) la siesta** to take a siesta, nap; **tomar una siesta** to take a siesta, nap

siete seven

significado meaning; significance

significar (qu) to mean

siguiente next, following; **al día siguiente** the next day

silenciar to silence

silencio silence

simpático/a nice, pleasant

simpatizar (c) to get along well together

sin *prep.* without; **sin embargo** nevertheless; **sin que** *conj.* without

sincero/a sincere

sino but (rather)

sinónimo synonym

sistema *m.* system

sitio site, place

situación *f.* situation

situado/a situated

sobre *n. m.* envelope; *prep.* about; on; **sobre todo** above all

sobrino/a nephew, niece; *pl.* nieces and nephews

sociedad *f.* society; **sociedad anónima (S.A.)** incorporated; stock company (Inc.)

socioeconómico/a socioeconomic

sol *m.* sun

solamente only

solas: a solas alone; in private

soldado soldier

soler (ue) + *inf.* to tend to be, be in the habit of (*doing something*)

sólo *adv.* only

solo/a *adj.* alone; sole

soltero/a single

solución *f.* solution

solucionar to solve

sombrero hat

sonar (ue) to sound; to ring

sonrisa smile

soñador(a) dreamy

soñar (ue) (con) to dream (about)

soportar to stand, bear

sorprender to surprise; **sorprenderse** to be surprised

sorprendido/a surprised

sorpresa surprise

sospechar to suspect

su(s) *poss.* his, her, its, your (*form. s., pl.*), their

subir (a) to go up

suceder to happen

suceso event

sucursal *f.* branch office

Sudamérica South America

suegro/a father-in-law, mother-in-law; *m. pl.* in-laws

sueño dream; sleep; **tener** (*irreg.*) **(mucho) sueño** to be (very) sleepy

suerte *f.* luck; **buena/mala suerte** good (bad) luck; **número de la suerte** lucky number; **por suerte** fortunately, luckily; **tener** (*irreg.*) **(buena) suerte** to be lucky, in luck; **tener** (*irreg.*) **mala suerte** to be unlucky

suficiente enough, sufficient

sufrir to suffer

sugerencia suggestion

sugerir (ie, i) to suggest

superar to get through; to overcome

suplicar (qu) to implore, pray

supuesto: por supuesto of course

sur *m.* south

surgir (j) to arise, come up

suroeste *m.* southwest

sustantivo (*gram.*) noun

sustituir (y) to substitute

sustituto/a *n., adj.* substitute

susto scare, fright

sutileza subtlety

suyo/a(s) *poss.* your, of yours (*form. s., pl.*) his, of his; her, (of) hers; its; their, of theirs

T

tabaco tobacco

tabla table, list (*of figures, etc.*); board

tal such (a); a certain (fellow) called; **como tal** as such; **con tal (de) que** so that; **¿qué tal?** how are you (doing)?; how about . . . ?; **¿qué tal si ... ?** what if . . . ?; **tal como** just as, exactly the same as; **tal vez** perhaps, maybe

talento talent

taller *m.* shop (*for manufacturing or repair*); repair shop (*automobiles*); **taller de reparaciones** repair shop

tamarindo tamarind (*tropical fruit used to make juice*)

también also, too

tampoco neither, not either

tan as, so; **tan ... como** as . . . as; **tan pronto como** as soon as

tanque *m.* tank

tanto *adv.* so much; **estar** (*irreg.*) **al tanto** to be informed, up to date; **mientras tanto** meanwhile; **no es para tanto** it's not that serious; **tanto como** as much as

tanto/a/os/as *adj.* as much/many; so much/many; **tanto/a/os/as ... como** as much/many . . . as

tapas hors d'œuvres (*Sp.*)

tardar to be long; to be or take a long time; **tardar (en)** + *inf.* to be or take a long time (to) (*do something*)

tarde *n. f.* afternoon, evening; **buenas tardes** good afternoon; **por la tarde** in the afternoon

tarde *adv.* late; **hacerse** (*irreg.*) **tarde** to be getting late; **llegar (gu) tarde** to arrive late; **más tarde** later; **se me hace tarde** it's getting late

tarjeta de crédito credit card

tarjeta postal postcard

tasa rate; **tasa de desempleo** unemployment rate

taxi *m.* taxicab

taxista *m., f.* taxicab driver

te *d.o.* you (*fam. s.*); *i.o.* to/for you (*fam. s.*); *refl. pron.* yourself (*fam. s.*)

teatro theater; **obra de teatro** play, dramatic work

telefonear to telephone

telefónico/a *adj.* telephone; **llamada telefónica** telephone call

teléfono telephone; **por teléfono** by telephone

telegrama *m.* telegram

tele(visión) *f.* television (*broadcasting medium*)

televisor *m.* television set

tema *m.* theme, topic

temer to fear, be afraid of

temperatura temperature; **tomarle (a alguien) la temperatura** to take (someone's) temperature

tener (*irreg.*) to have; **que tenga (un) buen viaje** have a nice trip; **tener ... años** to be . . . years old; **tener (buena) suerte** to be lucky, in luck; **tener celos (de)** to be jealous (of); **tener la culpa (de)** to be to blame (for); to be guilty (of); **tener en cuenta** to keep in mind; **tenerle envidia (a alguien)** to envy (someone); **tener éxito** to be successful; **tener una fiebre** to have a fever; **tener ganas de** + *inf.* to feel like (*doing something*); **tener hambre** to be hungry; **tener lugar** to take place; **tener miedo** to be afraid; **tener prisa (por** + *inf.*) to be in a hurry (*to do something*); **tener que** + *inf.* to have to (*do something*); **tener que ver con** to have to do with, be related to (*a topic*); **tener (toda la) razón** to be (absolutely) right

tenis *m.* tennis; **zapatos de tenis** tennis shoes

tensión *f.* tension

tenso/a tense

terapia therapy

terminar to end, be over; **al terminar ...** when . . . is/was over

ternura tenderness

terraza terrace

territorio territory

testamento will, testament

texto text

ti *obj of prep.* you (*fam. s.*); **contigo** with you

tiempo time; weather; (*gram.*) tense; **al mismo tiempo** at the same time; **al poco tiempo** shortly after; **¿qué tiempo hace?** what's the weather like?; **hace (muy) buen/mal tiempo** the weather's (very) good/bad; **todo el tiempo** all the time, the whole time, all along

tienda store, shop; **tienda de antigüedades** antique store; **tienda de comestibles** food store; **tienda de ropa para hombres/mujeres** men's/women's clothing store

tierra earth, land

tímido/a timid

tinto/a: vino tinto red wine

tío/a uncle, aunt; *m. pl.* uncles and aunts

típico/a typical

tipo type, kind; guy

titi *fam.* form of **tía**

título title; diploma, degree

tocar (qu) to touch; to play (*musical instrument*); **tocar la puerta** to knock on the door

todavía still, yet

todo *n.* whole; all, everything; **ante todo** above all; **sobre todo** above all

todo/a *adj.* all, every; **de todas formas** in any case; **por todas partes** all over, everywhere; **todo el tiempo** all the time, the whole time, all along; **todo el mundo** the whole world; everybody; **todos los días** every day

tolerar to tolerate
tomar to take; to have something to eat or drink; **tomar el aire** to get some fresh air, go for a walk; **tomar un autobús (barco, avión, taxi, tren)** to take a bus (ship, plane, taxi, train); **tomar una clase** to take a class; **tomar decisiones** to make decisions; **tomar en serio** to take seriously; **tomar una foto(grafía)** to take a picture, photograph; **tomar el pulso** to feel the pulse; **tomar una siesta** to take a siesta, nap; **tomarle (a alguien) la temperatura** to take (someone's) temperature; **tomarle cariño (a alguien)** to start to have affection for (someone)
tomate *m.* tomato
tormenta tempest, storm
torre *f.* tower
tortuga turtle, tortoise
totalmente totally
trabajador(a) *n.* worker; *adj.* hard working
trabajar to work; **trabajar de** to work as; **trabajar de noche** to work at night
trabajo work; school paper, report; job
tradicional traditional
traer (*irreg.*) to bring
tragamonedas: máquina tragamonedas slot machine
tragedia tragedy
traje *m.* suit; dress, costume
trance *m.* critical moment
tranquilidad *f.* tranquility
tranquilo/a calm, peaceful; quiet
transición *f.* transition
tras *prep.* after
trasladarse to move
tratar to treat; to deal with; **tratar de +** *inf.* to try to (*do something*); **tratar de tú** to use informal address (**tú**) in conversation; **tratarse de** to be a question of
traumático traumatic
través: a través de through, across
tren *m.* train; **estación** (*f.*) **del tren** train station
trimestre *m.* quarter, trimester
triste sad
tristeza sadness
triunfar to triumph
tropas troops
tu(s) *poss.* your (*fam. s.*)
tú *sub. pron.* you (*fam. s.*); **tratar de tú** to use informal address (**tú**) in conversation
tumba tomb, grave
túnel *m.* tunnel
turístico/a *adj.* tourist; **guía** (*m., f.*) **turístico/a** tourist guide; **plano turístico** map (*of a city*)
tutear to use the informal address (**tú**) in conversation
tuyo/a(s) *poss.* your, of yours (*fam. s.*)

U

u or (*used instead of* **o** *before words beginning with* **o** *or* **ho**)
último/a last, final, ultimate; latest; **por última vez** for the last time; **última vez** last time

un, uno/a one; a, an (*indefinite article*); *pl.* some, a few, several
único/a unique; only; **hijo/a único/a** only child
unido/a united; close-knit, close; **ser unido/a** to be united, close-knit, close; **Estados Unidos** United States
universidad *f.* university
universitario/a *adj.* university
urgencia: de urgencia emergency
urgente urgent
usar *v.* to use
usted (Ud., Vd.) *sub. pron.* you (*form. s.*); *obj. of prep.* you (*form. s.*)
ustedes (Uds., Vds.) *sub. pron.* you (*form. pl.*); *obj. of prep.* you (*form. pl.*)
útil *adj.* useful
utilizado/a used

V

vacaciones *f. pl.* vacation
vacilar to vacillate
vago/a vague
valentía bravery
valer (*irreg.*) to be worth; **(no) vale la pena** it's (not) worth the trouble
valor *m.* worth, value; *pl.* values
valorar to value
¿vamos? shall we go?; **¡vamos!** *interj.* let's go!
vanidoso/a vain, conceited
varios/as various; several
vasos sanguíneos blood vessels
vecino/a *n.* neighbor; *adj.* neighboring
veinte twenty
veinticinco twenty-five
vellón *m.* five-cent piece (*P.R.*); nickel (*U.S.*)
velorio wake
vendedor(a) salesclerk
vender to sell; **se vende(n)** for sale
venida arrival; return
venir (*irreg.*) to come; **que viene** coming, next
venta sale; **en venta** for sale
ventana window
ver (*irreg.*) to see; **a ver** let's see, let's have a look; **tener** (*irreg.*) **que ver con** to have to do with; be related to (*a topic*)
verano summer
verbo verb
verdad *f.* truth; **decir** (*irreg.*) **la verdad** to tell the truth; **¿verdad?** right?
verdadero/a true, real
verde green
verduras greens, vegetables
vergüenza shame; **tener** (*irreg.*) **vergüenza** to be embarrassed, ashamed
vestido dress; suit
veterinario/a veterinarian
vez *f.* (*pl.* **veces**) time, occasion; **a la vez** at the same time; **a veces** at times, sometimes; **alguna vez** ever; **de vez en cuando** sometimes; **érase una vez** once upon a time; **muchas veces** often; **otra vez** again; **(por) primera vez** (for the) first time; **(por) última vez** (for the) last time; **tal vez** perhaps, maybe; **última vez** last time; **una vez** once; **una vez más** one more time

viajar to travel
viaje *m.* trip; **hacer** (*irreg.*) **un viaje** to take a trip; **que tenga (un) buen viaje** have a nice trip
viajes: agencia de viajes travel agency; **agente** (*m., f.*) **de viajes** travel agent
vicepresidente/a vice-president
vicio bad habit, vice
vida life; **llevar una vida ...** to lead a . . . life; **vida diaria** daily life; **vida privada** personal life
viejo/a *n.* old woman, old man; *adj.* old
viernes *m. s., pl.* Friday
vino wine; **vino tinto** red wine
violado/a violated
violar to violate; to rape
violento/a violent
virar to turn (*P.R.*)
visión *f.* vision
visita *f.* visit; visitor
visitar to visit
vista view (of); sight; **amor** (*m.*) **a primera vista** love at first sight
viudo/a widower/widow
vivir to live; **vivir de** to live off of, support oneself by
vivo/a alive, live, living
vocación *f.* vocation
voluntad *f.* will, willingness
volver (ue) (*p.p.* **vuelto/a**) to return; **volver a +** *inf.* to do (*something*) again; **volverse** to become, turn into
vos *sub. pron. s.* you (*substitute for* **tú**) (*Arg.*)
vosotros/as *sub. pron.* you (*fam. pl. Sp.*); *obj. of prep.* you (*fam. pl. Sp.*)
voz *f.* (*pl.* **voces**) voice
vuelo flight
vuelta return; **a la vuelta** around the corner; **billete** (*m.*) **de ida y vuelta** round trip ticket; **estar** (*irreg.*) **de vuelta** to be back; to have returned; **pasaje** (*m.*) **de ida y vuelta** round trip fare
vuestro/a(s) *poss.* your (*fam. pl. Sp.*); of yours (*fam. pl. Sp.*)

X

X: rayos X X rays; **sacar (qu) rayos X** to take X rays
xenofobia xenophobia

Y

y and; **¿y qué?** so what?; what do you want me to do?
ya already; now; later, later on; right away, at once; at last; **ya lo creo** of course; **ya no** no longer; **ya que** since
yerno son-in-law
yo *sub. pron.* I

Z

zanahoria carrot
zapato shoe; **zapatos de tenis** tennis shoes

INDEX OF CHARACTERS

This index includes the names of most of the characters who appear in *Destinos,* alphabetized by their first names in most cases. Photographs are included for many characters as well, along with a brief description of them and a city in which they live.

Alfredo Sánchez, Madrid, España. A reporter who meets Raquel.

Ángel Castillo de Valle, Buenos Aires, Argentina. Son of Fernando Castillo Saavedra and Rosario del Valle.

Ángela Castillo Soto, San Juan, Puerto Rico. Daughter of Ángel Castillo and María Luisa Soto.

el Dr. Arturo Iglesias, Buenos Aires, Argentina. A psychiatrist and the son of Rosario and Martín Iglesias.

Blanca Núñez, San Juan, Puerto Rico. A real estate agent.

Carlitos Castillo, Miami, Florida. Son of Carlos and Gloria and grandson of don Fernando.

Carlos Castillo Márquez, Miami, Florida. One of don Fernando's sons and director of the Miami office of the family company.

Carlos Soto Contreras, San Juan, Puerto Rico. One of Ángela's uncles.

Carmen Contreras de Soto, San Germán, Puerto Rico. Ángela and Roberto's grandmother.

Carmen Márquez de Castillo, La Gavia, México. Second wife of don Fernando and mother of their four children, Ramón, Carlos, Mercedes, and Juan.

Carmen Soto, San Juan, Puerto Rico. One of Ángela's aunts.

el ciego, Sevilla, España. He sells lottery tickets.

Cirilo, Estancia Santa Susana, Argentina. A gaucho and ex-employee of Rosario.

Consuelo Castillo, La Gavia, México. Don Fernando's daughter-in-law, she lives at La Gavia with her husband Ramón and daughter Maricarmen.

Dolores Acevedo, San Germán, Puerto Rico. A longtime household employee of doña Carmen and her family.

Elena Ramírez de Ruiz, Sevilla, España. Daughter-in-law of Teresa Suárez and mother of Miguel and Jaime. Her husband is Miguel Ruiz.

Federico Ruiz Suárez, Madrid, España. Son of Teresa Suárez, Federico is a guitar maker.

Fernando Castillo Saavedra, La Gavia, México. Patriarch of the Castillo family, don Fernando initiates the investigation that is carried out by Raquel Rodríguez.

Flora, Buenos Aires, Argentina. Wife of José, a sailor.

Francisco (Pancho) Rodríguez Trujillo. *See* Pancho Rodríguez Trujillo.

Gloria Castillo, Miami, Florida. Carlos's wife and mother of Juanita and Carlitos.

Guillermo, New York, New York. Pati's assistant director at the university theater.

Héctor Condotti, Buenos Aires, Argentina. An experienced sailor and friend of Ángel.

Isabel Santiago, San Juan, Puerto Rico. A bank executive.

Jaime Ruiz Ramírez, Sevilla, España. Grandson of Teresa Suárez and son of Miguel Ruiz.

Jaime Soto Contreras, San Juan, Puerto Rico. One of Ángela's uncles.

Jorge Alonso, San Juan, Puerto Rico. Ángela's boyfriend and a professor of theater at the University of Puerto Rico.

José, Buenos Aires, Argentina. A sailor and friend of Héctor.

Juan Castillo Márquez, New York, New York. The youngest child of don Fernando and a professor of literature at New York University; married to Pati.

Juanita Castillo, Miami, Florida. Daughter of Carlos and Gloria.

el Dr. Julio Morelos, Toluca, México. The Castillo family physician.

Laura Soto, San Juan, Puerto Rico. One of Ángela's cousins and the daughter of tío Jaime.

Luis Villarreal, Los Angeles, California. The former boyfriend of Raquel.

Lupe, La Gavia, México. A household employee of the Castillo family at La Gavia.

Manuel Díaz, Sevilla/Madrid, España. A schoolteacher who meets Raquel.

Manuel Domínguez, New York, New York. The producer of Pati's current play.

María, Madrid, España. Federico's girlfriend, who teaches flamenco dancing.

María Luisa Soto de Castillo, San Juan, Puerto Rico. Daughter of doña Carmen and wife of Ángel Castillo.

María Orozco de Rodríguez, Los Angeles, California. Raquel's mother.

la Hermana María Teresa, un pueblo, México. A nun who gives Ángela and Raquel a place to rest and bathe.

Maricarmen Castillo, La Gavia, México. Daughter of Ramón and Consuelo.

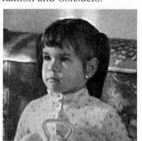

Mario, Buenos Aires, Argentina. A storekeeper in the La Boca district.

Martín Iglesias, Buenos Aires, Argentina. Second husband of Rosario, stepfather of Ángel Castillo, and father of Arturo Iglesias.

Mercedes Castillo Márquez, La Gavia, México. Don Fernando's only daughter, who lives at La Gavia with her father.

Miguel Ruiz Ramírez, Sevilla, España. Grandson of Teresa Suárez and son of Miguel Ruiz.

Miguel Ruiz Suárez, Sevilla, España. Son of Teresa Suárez and father of Miguel and Jaime.

Ofelia, Miami, Florida. Carlos's Cuban-born secretary.

Olga Soto Contreras, San Juan, Puerto Rico. One of Ángela's aunts.

Osito, Sevilla, España. A dog purchased by Miguel and Elena Ruiz for their sons, Miguel and Jaime.

Pancho Rodríguez Trujillo, Los Angeles, California. Raquel's father.

Pati Castillo, New York, New York. The wife of Juan and professor of theater at New York University, as well as a writer/director.

Pedro Castillo Saavedra, México, D.F., México. Law professor at the National University of México and brother of don Fernando.

Pepe, Sevilla, España. A barber in Sevilla.

Ramón Castillo Márquez, La Gavia, México. The oldest son of don Fernando. He runs Castillo Saavedra, S.A.

Raquel Rodríguez Orozco, Los Angeles, California. A lawyer contracted by Pedro Castillo to conduct the investigation.

Roberto Castillo Soto, San Juan, Puerto Rico. Son of Ángel Castillo and María Luisa Soto

Roberto García, Sevilla, España. A taxi driver from the Triana district.

el Padre Rodrigo, un pueblo, México. A priest who offers comfort to Raquel and Ángela.

Rosario del Valle de Iglesias, Buenos Aires, Argentina. First wife of don Fernando Castillo.

el Dr. Salazar, Guadalajara, México. A specialist who examines don Fernando.

Teresa Suárez, Madrid, España. Friend of Rosario who writes the letter to don Fernando that initiates the investigation.

Virginia López Estrada, México, D.F., México. A real estate agent.